ADOBE®
Photoshop® CS3
Introductory Concepts and Techniques

Gary B. Shelly
Thomas J. Cashman
Joy L. Starks

COURSE TECHNOLOGY
CENGAGE Learning™

Australia • Brazil • Japan • Korea • Mexico • Singapore • Spain • United Kingdom • United States

COURSE TECHNOLOGY
CENGAGE Learning

Adobe Photoshop CS3: Introductory Concepts and Techniques
Gary B. Shelly, Thomas J. Cashman, Joy L. Starks

Executive Editor: Alexandra Arnold

Marketing Manager: Tristen Kendall

Product Manager: Heather Hawkins

Associate Product Manager: Klenda Martinez

Developmental Editor: Laurie Brown

Editorial Assistant: Jon Farnham

Print Buyer: Julio Esperas

Production Editor: Heather Furrow

Proofreader: Harry Johnson

QA Manuscript Reviewer: Chris Scriver

Cover Artist: Joel Sadagursky

Composition: GEX Publishing Services

For product information and technology assistance, contact us at
Cengage Learning Academic Resource Center, 1-800-423-0563
For permission to use material from this text or product,
submit all requests online at **www.cengage.com/permissions**
Further permissions questions can be emailed to **permissionrequest@cengage.com**

The Shelly Cashman Series® is a registered trademark under license.

ISBN-13: 978-1-4239-1236-1
ISBN-10: 1-4239-1236-5

Course Technology
25 Thomson Place
Boston, MA 02210
USA

Cengage Learning products are represented in Canada by Nelson Education, Ltd.

For your lifelong learning solutions, visit **course.cengage.com**

Purchase any of our products at your local college store or at our preferred online store
www.ichapters.com

Printed in the United States of America
2 3 4 5 6 7 11 10 09 08

A D O B E

Photoshop CS3

Introductory Concepts and Techniques

Contents

iii

Preface

The Shelly Cashman Series® offers the finest textbooks in computer education. We are proud of the fact that our textbook series has been the most widely used in education. *Adobe® Photoshop® CS3: Introductory Concepts and Techniques* continues with the innovation, quality, and reliability that you have come to expect from the Shelly Cashman Series.

Adobe Photoshop CS3 is the standard in image editing software. Some of the ways that Adobe Photoshop CS3 enhances the work experience for users include: timesaving file handling with Adobe Bridge®; multiple layer control; customizable workspaces and menus; spot healing brush; and one-click red-eye reduction.

In this *Adobe Photoshop CS3* book, you will find an educationally sound and easy-to-follow pedagogy that combines a step-by-step approach with corresponding screens. All projects and exercises in this book are designed to introduce students to working with Adobe Photoshop CS3. The Other Ways and More About features provide greater knowledge of Adobe Photoshop CS3. The Learn It Online page presents a wealth of additional exercises to ensure your students have all the reinforcement they need. The chapter material is developed carefully to ensure that students will see the importance of learning Adobe Photoshop CS3 for future coursework.

Objectives of This Textbook

Adobe Photoshop CS3: Introductory Concepts and Techniques is intended for a course that offers an introduction to Photoshop and image editing. No previous experience with Adobe Photoshop CS3 is assumed, and no mathematics beyond the high school freshman level is required. The objectives of this book are:

- To teach the fundamentals of Adobe Photoshop CS3
- To expose students to image editing and graphic design fundamentals
- To develop an exercise-oriented approach that allows learning by doing
- To encourage independent study and help those who are working alone

The Shelly Cashman Approach

Features of the Shelly Cashman Series *Adobe Photoshop CS3* books include:

- **Project Orientation** Each chapter in the book presents a practical problem and complete solution using an easy-to-understand approach.
- **Step-by-Step, Screen-by-Screen Instructions** Each of the tasks required to complete a project is identified throughout the chapter. Full-color screens with callouts accompany the steps.
- **Thoroughly Tested Chapters** Unparalleled quality is ensured because every screen in the book is produced by the author only after performing a step, and then each chapter must pass Course Technology's award-winning Quality Assurance program.
- **Other Ways Boxes and Quick Reference** The Other Ways boxes displayed at the end of many of the step-by-step sequences specify the other ways to do the task completed in the steps. Thus, the steps and the Other Ways box make a comprehensive reference unit. The Quick Reference at the back of the book provides a quick reference to common keyboard shortcuts.
- **More About Feature** These marginal annotations provide background information and tips that complement the topics covered, adding depth and perspective to the learning process.
- **Integration of the World Wide Web** The World Wide Web is integrated into the Photoshop CS3 learning experience by (1) More About annotations that send students to Web sites for up-to-date information and alternative approaches to tasks; and (2) the Learn It Online page at the end of each chapter, which has chapter reinforcement exercises, learning games, and other types of student activities.

Organization of This Textbook

Adobe Photoshop CS3: Introductory Concepts and Techniques provides detailed instruction on how to use Adobe Photoshop CS3. The material is divided into three chapters, a special feature, three appendices, and a quick reference summary.

End-of-Chapter Student Activities

A notable strength of the Shelly Cashman Series *Adobe Photoshop CS3* books is the extensive student activities at the end of each chapter. Well-structured student activities can make the difference between students merely participating in a class and students retaining the information they learn. The activities in the Shelly Cashman Series *Adobe Photoshop CS3* books include the following:

- **What You Should Know** A listing of the tasks completed within a chapter together with the pages on which the step-by-step, screen-by-screen explanations appear.
- **Learn It Online** Every chapter features a Learn It Online page comprising ten exercises. These exercises include True/False, Multiple Choice, and Short Answer reinforcement questions, Flash Cards, Practice Test, Learning Games, Tips and Tricks, Expanding Your Horizons, and Search Sleuth.
- **Apply Your Knowledge** This exercise usually requires students to open and manipulate a file that is provided in the Data Files for Students. The Data Files for Students are available on the CD-ROM that ships with this textbook, or can be downloaded from the Web by following the instructions on the inside back cover.
- **In the Lab** Three in-depth assignments per chapter require students to utilize the chapter concepts and techniques to create additional Photoshop documents.
- **Cases and Places** Five unique real-world case-study situations, including one small-group activity.

Shelly Cashman Series Instructor Resources

The Shelly Cashman Series is dedicated to providing you with all of the tools you need to make your class a success. Information on all supplementary materials is available through your Course Technology representative or by callin g one of the following telephone numbers: Colleges, Universities, Continuing Education Departments, Post-Secondary Vocational Schools; Career Colleges, Business, Industry, Government, Trade, Retailer, Wholesaler, Library, and Resellers: 800-648-7450; K-12, Secondary Vocational Schools, Adult Education, and School Districts: 800-824-5179; Canada: 800-268-2222.

The Instructor Resources for this textbook include both teaching and testing aids. The contents of each item on the Instructor Resources CD-ROM (ISBN 1-4239-1239-x) are described below.

INSTRUCTOR'S MANUAL The Instructor's Manual is made up of Microsoft Word files, which include detailed lesson plans with page number references, lecture notes, teaching tips, classroom activities, discussion topics, and projects to assign.

SYLLABUS Sample syllabi, which can be customized easily to a course, are included. The syllabi cover policies, class and lab assignments and exams, and procedural information.

FIGURE FILES Illustrations for every figure in the textbook are available in electronic form. Use this ancillary to present a slide show in lecture or to print transparencies for use in lecture with an overhead projector. If you have a personal computer and LCD device, this ancillary can be an effective tool for presenting lectures.

POWERPOINT PRESENTATIONS PowerPoint Presentations is a multimedia lecture presentation system that provides slides for each chapter. Presentations are based on chapter objectives. Use this presentation system to present well-organized lectures that are both interesting and knowledge based. PowerPoint Presentations provides consistent coverage at schools that use multiple lecturers.

SOLUTIONS TO EXERCISES Solutions are included for the end-of-chapter exercises, as well as the Chapter Reinforcement exercises.

TEST BANK & TEST ENGINE The ExamView test bank includes 110 questions for every chapter (25 multiple-choice, 50 true/false, and 35 completion) with page number references, and when appropriate, figure references. A version of the test bank you can print also is included. The test bank comes with a copy of the test engine, ExamView, the ultimate tool for your objective-based testing needs. ExamView is a state-of-the-art test builder that is easy to use. ExamView enables you to create paper-, LAN-, or Web-based tests from test banks designed specifically for your Course Technology textbook. Utilize the ultra-efficient QuickTest Wizard to create tests in less than five minutes by taking advantage of Course Technology's question banks, or customize your own exams from scratch.

DATA FILES FOR STUDENTS All the files that are required by students to complete the exercises are included on the Instructor Resources CD-ROM and on a student CD-ROM that ships with the student book. You can also distribute the files on the Instructor Resources CD-ROM to your students over a network, or you can have them follow the instructions on the inside back cover of this book to obtain a copy of the Data Files for Students.

ADDITIONAL ACTIVITIES FOR STUDENTS These additional activities consist of Chapter Reinforcement Exercises, which are true/false, multiple choice, and short answer questions that help students gain confidence in the material learned.

Online Content

Blackboard is the leading distance learning solution provider and class management platform today. Course Technology has partnered with Blackboard to bring you premium online content. Instructors: Content for use with *Adobe Photoshop CS3: Introductory Concepts and Techniques* is available in a Blackboard Course Cartridge and may include topic reviews, case projects, review questions, test banks, practice tests, custom syllabi, and more. Course Technology also has solutions for several other learning management systems. Please visit http://www.course.com today to see what's available for this title.

CourseCasts Learning on the Go. Always Available...Always Relevant.

Want to keep up with the latest technology trends relevant to you? Visit our site to find a library of podcasts, CourseCasts, featuring a "CourseCast of the Week," and download them to your portable media player at http://coursecasts.course.com.

Our fast-paced world is driven by technology. You know because you are an active participant — always on the go, always keeping up with technological trends, and always learning new ways to embrace technology to power your life.

Ken Baldauf, the voice behind CourseCasts and a faculty member of the Florida State University (FSU) Computer Science Department, is responsible for teaching technology classes to thousands of FSU students each year. He knows what you know; he knows what you want to learn. He is also an expert in the latest technology and will sort through and aggregate the pertinent news and information so you can spend your time enjoying technology, rather than trying to figure it out.

Visit us at http://coursecasts.course.com to learn on the go!

CourseNotes

Course Technology's CourseNotes are six-panel quick reference cards that reinforce the most important widely used features of a software application in a visual and user-friendly format. CourseNotes will serve as a great reference tool during class and after the student completes the course.

About Our New Cover Look

Learning styles of students have changed, but the Shelly Cashman Series' dedication to their success has remained steadfast for over 30 years. We are committed to continually updating our approach and content to reflect the way today's students learn and experience new technology. This focus on the user is reflected in our bold new cover design, which features photographs of real students using the Shelly Cashman Series in their courses. Each book features a different user, reflecting the many ages, experiences, and backgrounds of all of the students learning with our books. When you use the Shelly Cashman Series, you can be assured that you are learning computer skills using the most effective courseware available. We would like to thank the administration and faculty at the participating schools for their help in making our vision a reality. Most of all, we'd like to thank the wonderful students from all over the world who learn from our texts and now appear on our covers.

Adobe Photoshop CS3 Trial Download

A copy of the Photoshop CS3 trial version can be downloaded from the Adobe Web site (www.adobe.com). You will need to register on Adobe's site to access Trial Downloads. Point to Downloads in the top navigation bar, click Trial Downloads, and then follow the on-screen instructions. Course Technology and Adobe provide no product support for this trial edition.

The minimum system requirements for the trial edition are an Intel® Pentium® 4, Intel Centrino®, Intel Xeon®, or Intel Core™ Duo (or compatible) processor; Microsoft® Windows® XP with Service Pack 2 or Windows Vista™ Home Premium, Business, Ultimate, or Enterprise (certified for 32-bit editions); 512MB of RAM; 64MB of video RAM; 1GB of available hard-disk space (additional free space required during installation); $1{,}024 \times 768$ monitor resolution with 16-bit video card DVD-ROM drive; QuickTime 7 software required for multimedia features.

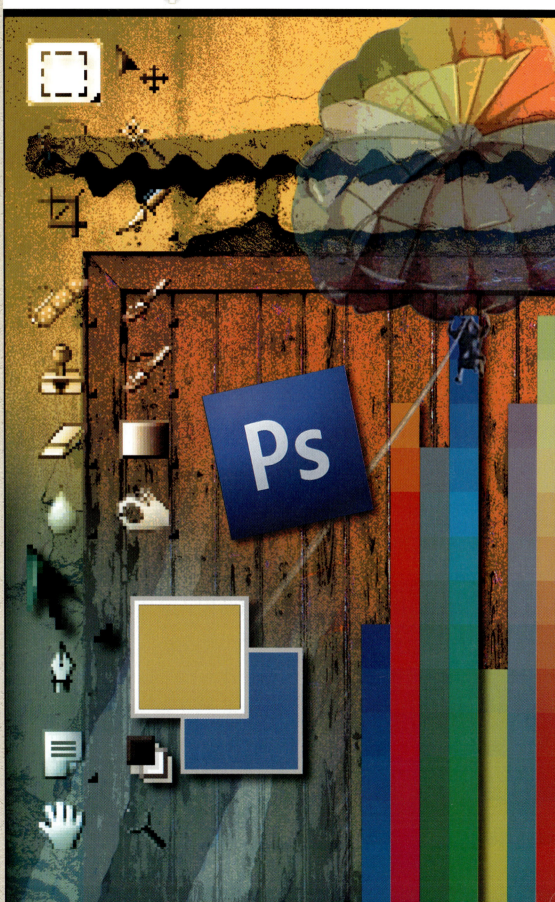

ADOBE
Photoshop CS3

Adobe PHOTOSHOP CS3

Editing a Photoshop Image

CHAPTER

CASE PERSPECTIVE

Ralph Hooton plans to open a parasailing attraction for island tourists. The new company, Up, Up & Away, will be located in the bustling harbor among cruise ship docks, and piers for sports fishing. He already has secured his business licenses, boats, sails, and financing.

Parasailing, also known as parascending, is a recreational activity where one or two people are towed behind a speedboat while attached to a parachute. As the boat accelerates, the wind causes the parachute to rise several hundred feet above the water. The parasailer needs no previous experience and has only to sit back and enjoy the view. Ralph's planned route will follow the coastline allowing the parasailer to see the most interesting parts of the island.

Ralph wants to advertise his parasailing business on the Up, Up & Away Web site and also with printed display-stand cards, known as rack cards. Rack cards typically measure 4 × 9 inches and are printed on both sides. Ralph knows of your interest in Adobe Photoshop and has asked you to begin work on a rack card by editing one of his many photographs. He would like the photograph to be more dramatic by eliminating much of the background sky, by focusing on the parasailers, and by adding a defining border. Ralph wants to use the eye-catching photograph in the upper portion on the front of the rack card, which he then will duplicate professionally on glossy card stock and distribute to local hotels and travel agencies.

As you discuss the project, you remind Ralph that the photograph used for print publications cannot always be in the same format as the one he might post on his Web site. You promise to investigate Photoshop's Web features.

As you read through this chapter, you will learn how to use Photoshop to load, edit, save, and print a photograph that displays a border. You also will save the image for use on the Web.

Editing a Photoshop Image

CHAPTER

Objectives

You will have mastered the material in this chapter when you can:

- Start Photoshop and customize the Photoshop window
- Open a photo
- Identify parts of the Photoshop window
- Explain file types
- Save a photo for both print and the Web
- Edit a photo using the Navigator palette and the Zoom Tool

- Crop and resize a photo
- Create a blended border
- Print a photo
- View files in Adobe Bridge
- Use Adobe Help
- Close a photo and quit Photoshop

What Is Photoshop CS3?

Photoshop CS3 is a popular image editing software application produced by Adobe Systems Incorporated. Image editing software refers to computer programs that allow you to create and modify **digital images**, or pictures in electronic form. One type of digital image is a digital **photograph** or **photo**, originally produced on light-sensitive film but now commonly captured and stored as a digitized array inside a camera. The photo then is converted into a print, a slide, or, if necessary, a digital file. Other types of digital images include scanned images or electronic forms of original artwork created from scratch. Digital images are used in graphic applications, advertising, publishing, and on the Web. Image editing software, such as Photoshop, can be used for basic adjustments such as rotating, cropping, or resizing, as well as more advanced manipulations, such as airbrushing, retouching, removing red-eye, changing the contrast of an image, balancing, or combining elements of different images. Because Photoshop allows you to save multilayered, composite images and then return later to extract parts of those images, it works well for repurposing a wide variety of graphic-related files.

Photoshop CS3 is part of the Adobe Creative Suite, but often it is used independently as a stand-alone application. Photoshop CS3 is available for both the PC and Macintosh computer systems. The chapters in this book are described using the PC platform running the Windows Vista operating system.

Chapter One — Editing a Photoshop Image

To illustrate the features of Photoshop CS3, this book presents a series of chapters that use Photoshop to edit photos similar to those you will encounter in academic and business environments, as well as photos for personal use. Chapter 1 uses Photoshop to enhance a photograph of parasailers to be used as an advertising piece for a para-sailing business. The original photo is displayed in Figure 1-1a. The edited photo is displayed in Figure 1-1b

(b) edited photo

(a) original photo

FIGURE 1-1

The enhancements will emphasize the sail and parasailers by focusing on the main object and positioning it to make the layout appear more visually dynamic. A rounded border will blend with the clouds in the photo. A light border color will enhance the image of the sail. Finally, the photo will be resized to fit in the upper portion of the 4 × 9 inch rack card and then optimized for the Web.

Starting and Customizing Photoshop

The steps on the next page, which assume Windows Vista is running, start Photoshop based on a typical installation. You may need to ask your instructor how to start Photoshop on your computer.

To Start Photoshop

1

• **Click the Start button on the Windows Vista taskbar, and then click All Programs at the bottom of the left pane on the Start menu.**

• **Scroll as necessary and then point to Adobe Photoshop CS3 in the All Programs list.**

Windows displays programs and folders on the Start menu above the Start button and displays the All Programs list (Figure 1-2). Your list of folders and files may differ.

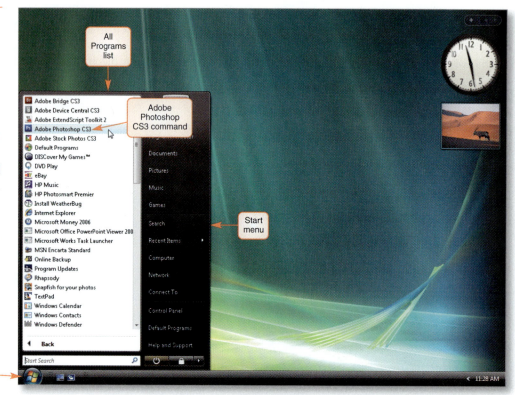

FIGURE 1-2

2

• **Click Adobe Photoshop CS3.**

Photoshop starts (Figure 1-3). While the program loads, Photoshop displays information about the version, owner, and creators.

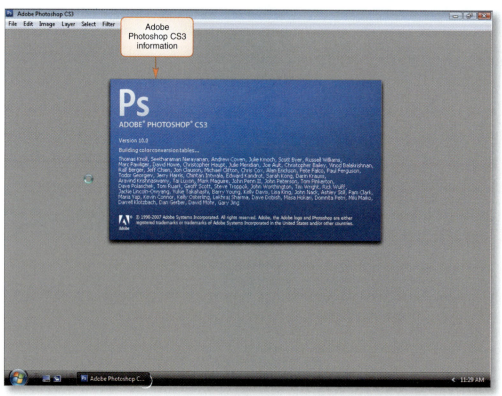

FIGURE 1-3

3

• **If the Adobe Photoshop window is not maximized, double-click its title bar to maximize it.**

The Adobe Photoshop window is displayed (Figure 1-4). The Windows taskbar displays the Adobe Photoshop button indicating that Photoshop is running.

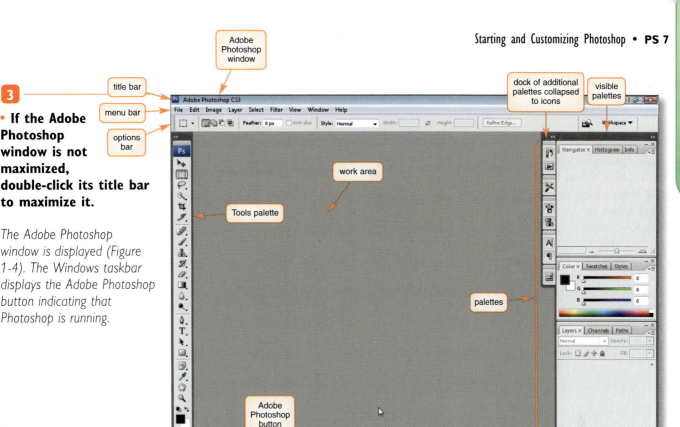

FIGURE 1-4

The screen in Figure 1-4 shows how the Photoshop window looks the first time you start Photoshop after installation on most computers. Photoshop does not open a blank or default photo automatically; rather, it displays a menu bar and a toolbar, called the options bar, across the top of the screen with a gray work area below the options bar. The Tools palette is displayed on the left; other palettes are displayed on the right. The gray work area, the options bar, and palettes are referred to collectively as the **workspace**. As you work in Photoshop, the palettes, the selected tool, and the options bar settings may change. Therefore, if you want your screen to match the figures in this book, you should reset the palettes, the selected tool, and the options bar settings. You also may need to change your computer's resolution to 1024 × 768. For more information about how to change the resolution on your computer, and other advanced Photoshop settings, read Appendix A.

The steps on the next page illustrate how to reset the palettes, reset the selected tool, and reset all tool settings.

Other Ways

1. Double-click Photoshop icon

More About

Creative Suite 3

The Adobe CS3 suite is available in several different packages that include different products. The Standard Design package includes Photoshop, InDesign, Illustrator, and Acrobat. The Premium package includes those same software programs as well as Flash and Dreamweaver. Other packages are available from adobe.com.

To Customize the Photoshop Window

1

• **Click Window on the Photoshop menu bar, and then point to Workspace on the Window menu.**

Photoshop displays the Window menu and the Workspace submenu (Figure 1-5).

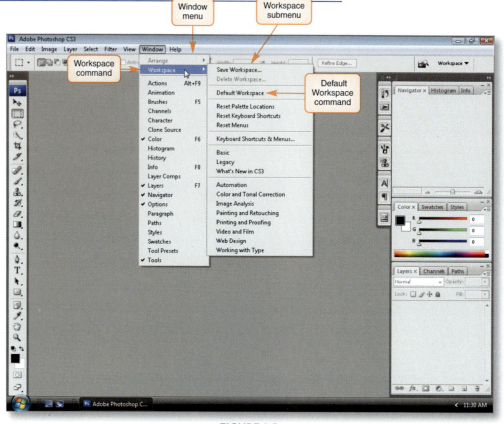

FIGURE 1-5

2

• **Click Default Workspace.**

After a few moments, Photoshop resets the placement of the palettes and toolbar (Figure 1-6). If Photoshop is a new installation on your system, you may notice few changes in the window.

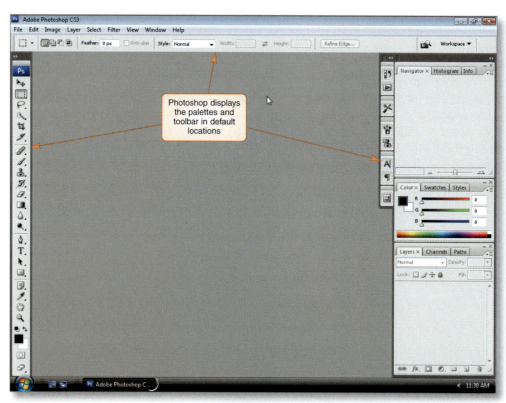

FIGURE 1-6

3

• **Right-click the second tool on the Tools palette.**

Photoshop displays a list of tools on the context menu (Figure 1-7).

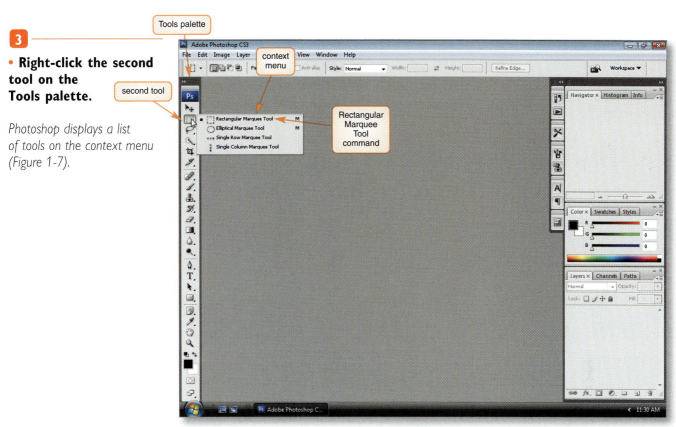

FIGURE 1-7

4

• **Click Rectangular Marquee Tool in the list.**

Photoshop displays the Rectangular Marquee Tool (M) on the Tools palette, in the tool tip, and on the options bar (Figure 1-8). Your screen may not reflect any change if the Rectangular Marquee Tool (M) already was selected.

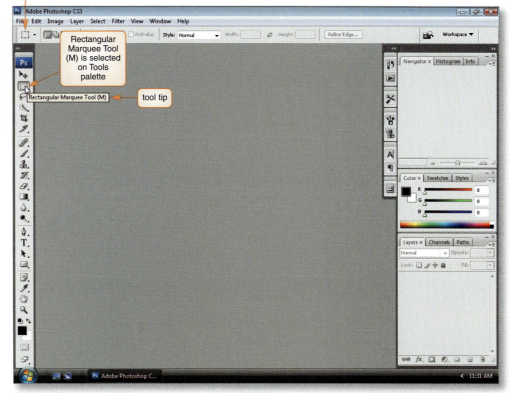

FIGURE 1-8

Photoshop Chapter 1

• **Right-click the Rectangular Marquee Tool button on the options bar.**

Photoshop displays the context menu (Figure 1-9).

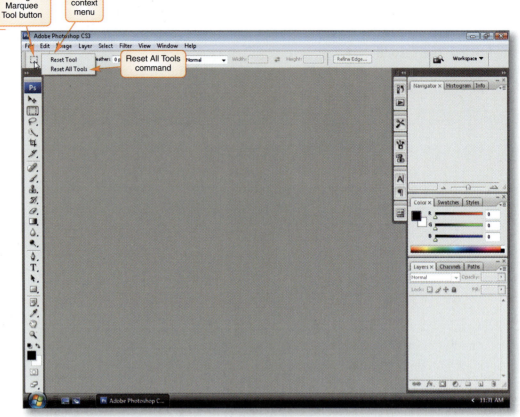

FIGURE 1-9

• **Click Reset All Tools.**

Photoshop displays a dialog box (Figure 1-10).

• **Click the OK button.**

The tools on the options bar, and other tool settings that are not currently visible, are reset to their default settings. On a new installation of Photoshop, you may not see any changes.

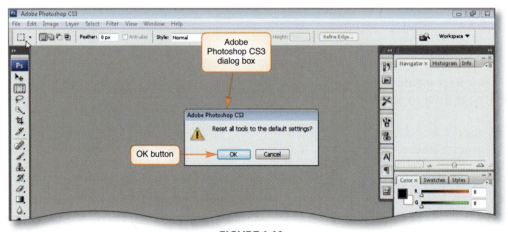

FIGURE 1-10

Other Ways

1. To reset the workspace, click Workspace button, click Default Workspace

As an alternative to Step 3 on the previous page, you can click a tool on the Tools palette and hold down the mouse button. In a few seconds, the tool's context menu will display. Whether you right-click, or click and hold to display the menu, depends on your personal preference.

When you point to many objects in the Photoshop window, such as a tool or button, Photoshop displays a tool tip. A **tool tip** is a short on-screen note associated with the object to which you are pointing. An example of a tool tip is shown in Figure 1-8. Some tool tips in Photoshop contain links leading to additional information about the tool. When you right-click some objects in the Photoshop window, Photoshop displays a context menu. A **context menu**, or **shortcut menu**, displays commands relevant to the active tool, selection, or palette.

Because of a default preferences setting, each time you start Photoshop, the Photoshop window is displayed the same way it was the last time you used Photoshop. If the palettes are relocated, then they will display in their new locations the next time you start Photoshop. Similarly, if values on the options bar are changed or a different tool is selected, they will remain changed the next time you start Photoshop. If you wish to return the screen to its default settings, follow the previous steps each time you start Photoshop. Appendix A discusses how to change more of these default settings.

As you work through the chapters, editing and creating photos, you will find that the options bar is **context sensitive**, which means it changes as you select different tools. You will learn about the palettes and the palette tabs as you use them.

Opening a Photo

To open a photo in Photoshop it must be stored as a digital file on your computer system or an external storage device. To **open** a photo, you bring a copy of the file from the storage location to the screen where you can **edit** or make changes to the photo. The changes do not become permanent, however, until you **save** or store them on a storage device. The photos used in this book are stored on a CD located in the back of the book. Your instructor may designate a different location for the photos.

The following steps illustrate how to open the file, Parasailing, from a CD located in drive E.

> **More About**
>
> ### Photos Online
> Many Web sites offer royalty free stock photos. Visit the Shelly Cashman More About Web site for a list of links to pages where you can search for free photos.

To Open a Photo

1

• Insert the CD that accompanies this book into your CD drive. After a few seconds, if Windows displays a dialog box, click its Close button.

• With the Photoshop window open, click File on the menu bar.

Photoshop displays the File menu (Figure 1-11).

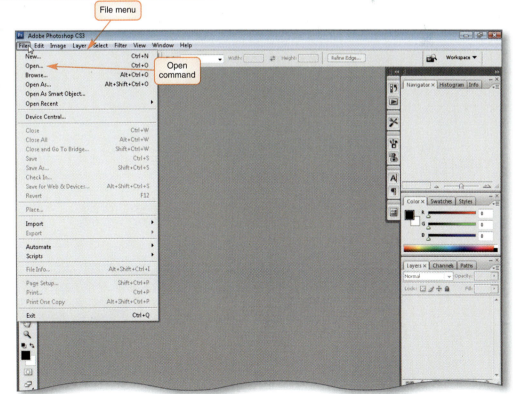

FIGURE 1-11

2

• **Click Open. When the Open dialog box is displayed, click the Look in box arrow.**

Photoshop displays the Open dialog box (Figure 1-12). A list of the available storage locations is displayed. Your list may differ depending on your system configuration.

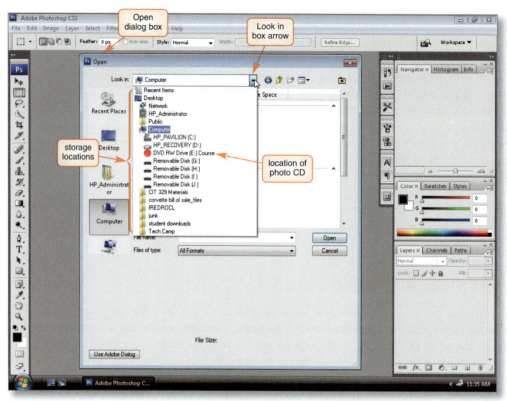

FIGURE 1-12

3

• **Click drive E or the drive associated with your CD.**

The folders located on the CD are displayed in the dialog box (Figure 1-13).

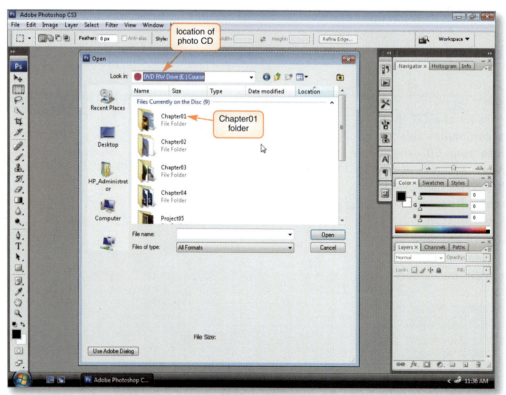

FIGURE 1-13

4

• **Double-click the Chapter01 folder and then click the file, Parasailing, to select it.**

The files located in the Chapter01 folder are displayed (Figure 1-14). Your list may display differently. Photoshop displays a preview in the Open dialog box.

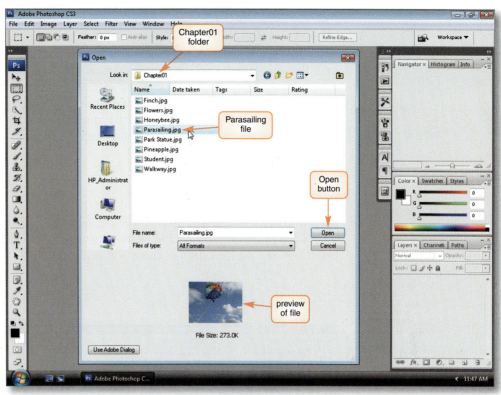

FIGURE 1-14

5

• **Click the Open button.**

Photoshop opens the file, Parasailing, from the CD in drive E. The photo is displayed in the Photoshop window (Figure 1-15).

Other Ways

1. In Windows, right-click file, click Open With, click Adobe Photoshop CS3
2. On options bar, click Go to Bridge button, double-click photo
3. Press CTRL+O, select File, click Open

FIGURE 1-15

Most of the images you will use in this book already will be stored in digital format; however, when you have a print copy of a picture that you wish to use in Photoshop, rather than a digital file stored on your system, it sometimes is necessary to scan the picture using a scanner. A **scanner** is a device used to convert an image into a digital form for storage, retrieval, or other electronic purposes. Photoshop allows you to bring a copy from the scanner, directly into the workspace. Make sure that your scanner is properly installed. Place your picture on the scanner and then click Import on the File menu. Your system's scanner will display on the Import submenu. Click your scanner. When the scanner dialog box is displayed, click the button related to starting a new scan.

The Photoshop Window

The **Photoshop window** (Figure 1-16) consists of a variety of components to make your work more efficient and to make your photo documents look more professional. The following sections discuss these components.

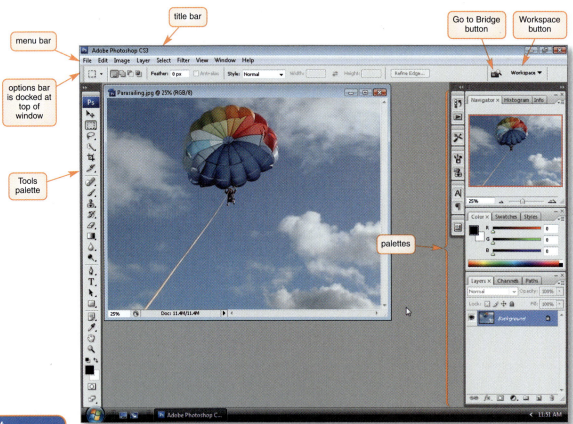

FIGURE 1-16

The Menu Bar and Options Bar

The menu bar and options bar display at the top of the screen just below the title bar (Figure 1-16).

MENU BAR The **menu bar** is a special toolbar that displays the Photoshop menu names. Each **menu** contains a list of commands you can use to perform tasks such as opening, saving, printing, and editing photos. When you point to a menu name on the menu bar, the area of the menu bar containing the name changes to a button. To display a menu, such as the Edit menu, click the Edit menu name on the menu bar. If you point to a command on a menu that has an arrow to its right edge, as shown in Figure 1-17, a **submenu**, or secondary menu, displays another list of commands.

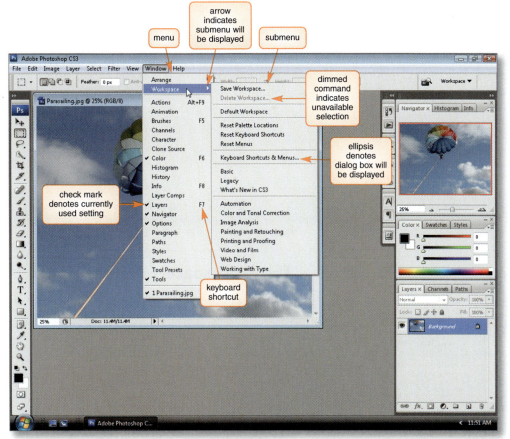

FIGURE 1-17

Menus may display **keyboard shortcuts** that indicate keys you can press on the keyboard to perform the same tasks as clicking a command on the menu. A **check mark** in a Photoshop menu means the setting is currently used or displayed. Three dots, called an **ellipsis**, follow some menu commands. When a command displaying an ellipsis is clicked, Photoshop will display a dialog box. Photoshop displays some **dimmed commands** that appear gray, or dimmed, instead of black, which indicates they are not available for the current selection.

When Photoshop first is installed, all of the menu commands display when you click a menu name. To hide seldom used menu commands, you can click Menus on the Edit menu and follow the on-screen instructions. A **hidden command** does not immediately display on a menu. If menu commands have been hidden, a Show All Menu Items command will display at the bottom of the menu list. Click the Show All Menu Items command, or press and hold CTRL when you click the menu name, to display all menu commands including hidden ones.

OPTIONS BAR The **options bar** is displayed below the menu bar. It contains buttons and boxes that allow you to perform tasks more quickly than using the menu bar and related menus. Most buttons on the options bar display words or images to help you remember their functions. When you point to a button or box on the options bar, a tool tip is displayed below the mouse pointer. The options bar changes to reflect the tool currently selected on the Tools palette. For example, a tool related to text may display a font box on the options bar, whereas a tool related to painting will display a brush button. The selected tool always is displayed as the first button on the options bar. On each tool's options bar is a Go to Bridge button to activate the file browsing and organization tool, Adobe Bridge, explained later in this chapter. On the far right of the options bar is a **Workspace button** that when clicked, displays some of the same commands as the Window menu. As each tool is discussed, the associated options bar will be explained in more detail.

You can move the options bar in the workspace by using the gray **gripper bar** on the left side of the options bar. You can dock the options bar at the top or bottom of the screen or float it in any other location in the workspace (Figure 1-18).

FIGURE 1-18

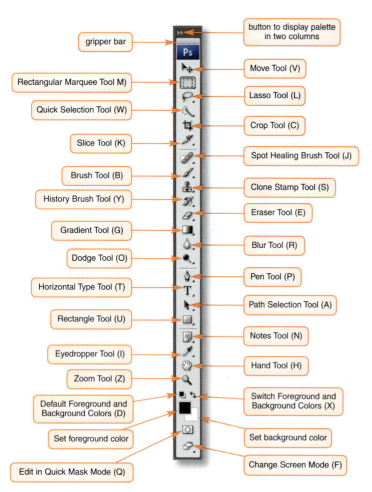

FIGURE 1-19

The Workspace

The Photoshop workspace is arranged to help you focus on creating and editing photos. The Tools palette, document window, and other palettes display on a gray background (Figure 1-16 on page PS 14).

The Tools Palette

On the left side of the workspace is the Photoshop **Tools palette**. The Tools palette is a group of **tools** or buttons, organized into a movable toolbar. In Photoshop the Tools palette is floating. You can move the Tools palette by dragging its gripper bar. You also can show or hide the Tools palette by clicking Tools on the Window menu. Each tool on the Tools palette displays a **tool icon**. When you point to the tool, a tool tip will display the name of the tool including its shortcut key. You can expand some tools to show hidden tools beneath them. Expandable tools display a small triangle in the lower-right corner of the tool icon. Click and hold the tool button or right-click a tool to see or select one of its hidden tools from the context menu. The default tool names are listed in Figure 1-19.

When you click a tool on the Tools palette to use it, Photoshop selects the button, changes the options bar as necessary, and changes the mouse pointer to reflect the selected tool. Some tools also open a dialog box.

The Tools palette is organized by purpose. At the very top of the palette is a button to display the palette in two columns, followed by the gripper bar and the Photoshop logo. Below that, the selection tools display, then the crop and slice tools, followed by retouching, painting, drawing and type, annotation, measuring, and navigation tools. At the bottom of the Tools palette are buttons to set default colors and screen modes.

More About

The Workspace

Pressing the TAB key toggles the display of palettes, and the options bar on and off. To hide or show all palettes except for the Tools palette and the options bar, press SHIFT+TAB.

The Document Window

The **document window** displays the active open file. The document window can be resized by dragging the border of the window. The document window contains the title bar, display area, scroll bars, and status bar (Figure 1-20).

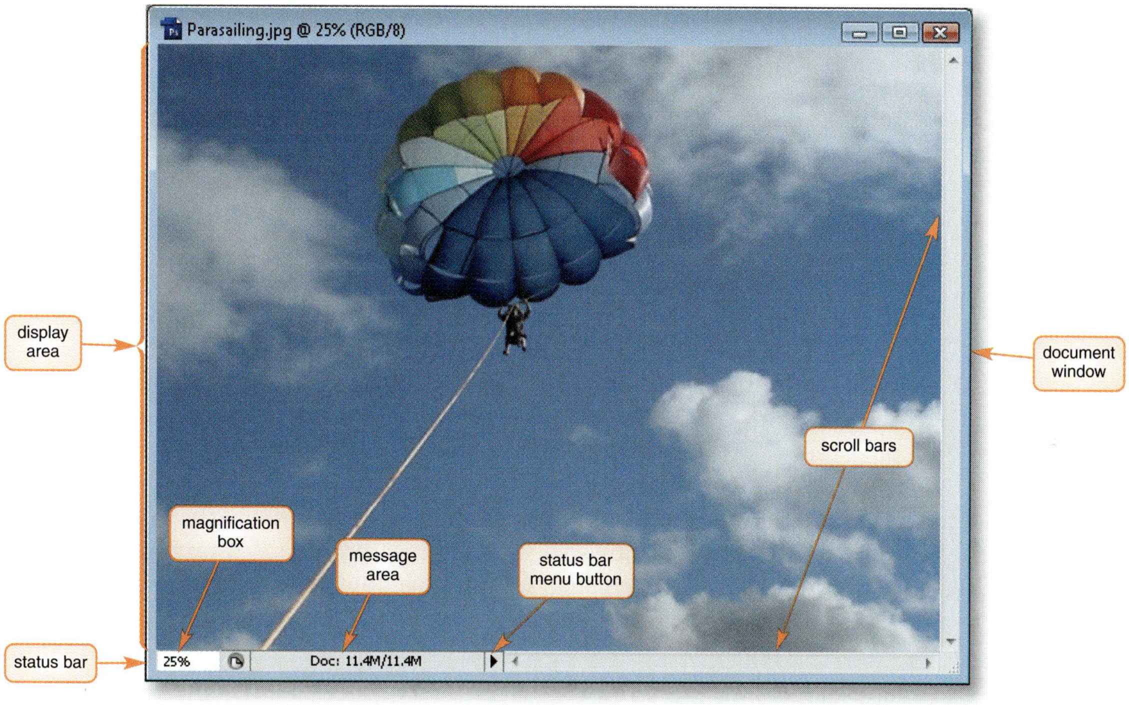

FIGURE 1-20

TITLE BAR The **title bar** of the document window displays the name of the file, the magnification, and the color mode. You can maximize the document window by double-clicking the title bar. When the document window is maximized, it fills the workspace between the palettes, the title bar no longer is displayed, the status bar docks to the bottom of the workspace, and the Minimize, Restore Down, and Close buttons are displayed on the right side of the menu bar.

DISPLAY AREA The **display area** is the portion of the document window that displays the photo or image. You perform most tool tasks and edit the photo in the display area.

SCROLL BARS **Scroll bars** display on the right side and bottom of the document window. When the photo is bigger than the document window, the scroll bars become active and display scroll arrows and scroll boxes to move the image up, down, left, and right.

STATUS BAR Across the bottom of the document window, Photoshop displays the **status bar**. The status bar contains a magnification box. **Magnification** refers to the percentage of enlargement or reduction on the screen. For example, 50% magnification in the box means the entire photo is displayed at 50 percent of its original size. Magnification does not change the size of the photo physically; it merely displays it on the screen at a different size. You can type a new percentage in the magnification box to zoom to a different view of the photo.

Next to the magnification box is the **message area**. Messages may display information about the file size, the current tool, or the document dimensions. On the right side of the status bar is the **status bar menu button**, that when clicked, displays a status bar menu. You use the status bar menu to change the message area or to change to other versions of the document.

Your installation of Photoshop may display rulers at the top and left of the document window. You will learn about rulers later in this chapter.

Palettes

A **palette**, named for the board that provides a flat surface on which artists mix paints, is a collection of graphically displayed choices and commands, such as those involving colors, brushes, actions, or layers. In Photoshop, some palettes display by default as stacked tabs in small windows on the right side of the workspace. These small windows contain a Minimize button and a Close button (Figure 1-21). Each palette has a palette menu button in the upper-right corner. Some palettes have a status bar across the bottom. A palette may display buttons, boxes, sliders, scroll bars, or drop-down lists. Palettes help you modify or monitor your photos.

You can arrange and reposition the available palettes either individually or in groups. To move them individually, drag their tabs; to move a stacked group drag the area above the tabs. Additionally, Photoshop allows you to drag each palette tab away from an existing group to create a separate window for that palette. The reverse also is true; you can **cluster** individual palettes into groups of your preference.

Palette groups are **expanded** when they display their contents. Palettes are **collapsed** when they display only an icon or name. To expand or collapse a palette group, click the black **Expand Dock button** or **Collapse to Icons button** located above the palette group. When you close a palette by clicking the Close button, it no longer is displayed. You can redisplay the palette by clicking the palette name on the Window menu.

Photoshop comes with 19 palettes as described in Table 1-1.

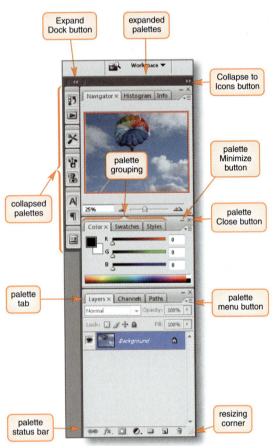

FIGURE 1-21

Labels around figure: Expand Dock button; expanded palettes; Collapse to Icons button; palette grouping; palette Minimize button; collapsed palettes; palette Close button; palette tab; palette menu button; resizing corner; palette status bar

Table 1-1 Photoshop Palettes

PALETTE NAME	PURPOSE	DEFAULT DISPLAY LOCATION
Actions	to record, play, edit, and delete individual actions	first collapsed grouping
Animation	to create a sequence of images, or frames, that is displayed over time	does not initially display
Brushes	to select preset brushes and design custom brushes	third collapsed grouping
Channels	to create and manage channels	third expanded grouping
Character	to provide options for formatting characters	fourth collapsed grouping
Clone Source	to set up and manipulate sample sources for the Clone Stamp tools or Healing Brush tools	third collapsed grouping
Color	to display the color values for the current foreground and background colors	second expanded grouping
Histogram	to view tonal and color information about an image	first expanded grouping
History	to jump to any recent state of the image created during the current working session	first collapsed grouping
Info	to display color values and document status information	first expanded grouping
Layer Comps	to display multiple compositions of a page layout	fifth collapsed grouping
Layers	to show and hide layers, create new layers, and work with groups of layers	third expanded grouping
Navigator	to change quickly the view of your artwork using a thumbnail display and to change the magnification	first expanded grouping
Paragraph	to change the formatting of columns and paragraphs	fourth collapsed grouping
Paths	to list the name and a thumbnail image of each saved path, the current work path, and the current vector mask	third expanded grouping
Styles	to view and select preset styles	second expanded grouping
Swatches	to store colors that you need to use often	second expanded grouping
Tools	to select tools	left side of workspace
Tool Presets	to save and reuse tool settings	second collapsed grouping

As each palette is introduced, its function and characteristics will be explained.

File Types

A **file type** refers to the internal characteristics of digital files; it designates the operational or structural characteristics of a file. Each digital file, graphic or otherwise, is stored with specific kinds of formatting related to how the file is displayed on the screen, how it prints, and the software it uses to do so. Computer systems use the file type to help users open the file with the appropriate software. File types are distinguished by a special file extension. **File extensions**, in most computer systems, are identified by a three- or four-letter specification after the file name. For example, Parasailing.jpg refers to a file named Parasailing with the extension and file type JPG. A period separates the file name and its extension. When you are exploring files on your system, you may see the file extensions as part of the file name or you may see a column of information about file types.

More About

Palettes

To collapse a palette group to display titles only, double-click the palette's tab, or click the Minimize button. You can open the palette menu even when the palette is collapsed.

Graphic files are created and stored using many different file types and extensions. The type of file sometimes is determined by the creating hardware or software. Other times, when the user has a choice in applying file types, it commonly is decided by the intended purpose of the graphic file, such as whether or not the file is to be used on the Web, the file size, or the desired color mode. **Color modes**, or **color models**, use a numerical method to determine how to display and print colors. You may have heard of the RGB color model that creates its colors based on combinations of red, green, and blue. You will learn more about color models in a later chapter.

A few common graphic file types are listed in Table 1-2.

Table 1-2 Graphic File Types

FILE EXTENSION	FILE TYPE	DESCRIPTION
BMP	Bitmap	BMP is a standard Windows image format used on DOS and Windows-compatible computers. BMP format supports many different color modes.
EPS	Encapsulated PostScript	EPS files can contain both bitmap and vector graphics. They are supported by almost all graphics, illustration, and page-layout programs. EPS format can be used to transfer PostScript artwork between applications. While editing of EPS files is limited, Photoshop allows users to save any photo as an EPS file for use in other programs.
GIF	Graphics Interchange Format	GIF commonly is used to display graphics and images on Web pages. It is a compressed format designed to minimize file size and electronic transfer time.
JPG OR JPEG	Joint Photographic Experts Group	JPG files commonly are used to display photographs on Web pages. JPG format supports many different color modes. JPG retains all color information in an RGB image, unlike GIF format. JPG compresses file size by selectively discarding data. Most digital cameras produce JPG files.
PDF	Portable Document	PDF is a flexible file format based on the PostScript imaging model that is cross-platform and cross-application. PDF files accurately display and preserve fonts, page layouts, and graphics. PDF files can contain electronic document search and navigation features such as hyperlinks. While editing of PDF files is limited, Photoshop allows users to save any photo as a PDF file for use in other programs.
PSD	Photoshop Document	PSD format is the default file format in Photoshop and the only format that supports all Photoshop features. Other Adobe applications can import PSD files directly and preserve many Photoshop features due to the tight integration between Adobe products.
RAW	Photoshop Raw	RAW format is a flexible file format used for transferring images between applications and computer platforms. There are no pixel or file size restrictions in this format. Documents saved in the Photoshop Raw format cannot contain layers.
TIF OR TIFF	Tagged Image File Format	TIF is a flexible bitmap image format supported by almost all paint, image-editing, and page-layout applications. This format often is used for files that are to be exchanged between applications or computer platforms. Most desktop scanners can produce TIF images.

To preserve the most features such as layers, effects, masks, and styles, Photoshop encourages the use of its own format, **PSD**, which stands for Photoshop Document format. Similarly to most file formats, PSD supports files up to 2 gigabytes (GB) in size. As you complete the chapters in this book, you will examine file types more closely.

Table 1-3 displays information about the parasailing photo. It was created by a digital camera and is stored as a JPG file. **JPG**, or **JPEG**, stands for Joint Photographic Experts Group, a standard format used by photo hardware devices that supports many different color modes, and one that can be used on the Web.

Table 1-3 Parasailing Photo Characteristics	
File Name	Parasailing
File Type	JPG
Document Size	7.68 × 5.76 inches
Color Mode	RGB
Resolution	300 pixels/inch
File Size	274 KB

Saving a Photo

As you make changes to a file in Photoshop, the computer stores it in memory. If you turn off the computer or if you lose electrical power, the document in memory is lost. If you plan to use the photo later, you must save it on a storage device such as a USB flash drive, or hard disk. The following steps illustrate how to save a file on a USB flash drive using the Save As command on the File menu.

You will save the photo with a new file name and in a new location. Even though you have yet to edit the photo, it is a good practice to save the file on your personal storage device early in the process. You will name the file Parasailing Edited. The following steps illustrate how to save a photo.

To Save a Photo

1

• **With your USB flash drive connected to one of the computer's USB ports, click File on the menu bar.**

Photoshop displays the File menu (Figure 1-22).

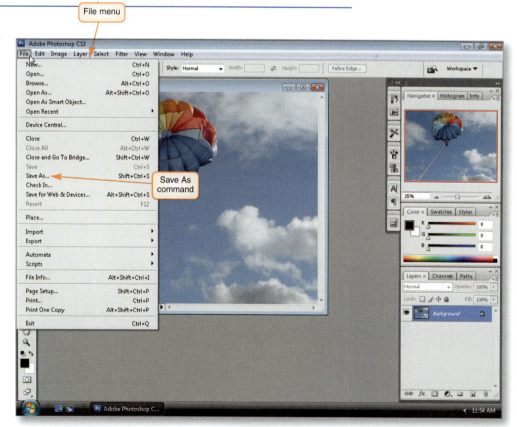

FIGURE 1-22

2

• **Click Save As. When the Save As dialog box is displayed, type** Parasailing Edited **in the File name text box. Do not press the ENTER key after typing the file name.**

The file name Parasailing Edited is displayed in the File name text box (Figure 1-23).

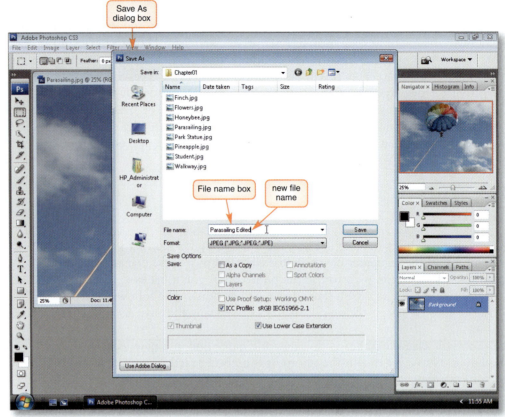

FIGURE 1-23

3

• **Click the Save in box arrow and then click USB (F:), or the location associated with your USB flash drive, in the list.**

If you have folders or files on your flash drive, Photoshop displays the folders and files in the Save As dialog box (Figure 1-24).

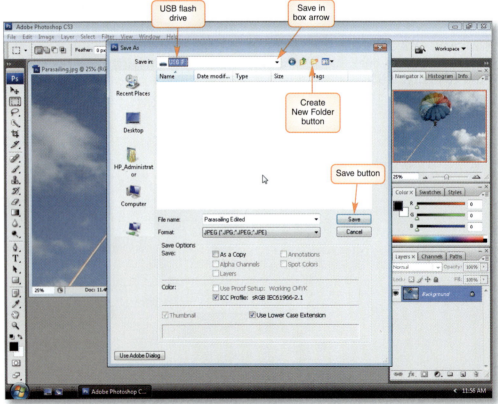

FIGURE 1-24

4

• **Click the Save button in the Save As dialog box. If Photoshop displays a JPEG Options dialog box, click its OK button.**

Photoshop saves the file on the USB flash drive with the file name Parasailing Edited and displays the new name on the document window title bar (Figure 1-25). Although the photo is saved on a storage device, it also remains in main memory and is displayed on the screen.

FIGURE 1-25

You may wish to create a folder for each chapter in this book. If so, click the Create New Folder button in the Save As dialog box (Figure 1-24). When the new folder is displayed, type a chapter name such as Chapter01. Double-click the new folder to open it and then click the Save button in the Save As dialog box.

Editing the Photo

Editing, or making corrections and changes to photos, involves a wide variety of tasks such as changing the focus of interest, recoloring portions of the photo, correcting defects, and changing the file type for specific purposes. Table 1-4 on the next page suggests typical categories and types of edits you might perform on photos; there are many others. These edits commonly overlap, and, when performed in combination, they may create new editing varieties. You will learn more about edits as you work through the chapters in this book.

Table 1-4 Photo Edits

CATEGORY	TYPES OF EDITS
Resize and Focus	cropping, shrinking, enlarging, slicing, changing the aspect, rotating, leveling, mirroring, collinearity editing
Enhancements and Layering	filters, layers, clones, borders, artwork, text, animation, painting, morphing, ordering, styles, masks, cut aways, selections, depth perception, anti-aliasing, move, warp, shapes, rasterizing
Color	correction, contrast, blending, modes and systems, separations, resolution, screening, levels, ruling, trapping, matching, black and white
Correction	sharpening, red eye, tears, correcting distortion, retouching, reducing noise
File Type	camera raw, print, Web, animated images

Editing always should be performed with design principles in mind. From a design point of view, the parasailing photo would serve the customer better if more emphasis were placed on the parasailers. If you want to emphasize a single object on a fairly solid background, it is important to bring that object closer and trim extraneous space around the object. When movement or motion needs to be portrayed, it is common for designers to place a central object slightly toward one edge of the photo, whereas static photos such as a headshot for a yearbook could be displayed centered. Adding a border or decorative frame around a photo sometimes can be an effective way to highlight or make the photo stand out on the page. Using a border color that complements one of the colors already in the photo creates a strong, visually connected image.

Editing the parasailing photo to emphasize, to create motion, and to highlight will involve three parts. First, you will zoom in and crop the photo to remove excessive background. Next, you will add a border, smooth its edges, and fill it with color. Finally, you will resize the photo to fit the intended use and size requirements.

Zooming

In order to make careful edits in a photo, you sometimes need to change the magnification or **zoom** to a certain portion of the photo. Zooming allows you to focus on certain parts of the photo, such as a specific person in a crowd scene or details in a complicated picture. Magnification is measured by a percentage that is displayed on the document window title bar. A magnification of 100 percent means the photo is displayed in its actual size. Zooming in enlarges the magnification and percentage of the photo; zooming out reduces the magnification.

The **Zoom Tool (Z) button** displays a magnifying glass icon on the Photoshop Tools palette. When you use the Zoom tool, each click magnifies the image to the next preset percentage and centers the display at the point you click. Right-clicking with the Zoom tool in the photo allows you to choose to zoom in or zoom out on a shortcut menu.

The following steps illustrate how to use the Zoom Tool (Z) button on the Tools palette to zoom in on the parasail for careful editing later in the chapter.

To Use the Zoom Tool

1

• **Click the Zoom Tool (Z) button on the Tools palette. Point to the center of the parasail.**

The mouse pointer changes to a magnifying glass with a plus sign in it (Figure 1-26). The options bar displays choices associated with zooming. Notice the current magnification is 25%.

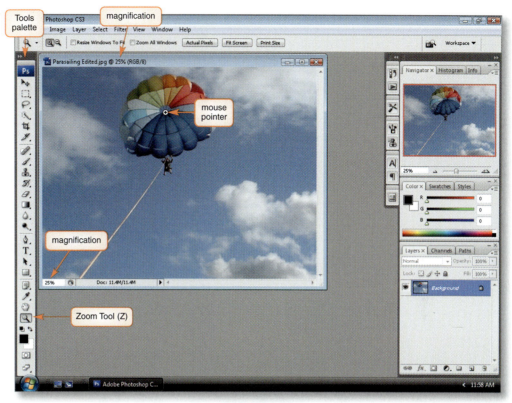

FIGURE 1-26

2

• **Click the parasail.**

The magnification increases to 33.33% (Figure 1-27).

FIGURE 1-27

On the options bar, you can cause the Zoom tool to reduce the magnification by clicking the Zoom Out button. In the case of Zoom Out, the mouse pointer displays a magnifying glass with a subtraction sign. Other options include fitting the photo on the screen, displaying the actual pixels, and displaying the photo at its print size.

The Navigator Palette

Another convenient way to zoom and move around the photo is to use the Navigator palette. The **Navigator palette** (Figure 1-28) is used to change the view of your artwork using a thumbnail display. The colored box in the Navigator palette is called the **proxy view area** or **view box**, which outlines the currently viewable area in the window. Dragging the proxy view area changes the portion of the picture that is displayed in the document window. When you click the **palette menu button**, Photoshop displays a menu with choices specific to that palette. In Figure 1-28, the Navigator palette menu displays choices to dock the palette to the menu well and to change the outline color of the proxy view area. In the lower portion of the Navigator palette, you can type in the desired magnification, or you can use the slider or buttons to increase or decrease the magnification. To move the palette, drag its title bar. To change the size of the palette, drag its border.

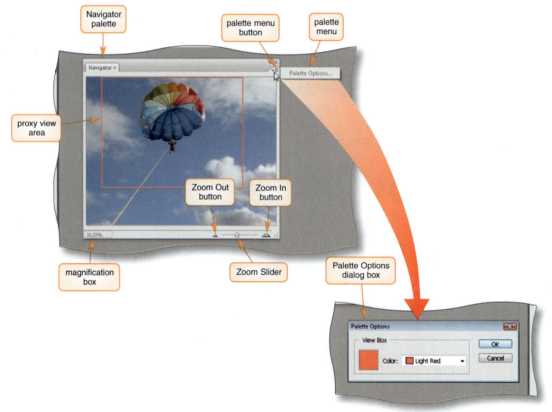

FIGURE 1-28

The following step uses the Navigator palette to position the view in the document window.

To Use the Navigator Palette

1

• **Drag the proxy view area to the top and left.**

The document window displays the reposition (Figure 1-29). When the mouse pointer is positioned over the proxy view area, it displays a hand.

FIGURE 1-29

Other Ways

1. Use scroll bars in document window

When you are using a different tool on the Tools palette, such as a text or brush editing tool, it is easier to use the Navigator palette to zoom and move around in the photo. That way, you do not have to change to the Zoom tool, perform the zoom, and then change back to your editing tool.

The Hand tool also can be used to move around in the photo, if the photo has been magnified to be larger than the document window. To use the Hand tool, click the **Hand Tool (H) button** on the Tools palette (Figure 1-29) and then drag in the display area of the document window.

Viewing Rulers

In order to make careful edits in a photo, sometimes it is necessary to use precise measurements, in addition to zooming and navigating. In these cases, changing the Photoshop document window in order to view the rulers is important. **Rulers** display on the top and left sides of the document window. Rulers help you position images or elements precisely. As you move your mouse over a photo, markers in the ruler display the mouse pointer's position.

The steps on the next page describe how to view the rulers.

To View Rulers

1

• **Click View on the menu bar.**

Photoshop displays the View menu (Figure 1-30).

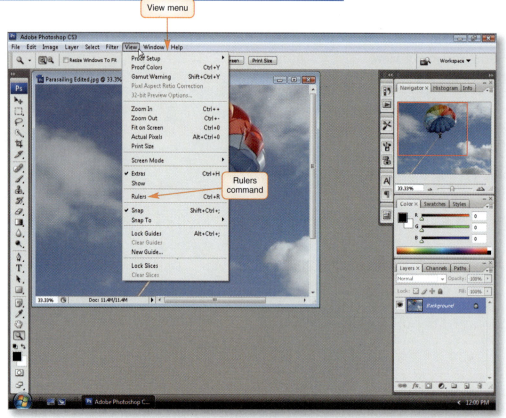

FIGURE 1-30

2

• **Click Rulers.**

Photoshop displays the rulers on the top and left of the document window (Figure 1-31).

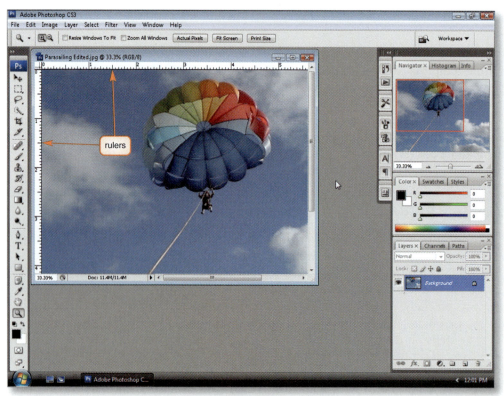

FIGURE 1-31

Other Ways

1. Press CTRL+R

Rulers display inches by default, but you can right-click a ruler to change the measurement to pixels, centimeters, or other measurements. You can drag the mouse from a ruler to any position in the photo to display a **ruler guide**, or green line, which helps you straighten or align objects by providing a visual cue. Ruler guides do not print.

Cropping

The next step in editing the parasailing photo is to **crop** or trim away some of the blue sky so the photo focuses on the parasail and the parasailers. Photographers try to compose and capture images full-frame, which means the object of interest fills the dimensions of the photo. When that is not possible, photographers and graphic artists crop the image either to create an illusion of full-frame, to fit unusual shapes in layouts, or to make the image more dramatic. From a design point of view, sometimes it is necessary to crop a photo to straighten an image, remove distracting elements, or enlarge small portions. The goal of most cropping is to make the most important feature in the original photo stand out. Cropping sometimes is used to convert a digital photo's proportions to those typical for traditional photos.

Many photographers and graphic artists use the **rule of thirds** when placing the focus of interest. Imagine that the scene is divided into thirds both vertically and horizontally. The intersections of these imaginary lines suggest four positions for placing the focus of interest (Figure 1-32). The position you select depends on the subject and how you would like that subject to be presented. For instance, there may be a shadow, path, or line of sight you wish to include; or, in the case of moving objects, you generally should leave space in front of them into which they can move.

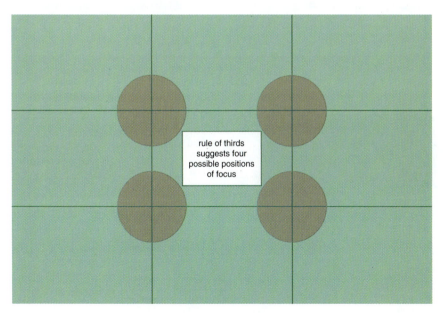

rule of thirds suggests four possible positions of focus

FIGURE 1-32

The **Crop Tool (C) button** on the Tools palette is used to drag or select the portion of the photo you wish to retain. Then, when you press the ENTER key, the rest of the photo is trimmed away or cropped. The steps on the next page demonstrate cropping the photo to place the parasail to the right and slightly above center while still leaving some blue sky on all edges. Using the rule of thirds, the middle of the sail will be centered in the upper-right to emphasize the sail and to indicate motion.

To Crop a Photo

1

• **Click the Crop Tool (C) button on the Tools palette.**

The Crop Tool (C) button is selected indicating the active editing tool (Figure 1-33). The options bar also reflects the tool.

FIGURE 1-33

2

• **Using the rulers as guides, drag a rectangle beginning at the top of the photo, approximately 1 inch from the left edge. Continue dragging right to approximately 5⅛ inches on the horizontal ruler, and down to approximately 3¼ inches on the vertical ruler. Do not release the mouse button.**

Photoshop displays the cropping selection. The mouse pointer changes to a cropping symbol when using the Crop tool (Figure 1-34).

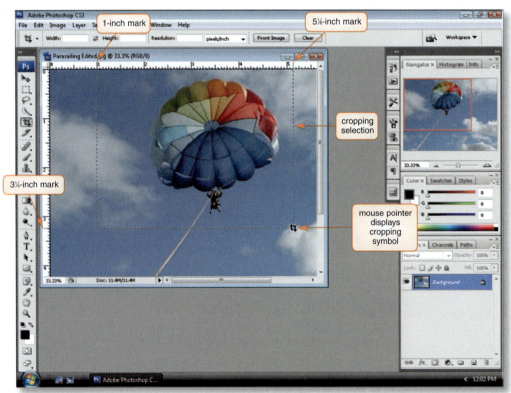

FIGURE 1-34

3

• **Release the mouse button.**

Photoshop displays the area to crop darker than the selection (Figure 1-35). The selection indicator sometimes is called a marquee or marching ants.

FIGURE 1-35

4

• **Press the ENTER key.**

Photoshop crops the photo (Figure 1-36). Cropping reduces the size of the document as shown on the document window status bar.

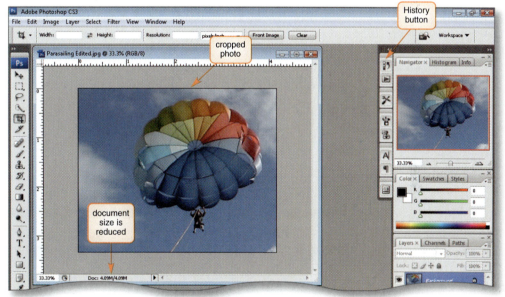

FIGURE 1-36

If you make a mistake while dragging the cropping area and want to start over, you can press the ESC key which cancels the selection.

If you already have performed the crop and change your mind, you have several choices. You can click the **Undo command** on the Edit menu, or you can press CTRL+Z to undo the last edit. Additionally, Photoshop keeps track of all your edits in the History palette. To display the History palette, you click the History button (Figure 1-36). Each edit or state of the photo is recorded sequentially in the History palette. If you want to step back through the edits or go back to a particular state, such as the previous crop, click the state in the History palette. You will learn more about the History palette in a future chapter.

Creating a Blended Border

A **border** is a decorative edge on a photo or a portion of a photo. Photoshop provides several ways to create a border, ranging from simple color transformations around the edge of the photo, and predefined decorated layers, to styled photo frames. A border helps define the edge of the photo especially when the photo may be placed on colored paper or on a Web page with a background texture. A border visually separates the photo from the rest of the page. Rounded borders soften the images in a photo. Square borders are more formal. Decorative borders on a static photo can add interest and amusement, but can easily detract from the focus on a busier photo. Blended borders are not a solid fill; they blend a fill color from the outer edge toward the middle. A border that complements the photo in style, color, and juxtaposition is best.

To add a border to the parasailing photo, you first will select pixels along the edge of the image. A **pixel** is an individual dot of light that is the basic unit used to create digital images. After you select pixels along the edges, you then will smooth the corners. Finally, you will blend the color white into the border pixels creating an appropriate frame for the photo.

Making Selections

Specifying or isolating an area of your photo for editing is called making a **selection**. By selecting specific areas, you can edit and apply special effects to portions of your image while leaving the unselected areas untouched. Selections can be simple shapes such as rectangles or ovals, or unusually shaped areas of a photo outlining specific objects. Selections can be the entire photo or as small a portion as one pixel. Photoshop has many commands to help users make selections. In the case of the parasailing photo, the region you wish to edit by adding a border is the entire photo. The following steps show how to use the Select menu to select all of the photo.

To Select All

1

• Click Select on the menu bar (Figure 1-37).

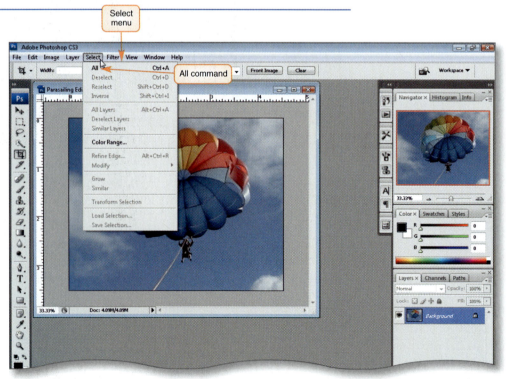

FIGURE 1-37

2

• **Click All on the Select menu.**

Photoshop displays the selection (Figure 1-38).

Selection indicator or marquee

Entire photo is selected

FIGURE 1-38

Other Ways

1. To select all, press CTRL+A
2. To select areas, use selection tools

When you select all, Photoshop displays the photo with a selection around all four edges. The selection tools on the Tools palette also can help you make selections in the photo. The Rectangular Marquee, Lasso, Quick Selection, and Magic Wand tools will be discussed in Chapter 2.

Modifying the Border

Selections can be outlined in Photoshop with simple lines or wider borders. When modifying a border, you must identify how many pixels wide the border should be as described in the following steps.

To Modify a Border

1

• **Click Select on the menu bar, and then point to Modify.**

Photoshop displays the Modify submenu (Figure 1-39).

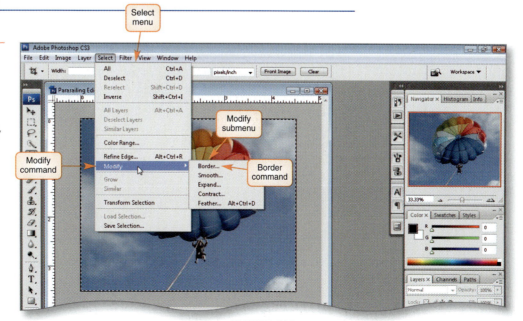

Select menu

Modify submenu

Modify command

Border command

FIGURE 1-39

2

• **Click Border on the Modify submenu.**

• **In the Border Selection dialog box, type** 100 **in the Width box.**

Photoshop displays the Border Selection dialog box (Figure 1-40). Entering 100 pixels will cause the selection to create a border around the edge of the photo.

FIGURE 1-40

3

• **Click the OK button in the Border Selection dialog box.**

The selection now contains 100 pixels on each edge (Figure 1-41).

FIGURE 1-41

Smoothing the Border

Smoothing the border adjusts the radius of the pixels at the inner corners of the border and adds them to the selection, resulting in a rounded, rectangular border selection. The following steps illustrate how to smooth the border.

To Smooth the Border

1

• Click Select on the menu bar, and then point to Modify.

Photoshop again displays the Modify submenu (Figure 1-42).

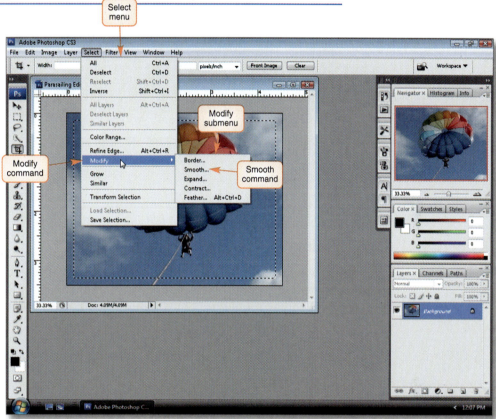

FIGURE 1-42

2

• Click Smooth on the Modify submenu.

• In the Smooth Selection dialog box, type 50 in the Sample Radius box.

Photoshop displays the Smooth Selection dialog box (Figure 1-43). The Sample Radius box accepts a pixel unit of measure.

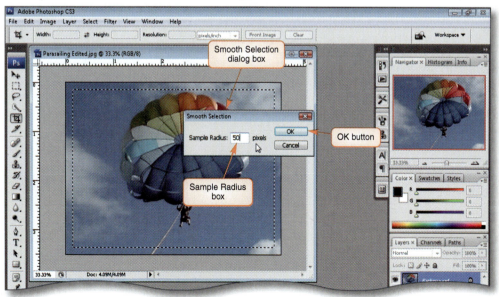

FIGURE 1-43

3

• **Click the OK button in the Smooth Selection dialog box.**

After a few moments, Photoshop adjusts the corners of the selection (Figure 1-44).

FIGURE 1-44

Filling a Selection

When you **fill** a selection, you **blend** a color or a pattern into the selection area. Photoshop allows you to choose a color, a blending mode, and a percentage of opacity. **Blending modes** are the ways in which pixels in the image are affected by a color. Examples of blending modes include normal, lighten, darken, and other color manipulations. **Opacity** refers to the level at which you can see through the color to reveal the paper or layer beneath it. For example, 1% opacity appears nearly transparent, whereas 100% opacity appears completely opaque.

The following steps fill the border selection with white using a Normal blending mode.

To Fill a Selection

1

• **Click Edit on the menu bar.**

Photoshop displays the Edit menu (Figure 1-45).

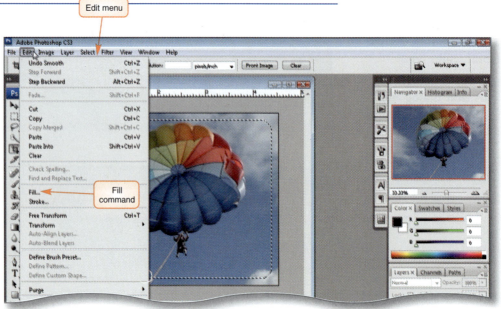

FIGURE 1-45

Photoshop Chapter 1

2

• **Click Fill on the Edit menu.**

• **Click the Use box arrow in the Fill dialog box.**

Photoshop displays the Fill dialog box (Figure 1-46). The Use box allows you to choose colors or patterns to fill the border selection.

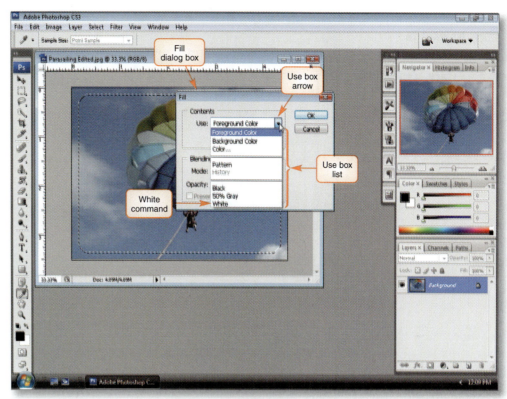

FIGURE 1-46

3

• **Click White in the Use box list.**

• **Click the Mode box arrow.**

The Mode box allows you to choose a blending mode (Figure 1-47).

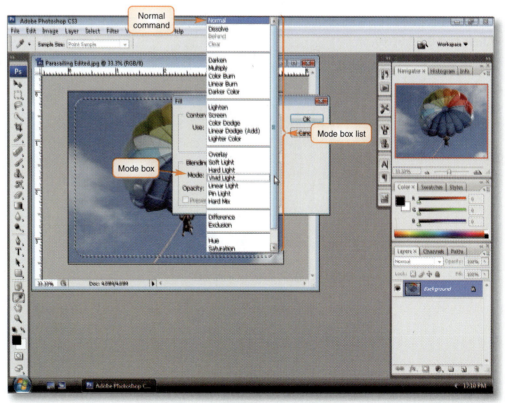

FIGURE 1-47

4

• **Click Normal in the list.**

• **If necessary, type** 100% **in the Opacity box.**

Photoshop will use a white color with a normal blend (Figure 1-48).

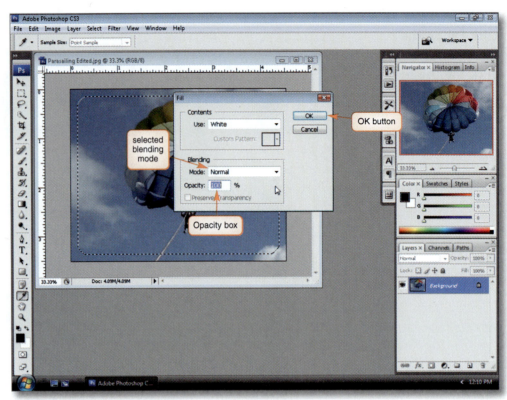

FIGURE 1-48

5

• **Click the OK button in the Fill dialog box.**

A white, blended border with smooth corners is displayed around the photo (Figure 1-49).

FIGURE 1-49

Other Ways

1. To display the Fill dialog box, press SHIFT+F5

Deselecting

When you are done editing a selection, you should remove the selection indicator so it no longer is displayed. To **deselect** a previous selection, click the document window away from the selection as described in the following step.

To Deselect

1

• **Click anywhere in the document window to remove the selection.**

The selection indicator no longer is displayed (Figure 1-50).

selection indicator no longer is displayed

FIGURE 1-50

Saving a Photo with the Same File Name

Because you have made many edits to the photo, it is a good idea to save the photo again. When you saved the document the first time, you assigned a file name to it (Parasailing Edited). When you use the following procedure, Photoshop automatically assigns the same file name to the photo and it is stored in the same location.

To Save a Photo with the Same File Name

1 **Click File on the menu bar.**

2 **Click Save on the File menu. If Photoshop displays a JPEG Options dialog box, click the OK button.**

Photoshop saves the photo on a USB flash drive using the currently assigned file name, Parasailing Edited.

Changing Image Sizes

Sometimes it is necessary to resize an image to fit within certain space limitations. **Resize** means to scale or change the dimensions of the photo. Zooming in or dragging a corner of the document window to change the size is not the same as actually changing the dimensions of the photo. Resizing in a page layout program, such as Publisher or InDesign, merely stretches the pixels. In Photoshop, resizing means adding or subtracting the number of pixels.

Photoshop uses a mathematical process called **interpolation**, or **resampling**, when it changes the number of pixels. The program interpolates or calculates how to add new pixels to the photo to match those already there. Photoshop samples the pixels and reproduces them to determine where and how to enlarge or reduce the photo.

When you resize a photo, you must take many things into consideration, such as the type of file, the width, the height, and the resolution. **Resolution** refers to the number of pixels per inch, printed on a page. Not all photos lend themselves to resizing. Some file types lose quality and sharpness when resized. Fine details cannot be interpolated from low resolution photos. Resizing works best for small changes where exact dimensions are critical. If possible, it usually is better to take a photo at the highest feasible resolution or rescan the image at a higher resolution rather than resizing it later.

Resizing the Image

In those cases where it is impossible to create the photo at the proper size, Photoshop helps you resize or scale your photos for print or online media. Because the photo will be printed on a rack card of a specific size, you will change the width to 4 inches wide. The next steps describe how to resize the image to create a custom-sized photo for printing.

To Resize the Image

1

• **Click Image on the menu bar.**

Photoshop displays the Image menu (Figure 1-51).

FIGURE 1-51

2

• **Click Image Size.**

Photoshop displays the Image Size dialog box (Figure 1-52).

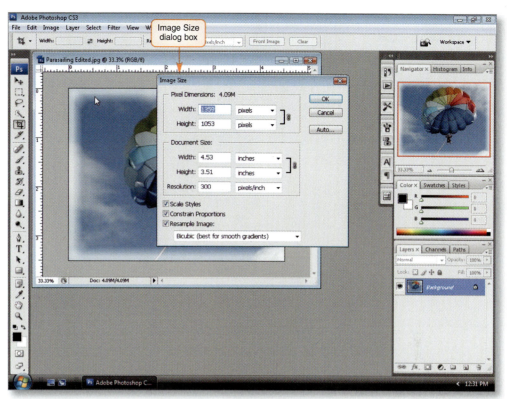

FIGURE 1-52

3

• **In the Document Size area, double-click the value in the Width box and then type** 4 **to replace the previous value.**

The new width is displayed (Figure 1-53). When you enter the width, the height automatically is adjusted to maintain the proportions of the photo. Your exact height may differ slightly depending on how closely you cropped the original photo.

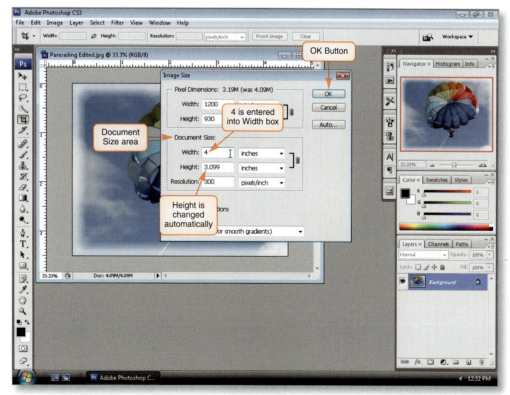

FIGURE 1-53

4

• **Click the OK button.**

*The resized image is displayed
(Figure 1-54).*

document
file size is
reduced

FIGURE 1-54

5

• **Click the status bar
menu button.**

*The status bar menu is
displayed (Figure 1-55).*

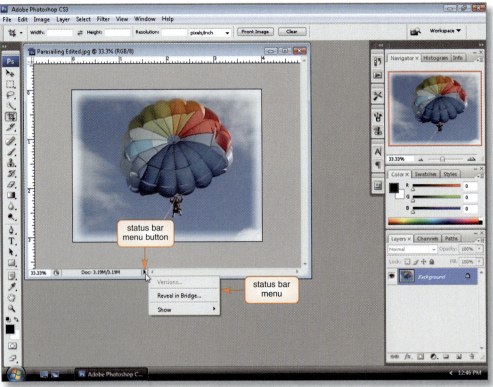

status bar
menu button

status bar
menu

FIGURE 1-55

6

• **Point to Show.**

The Show submenu lists options for displaying different kinds data in the message area (Figure 1-56).

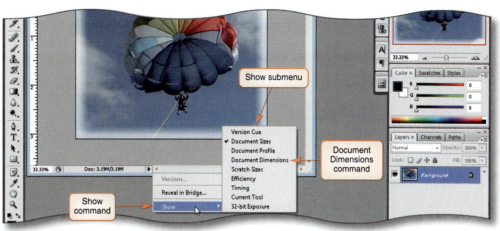

FIGURE 1-56

7

• **Click Document Dimensions.**

The status bar displays the document dimensions in the message area (Figure 1-57).

FIGURE 1-57

The photo now can be printed, saved, taken to a professional print shop, or sent online to a printing service. In this chapter, you will print the resized photo, save it, and then close it — returning to the original photo to prepare a Web version.

Printing a Photo

The next step is to print a copy of the resized photo. A printed version of the photo is called a hard copy or printout. The steps on the next page show how to print the photo created in this chapter.

To Print a Photo

1

• **Ready the printer according to the printer instructions.**

• **Click File on the menu bar.**

Photoshop's Print commands are available on the menu or by using shortcut keys (Figure 1-58). There is no Print button on the options bar.

FIGURE 1-58

2

• **Click Print One Copy on the File menu. If Photoshop displays a dialog box about print settings, click the OK button.**

The mouse pointer briefly changes to the Working in Background shape as Photoshop prepares to print the photo. While the photo is printing, a printer icon is displayed in the notification area on the Window taskbar as shown in Figure 1-59.

Other Ways

1. To print one copy, press ALT+SHIFT+CTRL+P
2. To display the Print dialog box, press CTRL+P

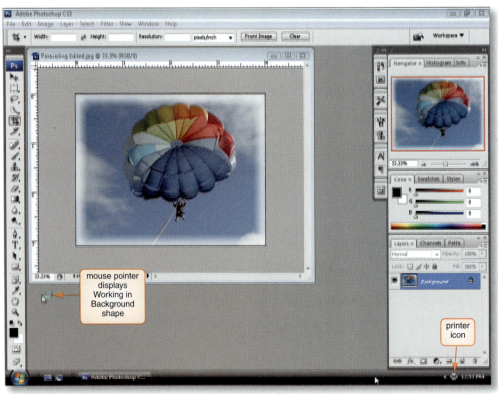

FIGURE 1-59

When you use the Print One Copy command to print a document, Photoshop prints the photo automatically using preset options. You then may distribute the printout or keep it as a permanent record of the photo.

If you wanted to print multiple copies of the document, display the Print dialog box by clicking File on the menu bar, clicking Print and entering the number of copies you want to print. In addition to the number of copies, the Print dialog box has several printing options. The Page Setup and Print With Preview commands also display options specific to your printer, printer drivers, and operating system with color management options. Print Online allows you to send your print file directly to an online service, if it is available, that will do the printing for you.

Saving the Resized Photo

Many graphic designers will save multiple copies of the same photo with various edits. Because this photo has been resized to print properly, you need to save it with a different name as described in the following steps.

To Save the Resized Photo

1
• Click File on the menu bar and then click Save As.

2
• When Photoshop displays the Save As dialog box, type `Parasailing for Print` in the File name box.

• If necessary, click the Save in box arrow and then click USB (F:), or the location of your USB flash drive and appropriate folder in the list.

The photo will save on the USB flash drive (Figure 1-60).

3
• Click the Save button.

• If Photoshop displays a JPEG Options dialog box, click the OK button without making any further changes.

The file is saved in the same location with the name Parasailing for Print.

FIGURE 1-60

Other Ways
1. Press SHIFT+CTRL+S

Saving a Photo for the Web

When preparing photos for the Web, you often need to compromise between display quality and file size. Web users do not want to wait while large photos load from the Web to their individual computer systems. Photoshop provides several commands to compress the file size of an image while optimizing its online display quality. **Optimization** is the process of changing the photo to make it most effective for its purpose. The Save for Web & Devices command allows you to preview optimized images in different file formats, and with different file attributes, for precise optimization. You simultaneously can view multiple versions of a photo and modify settings as you preview the image. Photoshop allows you to save the photo in a variety of formats such as **GIF**, which is a compressed graphic format designed to minimize file size and electronic transfer time, or as an **HTML** (Hypertext Markup Language) file, which contains all the necessary information to display your photo in a Web browser.

You have two choices in Photoshop CS3 for creating Web images, the Zoomify command and the Save for Web & Devices command. The **Zoomify command** allows you to create a high-resolution image for the Web, complete with a background and tools for navigation, panning, and zooming. Download times for this HTML-based solution are approximately equivalent to JPG files. To use the Zoomify command, click Export on the File menu and then click Zoomify. In the Zoomify Export dialog box you set various Web and export options. Photoshop creates the HTML code and files for you to upload to a Web server.

If you do not want the extra HTML files for the background, navigation, and zooming, you can create a single HTML file using the **Save for Web & Devices command**. The resulting HTML file can be used on the Web or on a variety of mobile devices. In the Save For Web & Devices dialog box you can preview how your file will display and set output options.

Using the Save for Web & Devices Command

To optimize the parasailing photo for use on the Web, you need to make decisions about the file size and how long it might take to load on a Web page. These kinds of decisions must take the audience and the nature of the Web page into consideration. For example, Web pages geared for college campuses probably could assume a faster download time than those who target a wide range of home users. An e-commerce site that needs high-quality photography to sell its product will make certain choices in color and resolution. The hardware and software of Web users also is taken into consideration. For instance, if a Web photo contains more colors than the user's monitor can display, most browsers will **dither**, or approximate, the colors that it cannot display by blending colors that it can. Many other appearance settings play a role in the quality of Web graphics, some of which are subjective in nature. As you become more experienced in Photoshop, you will learn how to make choices about color, texture, and layers, which also play a role in Web pages.

The followings steps describe using the Save for Web & Devices command to display previews for four possible Web formats, to choose a connection speed, and to save the photo as a GIF.

To Save for Web & Devices

1

• **With the Parasailing for Print photo selected in the workspace, click File on the menu bar.**

Photoshop displays the File menu (Figure 1-61).

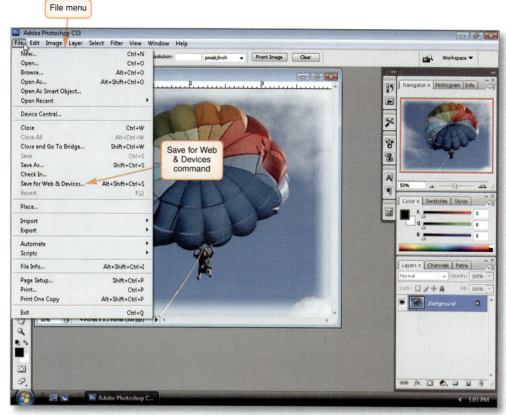

FIGURE 1-61

2

• **Click Save for Web & Devices.**

• **When Photoshop displays the Save For Web & Devices dialog box, if necessary, click the 4-Up tab.**

• **Click the Zoom Level box arrow.**

Photoshop displays 4 previews — the original photo and three others converted to different resolutions to optimize download times on the Web (Figure 1-62). The Zoom Level list displays many magnifications at which to display the previews.

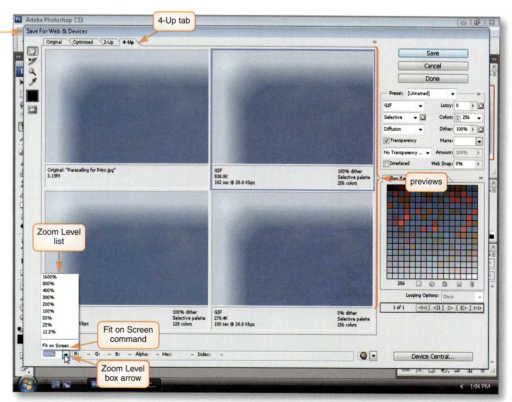

FIGURE 1-62

3

• **Click Fit on Screen in the list.**

• **Click the upper-right preview, if necessary.**

• **Click the Colors box arrow.**

The previews now display the entire photo (Figure 1-63). Your display may differ. The Colors list displays the number of colors to use for the Web version of the photo. The default file type is GIF.

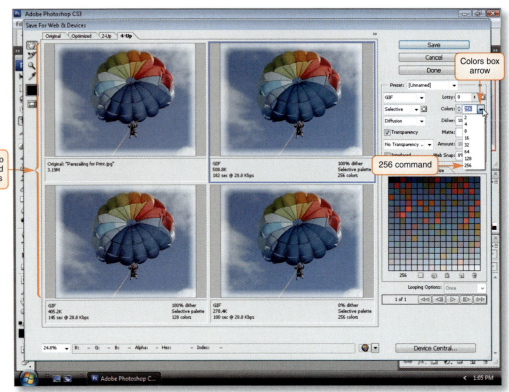

FIGURE 1-63

4

• **Click 256 in the list, if necessary.**

• **Right-click the upper-right preview.**

The colors of the preview change and the shortcut menu displays different connection speeds (Figure 1-64). Your list may differ.

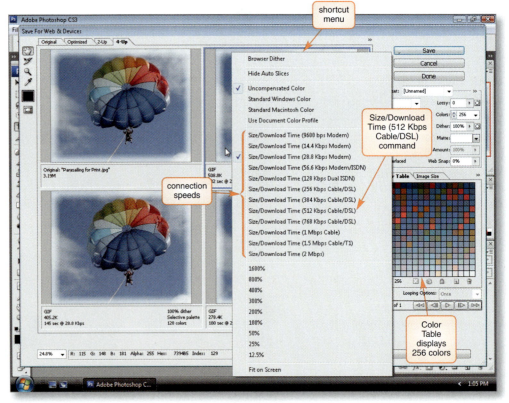

FIGURE 1-64

5

• **Click Size/Download Time (512 Kbps Cable/DSL) in the list.**

• **Click the Image Size tab.**

• **Double-click the Width box and type** 500 **to replace the width value.**

At 512 kilobytes per second, the upper-right preview will load on the Web in 11 seconds (Figure 1-65). Your load time may differ. The selected preview displays with a blue box. The height automatically adjusts proportionally when you enter a width.

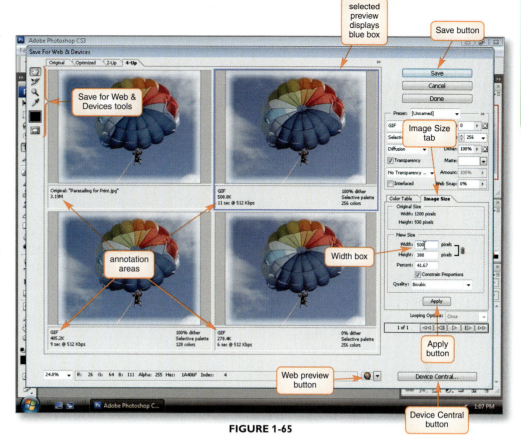

FIGURE 1-65

6

• **Click the Apply button.**

• **Click the Save button.**

• **When the Save Optimized As dialog box is displayed, type** Parasailing-for-Web **in the File name box.**

• **If necessary, click the Save in box arrow and then click USB (F:), or the location of your USB flash drive and appropriate folder in the list.**

Photoshop displays the Save Optimized As dialog box (Figure 1-66). Notice that the words in the default file name are hyphenated as is standard for Web graphics.

 7

Click the Save button.

The file saves in the specified location.

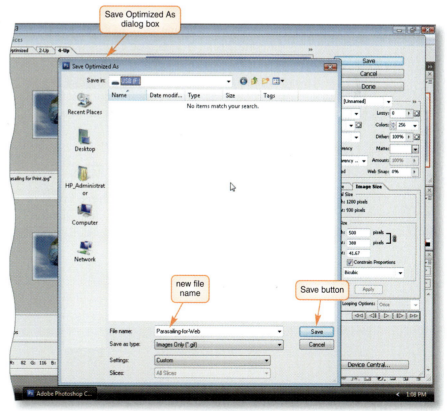

FIGURE 1-66

More About

CS3 Device Central

Device Central enables you to preview how Photoshop files will look on a variety of mobile devices. When you click the Device Central button (Figure 1-65 on the previous page), you can choose the specific mobile device and preview how the file will look. An emulator or mock-up displays the device. Photoshop supports most cell phone displays, portable electronic devices, and MP3 players with video. In the Device Central window, you can adjust settings for lighting, scaling, and alignment.

The annotation area (Figure 1-65 on the previous page) below each image in the Save For Web & Devices dialog box provides optimization information such as the size of the optimized file, and the estimated download time using the selected modem speed.

On the left side of the Save For Web & Devices dialog box, Photoshop provides several tools to move, zoom, select colors, and slice a portion of the selected preview.

Along the bottom of the Save For Web & Devices dialog box are zoom levels, color indicators, and a Web preview button.

If you choose a preview other than the original located on the upper-left, the Save For Web dialog box displays options in the Preset area on the right. The Preset area lets you make changes to the selected preview such as the file type, the number of colors, transparency, dithering, and photo finishes. Fine-tuning theses kinds of optimization settings allows you to balance the image quality and file size.

Below the Preset area are two tabs. The Color Table tab displays the Color Table Panel. Based on the choices you made in the Preset area, the colors used in the selected preview can be locked, deleted, set to transparent, or adjusted for standard Web palettes. The Image Size tab allows you to make changes to the size of the image similar to those changes you made using the Resize Image Wizard. Changing the image size affects all four previews. The settings are not permanent until you click the Save button.

The resulting optimized Web photo then can be referenced in HTML code or inserted into a page layout generated with Web development software. The photo must be uploaded to a file server along with the Web page or code.

Adobe Bridge

Adobe **Bridge** is a file exploration tool similar to Windows Explorer. Bridge replaces previous file browsing techniques and can be used with any of the software programs in the suite. Using Bridge, you can locate, drag, organize, browse, and standardize color settings across your content for use in print, on the Web, and even on mobile devices. A useful Bridge tool allows you to attach or assign keywords, or **metadata**, used for searching and categorizing photos. Metadata is divided into three categories: file information, image usage, and image creation data. The Bridge interface is explained in detail in Appendix C.

Using Bridge to View Files

So far in this chapter, you have saved the original parasailing photo, the edited photo, a version for printing, and a version for the Web. The following steps show how to view those files as thumbnails and then with details.

To Use Bridge to View Files

1

• **Click the Go to Bridge button on the options bar.**

• **When the Desktop - Adobe Bridge window is displayed, click the Location box arrow.**

Adobe Bridge opens in a new window (Figure 1-67). Your location and displayed files may differ.

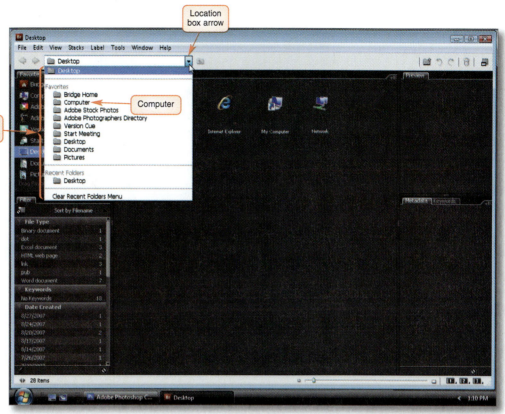

FIGURE 1-67

2

• **Click Computer in the list.**

The storage locations on your system are displayed (Figure 1-68). You can change the size of the thumbnails by dragging the slider in the status bar.

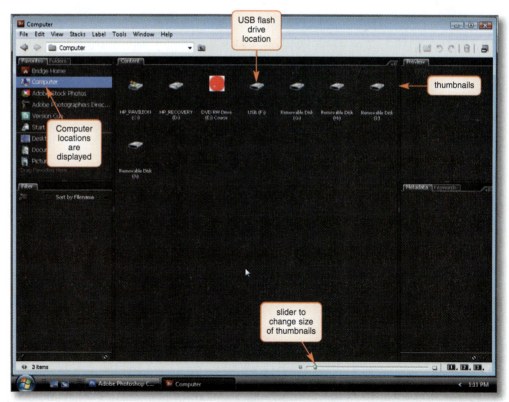

FIGURE 1-68

3

• **Double-click your USB flash drive location.**

• **If you created a Chapter01 folder, double-click the Chapter01 folder.**

• **Click View on the menu bar and then click As Details.**

The files you have saved in the chapter are displayed in As Details view (Figure 1-69).

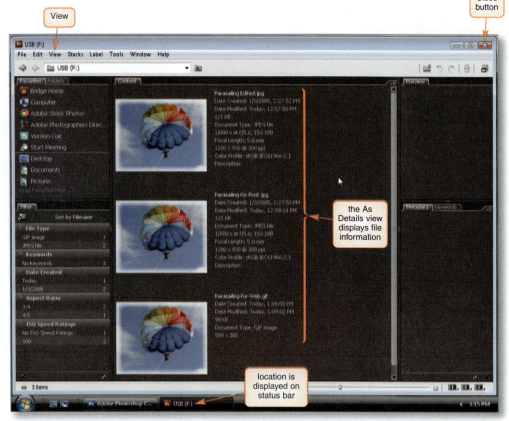

FIGURE 1-69

You can use Bridge to organize your photos into folders, to set keywords for future searching, or simply to open a file by double-clicking the thumbnail. In Thumbnails view, the files that are currently open in Photoshop display a small, round icon in the lower-right corner of the thumbnail. Bridge is like a database for your photos.

Closing Adobe Bridge

The next step illustrates how to close Adobe Bridge.

To Close Bridge

1

• **Click the Close button on the right of the Adobe Bridge title bar (Figure 1-69).**

Adobe Bridge closes and returns you to Photoshop.

If you are working with multiple photos, or organizing your photos, it may be more convenient to use the Bridge tool to open files. In other cases, use the Open command on the Photoshop File menu if you only want to open a single photo for editing.

Adobe Help

At anytime while you are using Photoshop you can get answers to questions using **Adobe Help**. You activate Adobe Help either by clicking Help on the menu bar or pressing F1. The Help menu includes commands to display more information about your copy of Photoshop as well as a list of how-to guides for common tasks. Once inside Adobe Help, a wealth of assistance is available including tutorials with detailed instructions accompanied by illustrations and videos.

Used properly, this form of online assistance can increase your productivity and reduce your frustration by minimizing the time you spend learning how to use Photoshop.

The following section shows how to obtain answers to your questions in Adobe Help by using the Search box. Additional information about using Adobe Help is available in Appendix B.

Using the Search Box

The **Search box**, located on the right side of the Adobe Help menu bar (Figure 1-71 on the next page), allows you to type words or phrases about which you want additional information and help, such as cropping or printing images. When you press the ENTER key, Photoshop responds by displaying a list of topics related to the word or phrase you typed. The following steps show how to use the Search box to obtain information about the Tools palette.

To Use Help

1

• **Click Help on the menu bar.**

Photoshop displays the Help menu (Figure 1-70). When clicked, the Photoshop Help command will open Adobe Help in a new window, as will the various How to commands.

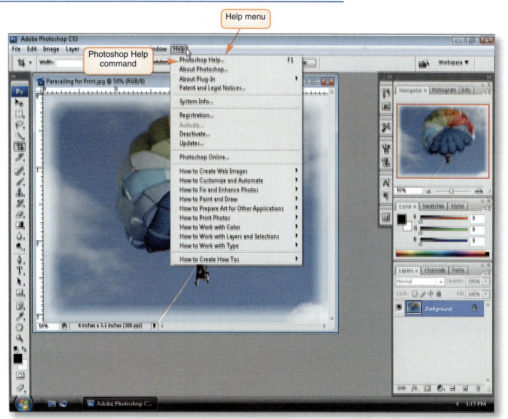

FIGURE 1-70

• **Click Photoshop Help.**

• **When the Adobe Help Viewer 1.1 window is displayed, double-click its title bar to maximize the window.**

• **Click the Search box on the right side of the menu bar and then type** Tools palette **(Figure 1-71).**

The Adobe Help Viewer 1.1 window is displayed. Because Adobe Help was activated from Photoshop, Adobe Photoshop CS3 is displayed in the Browse box.

FIGURE 1-71

• **Press the ENTER key.**

• **When Photoshop displays the results, click the third topic, Use a tool.**

When the Use a tool link is clicked, Photoshop displays information about the topic in the main window (Figure 1-72).

• **Click the Close button on the Adobe Help Viewer 1.1 title bar.**

Adobe Help closes and the Adobe Photoshop window again is active.

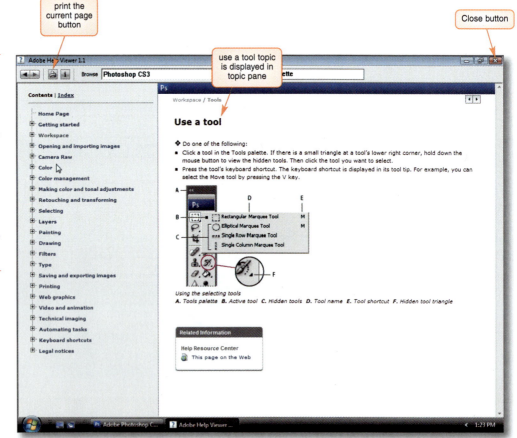

FIGURE 1-72

Other Ways

1. Press F1, enter search topic

Use the buttons in the upper-left corner of the Adobe Help Viewer 1.1 window (Figure 1-72) to move back and forth through the Help system pages or print the contents of the window. To navigate the help topics in order, use the previous and next buttons in the upper-right corner of the topic pane.

Quitting Photoshop

After you create, save, and print the photo, Chapter 1 is complete. The following steps show how to quit Photoshop and return control to Windows.

To Quit Photoshop

1

• **Point to the Close button on the right side of the Photoshop title bar (Figure 1-73).**

2

• **Click the Close button.**

• **If Photoshop displays a dialog box asking you to save changes, click the No button.**

The Photoshop window closes.

Close button

FIGURE 1-73

Other Ways

1. On File menu, click Exit
2. Press CTRL+Q

When you quit Photoshop, a dialog box may display asking if you want to save the changes. This occurs if you make changes to the photo since the last save. Clicking the Yes button in the dialog box saves the changes; clicking the No button ignores the changes; and clicking the Cancel button returns to the photo. If you did not make any changes since you saved the photo, this dialog box usually is not displayed.

Chapter Summary

In editing the parasailing photo in this chapter, you gained a broad knowledge of Photoshop. First, you were introduced to starting Photoshop. You learned about the Photoshop window. You learned how to open a photo and zoom in. You learned about design issues related to the placement of points of interest. You then learned how to crop a photo to eliminate extraneous background. After you added a border, you resized the image for printing.

Once you saved the photo, you learned how to print it. You used the Save for Web & Devices command to optimize and save a Web version. You learned how to use Adobe Bridge to view files, and Adobe Help to research specific help topics. Finally, you learned how to quit Photoshop.

What You Should Know

Having completed this chapter, you should be able to perform the tasks below. The tasks are listed in the same order they were presented in this chapter. For a list of the buttons, menus, toolbars, and other commands introduced in this chapter, see the Quick Reference Summary at the back of this book and refer to the Page Number column.

1. Start Photoshop (PS 6)
2. Customize the Photoshop Window (PS 8)
3. Open a Photo (PS 11)
4. Save a Photo (PS 21)
5. Use the Zoom Tool (PS 25)
6. Use the Navigator Palette (PS 27)
7. View Rulers (PS 28)
8. Crop a Photo (PS 30)
9. Select All (PS 32)
10. Modify a Border (PS 33)
11. Smooth the Border (PS 35)
12. Fill a Selection (PS 36)
13. Deselect (PS 39)
14. Save a Photo with the Same File Name (PS 39)
15. Resize the Image (PS 40)
16. Print a Photo (PS 44)
17. Save the Resized Photo (PS 45)
18. Save for Web & Devices (PS 47)
19. Use Bridge to View Files (PS 51)
20. Close Bridge (PS 52)
21. Use Help (PS 53)
22. Quit Photoshop (PS 55)

Learn It Online

Instructions: To complete the Learn It Online exercises, start your browser, click the Address bar, and then enter the Web address scsite.com/pscs3/learn. When the Photoshop CS3 Learn It Online page is displayed, follow the instructions in the exercises below. Each exercise has instructions for printing your results, either for your own records or for submission to your instructor.

1 Chapter Reinforcement TF, MC, and SA

Below Photoshop Chapter 1, click the Chapter Reinforcement link. Print the quiz by clicking Print on the File menu for each page. Answer each question.

2 Flash Cards

Below Photoshop Chapter 1, click the Flash Cards link and read the instructions. Type 20 (or a number specified by your instructor) in the Number of playing cards text box, type your name in the Enter your Name text box, and then click the Flip Card button. When the flash card is displayed, read the question and then click the ANSWER box arrow to select an answer. Flip through Flash Cards. If your score is 15 (75%) correct or greater, click Print on the File menu to print your results. If your score is less than 15 (75%) correct, then redo this exercise by clicking the Replay button.

3 Practice Test

Below Photoshop Chapter 1, click the Practice Test link. Answer each question, enter your first and last name at the bottom of the page, and then click the Grade Test button. When the graded practice test is displayed on your screen, click Print on the File menu to print a hard copy. Continue to take practice tests until you score 80% or better.

4 Who Wants to Be a Computer Genius?

Below Photoshop Chapter 1, click the Computer Genius link. Read the instructions, enter your first and last name at the bottom of the page, and then click the PLAY button. When your score is displayed, click the PRINT RESULTS link to print a hard copy.

5 Wheel of Terms

Below Photoshop Chapter 1, click the Wheel of Terms link. Read the instructions, and then enter your first and last name and your school name. Click the PLAY button. When your score is displayed, right-click the score and then click Print on the shortcut menu to print a hard copy.

6 Crossword Puzzle Challenge

Below Photoshop Chapter 1, click the Crossword Puzzle Challenge link. Read the instructions, and then enter your first and last name. Click the SUBMIT button. Work the crossword puzzle. When you are finished, click the Submit button. When the crossword puzzle is redisplayed, click the Print Puzzle button to print a hard copy.

7 Tips and Tricks

Below Photoshop Chapter 1, click the Tips and Tricks link. Click a topic that pertains to Chapter 1. Right-click the information and then click Print on the shortcut menu. Construct a brief example of what the information relates to in Photoshop to confirm you understand how to use the tip or trick.

8 Expanding Your Horizons

Below Photoshop Chapter 1, click the Expanding Your Horizons link. Click a topic that pertains to Chapter 1. Print the information. Construct a brief example of what the information relates to in Photoshop to confirm you understand the contents of the article.

9 Search Sleuth

Below Photoshop Chapter 1, click the Search Sleuth link. To search for a term that pertains to this project, select a term below the Chapter 1 title and then use the Google search engine at google.com (or any major search engine) to display and print two Web pages that present information on the term.

10 Photoshop Online Training

Below Photoshop Chapter 1, click the Photoshop Online Training link. When your browser displays the Web page, click one of the Photoshop tutorials that covers one or more of the objectives listed at the beginning of the chapter on page PS 4. Print the first page of the tutorial before stepping through it.

Apply Your Knowledge

1 Editing and Printing a Photo

Instructions: The following steps start Photoshop, reset the workspace and tool settings, and then open a photo. The required photo can be found on the CD that accompanies this book in the Chapter01 folder, or in a location specified by your instructor.

The photo you open is a picture of Black-Eyed Susan flower with a honeybee. You are to edit the photo to focus on the honeybee and save it so it looks like Figure 1-74. You will prepare both a print and Web version of the photo.

FIGURE 1-74

1. Start Photoshop. Click Workspace on the Window menu and then click Default Workspace.
2. On the Tools palette, right-click the second tool and then click Rectangular Marquee Tool in the list.
3. On the options bar, right-click the Rectangular Marquee Tool (M) button and then click Reset All Tools. When the Reset All Tools dialog box is displayed, click the OK button.
4. Using the Open command on the File menu, open the file, Honeybee.
5. On the File menu, click Save As. When the Save As dialog box displays, type the file name `Honeybee Edited`. Do not press the ENTER key. Click the Save in box arrow and choose your USB flash drive from the list. Click the Save button. If Photoshop displays a JPEG Options dialog box, click the OK button.
6. Click the Zoom Tool (Z) button on the Photoshop Tools palette. Click the flower with the honeybee until the magnification is 150 percent.
7. In the Navigator palette, drag the proxy view area to display the honeybee in the upper-right third of the photo.
8. Click the Crop Tool (C) button on the Photoshop Tools palette. Drag an area to crop, where the focus will be on the honeybee and the flower it sits on. Include as few of the other flowers as possible.
9. Press the ENTER key to complete the crop.
10. Save the file again, by clicking Save on the File menu. If Photoshop displays a JPEG Options dialog box, click the OK button.
11. Click the Go to Bridge button on the options bar. When the Adobe Bridge window is displayed, click the box arrow in the Bridge toolbar and then click Computer in the list.
12. When the list of locations is displayed, double-click your USB flash drive location.
13. At the bottom of the window, use the slider on the right side of the Bridge status bar to change the size of the display. Use the View menu to view the photos as thumbnails and then with details.
14. Close the Adobe Bridge window to return to the Adobe Photoshop window.
15. Press the F1 key to access Adobe Help. When the Adobe Help Viewer 1.1 window is displayed, click the Search box and then type `desktop printing`. Press the ENTER key.
16. When Photoshop displays the help topics on desktop printing, click three different topics, one at a time. Read each one. Choose one of the help topics to print, and then click the Print the current page button (Figure 1-72 on page PS 54) on the Adobe Help toolbar.
17. Close the Adobe Help window. When Photoshop again displays the Honeybee Edited photo, click Print One Copy on the File menu.
18. Turn in the hard copies of the photo and the help topic to your instructor.
19. Quit Photoshop.

In the Lab

1 Using Precise Measurements to Crop and Resize a Photo

Problem: As a member of your high school reunion committee, it is your task to assemble the class photo directory. You are to edit the photo of a high school picture and prepare it for print in the reunion directory. The photo needs to fit in a space 1.75 inches high and 1.33 inches wide. Each photo needs to have approximately the same amount of space above the headshot — .25 inches. The edited photo is displayed in Figure 1-75.

FIGURE 1-75

Instructions:

1. Start Photoshop. Perform the customization steps found on pages PS 8 through PS 10.
2. Open the file, Student, from the Chapter01 folder on the CD that accompanies this book, or in a location specified by your instructor.
3. Use the Save As command on the File menu to save the file on your storage device with the name, Student Edited. If Photoshop displays a JPEG Options dialog box, click the OK button.
4. Use the Navigator palette to zoom the photo to 50 percent magnification, if necessary.
5. If the rulers do not display, press CTRL+R to view the rulers.
6. Drag from the horizontal ruler down into the photo until the green ruler guide touches the top of the student's head. Obtain the vertical measurement of the top of the student's head by measuring where the line touches the vertical ruler. Drag a second ruler guide to a position .25 inches above the first one. If you make a mistake while dragging a ruler guide, click Undo New Guide on the Edit menu.
7. Select the Crop tool. Drag from the left margin at the upper green line, down and to the right to include all the lower portion of the photo. *Hint:* If your selection is not perfect, press the ESC key and then drag again.
8. Press the ENTER key. If your crop does not seem correct, click the Undo command on the Edit menu and repeat Steps 6 and 7.
9. Once your photo has .25 inches of space above the student's head, save the photo again.
10. Click the Image Size command on the Image menu. When the Image Size dialog box is displayed in the Document Size area, type 1.75 in the Height box. Click the OK button.
11. Save the resized file with a new file name, Student for Print. If a JPEG Options dialog box is displayed, click the OK button.
12. Use the Print One Copy command on the File menu to print a copy of the photo.
13. Quit Photoshop.
14. Send the photo as an e-mail attachment to your instructor, or follow your instructor's directions for submitting the lab assignment.

In the Lab

2 Creating a Border

Problem: The owner of Birdhouses Incorporated is preparing a booklet to ship along with the custom ordered birdhouses he creates for his clientele. He would like you to take one of the pictures he has taken of a finch atop a tree and create a bordered photo of just the finch. The blended border should be black with a normal blend and 30 pixels wide to match the other bird photos in the booklet.

   The edited photo is displayed in Figure 1-76.

Instructions:

1. Start Photoshop. Perform the customization steps found on pages PS 8 through PS 10.
2. Open the file, Finch, from the Chapter01 folder on the CD that accompanies this book, or in a location specified by your instructor.
3. Use the Save As command on the File menu to save the file on your storage device with the name, Finch Edited. If a JPEG Options dialog box is displayed, click the OK button.
4. Click the Zoom Tool (Z) button on the Tools palette. Click the bird to center it in the display. Zoom in as necessary so you can make precise edits.
5. Crop the picture with approximately .75 inches on all four sides of the bird. Use the ruler to help you determine how much room to leave around the bird.
6. Save the photo again.
7. Press CTRL+A to select all of the photo.
8. To create the border, do the following:
   a. On the Select menu, point to Modify, and then click Border.
   b. When the Border Selection dialog box is displayed, type 50 in the Width Box. Click OK.
   c. Press SHIFT+F5 to access the Fill command.
   d. When the Fill dialog box is displayed, click the Use box arrow and then click Black in the list.
   e. Click the Mode box arrow and then click Normal in the list, if necessary.
   f. If necessary, type 100 in the Opacity box. Click the OK button.
9. Save the photo again.
10. Use the Print One Copy command on the File menu to print a copy of the photo.
11. Close the document window.
12. Quit Photoshop.
13. Send the photo as an e-mail attachment to your instructor, or follow your instructor's directions for submitting the lab assignment.

FIGURE 1-76

In the Lab

3 Preparing a Photo for the Web

Problem: As an independent consultant in Web site design, you have been hired by the Pineapple Growers Association to prepare a photo of an exotic pineapple growing in a field for use on the association's Web site. The edited photo is displayed in Figure 1-77.

Instructions:

1. Start Photoshop. Perform the customization steps found on pages PS 8 through PS 10.
2. Open the file, Pineapple, from the Chapter01 folder on the CD that accompanies this book, or in a location specified by your instructor.
3. Resize the photo to 500 pixels wide.
4. Use the Save As command on the File menu to save the file on your storage device with the name, Pineapple Edited. If Photoshop displays a JPEG Options dialog box, click the OK button.
5. On the Help menu, click Photoshop Help. Search for the word, Optimization. Read about optimizing for the Web. Print a copy of the help topic and then close the Adobe Help window.
6. When the Photoshop window again is displayed, click Save for Web & Devices on the File menu.
7. When the Save For Web & Devices dialog box is displayed, click the 4-Up tab.
8. Click the Zoom Level box arrow in the lower-left corner of the dialog box and then click Fit on Screen.

FIGURE 1-77

9. Right-click any of the previews and choose the connection speed of your Internet connection. See your instructor if you are not sure of your connection speed.
10. Click the preview that looks the best on the screen.
11. Make the following changes to the Save for Web & Devices settings at the right side of the Save For Web & Devices dialog box. Some of the settings already may be set correctly. If you are unsure of a setting, point to the setting to display its tool tip.
    a. Click the Color reduction algorithm box arrow, and then click Selective in the list.
    b. Click the Specify the dither algorithm box arrow, and then click Noise in the list.
    c. Click the Maximum number of colors in the Color Table box arrow, and then click 256 in the list.
12. For extra credit, create a Web page by doing the following lettered steps. Otherwise skip to Step 13.
    a. Click the Preview in Default Browser button in the lower-right corner on the Save For Web status bar.
    b. The Web preview will open a browser window. In the lower portion of the window, the browser will display the HTML code necessary to display the picture as a Web page. Drag the code to select it. Press CTRL+C to copy it.
    c. Open a text editor program such as Notepad or TextPad and press CTRL+V to paste the code into the editing window. Save the file as Pineapple.html in the same folder as your photo. Close the text editor.
    d. Click the Close button in the browser window.

(continued)

Preparing a Photo for the Web *(continued)*

13. Click the Save button in the Save For Web & Devices dialog box. When the Save Optimized As dialog box is displayed, click the Save button.
14. Close the document window and quit Photoshop.
15. Send the GIF file to your instructor.
16. If you did the extra credit, view your HTML file as a Web page. See your instructor for instructions on uploading the GIF and HTML files to a server or other ways to submit your assignment.

Cases and Places

The difficulty of these case studies varies:
🔶 are the least difficult and 🔶🔶 are the most difficult. The last exercise is a group exercise.

1 🔶 Your cousin Steve has dropped by to tell you about his recent vacation. While you look at his photos, Steve admits he is not the best photographer. He asks you if you can enhance one of his photos on the computer. After starting Photoshop, you select the photo, Park Statue, from the Chapter01 folder on the CD that accompanies this book. Save the photo on your USB flash drive storage device as Park Statue Edited. Crop the photo to remove the excess sky and add a black border of approximately 100 pixels. Save the photo again and print a copy for your instructor.

2 🔶 You are an intern with the Chamber of Commerce. In cooperation with the town, the old historic district has been revitalized. The Chamber of Commerce wants to publish a brochure about the old historic district with high-quality photos to help attract tourism. The photo submitted by the Chamber of Commerce is named Walkway and is located in the Chapter01 folder on the CD that accompanies this book. Crop the photo at both the bottom and right to focus attention on the many store fronts. Keep the old-fashioned light fixture and the oval wall plaque in the photo.

3 🔶🔶 Use a scanner to scan a favorite photo. Using the scanner's software, save the photo in the highest possible resolution, using the most color settings. Bring the picture into Photoshop and save it on your storage device. Crop it to remove extra background images. Use the rule of thirds to focus on the main point of interest. Resize the photo to fit your favorite frame. Add a blended border if it will not detract from the images in the photo. Send the edited photo via e-mail to a friend or use it in a page layout program to create a greeting card.

4 🔶🔶 Look through magazines or newspapers for color photos that might be cropped. If possible, cut out three photos and mark them with cropping lines. Write a short paragraph for each one describing why you think the photo could benefit from cropping. If the cropped photo needs to be resized, give the exact dimensions. List at least two uses for the photo, other than the one in which it was displayed. Attach the photos to the descriptions and submit them to your instructor.

5 🔶🔶 **Working Together** Your school would like to display a picture of the main building or student center on the Web site's home page. Your team has been assigned to take the photo and optimize it for the Web. Using a digital camera or camera phone, each team member should take a picture of the building from various angles. As a team, open each digital file and choose one or two that best incorporate the styles and suggestions in this chapter. Choose a border that highlights the color and dynamic of the photo. Resize the photo to less than 500 x 500 pixels. As a group, make decisions in the Save For Web & Devices dialog box on the 4-Up tab as to which optimization would best suit the school's needs. Show the final products to another person or group in your class for suggestions. Submit the best one to your instructor.

ADOBE
Photoshop CS3

Using Selection Tools

CHAPTER

2

CASE PERSPECTIVE

Kevin Bernard leads the graphic design team at Achievement Advertising Agency, a medium-sized firm that caters to small business accounts. As an aggressive and versatile firm, they believe in the fundamentals of communication strategies and have developed a reputation for effective, on-target marketing. The agency's marketing strategy is to maximize exposure and response to the client's products and needs.

Kevin has hired you as a graphic design intern with the company. Your first assignment is to work on a gift shop catalog the ad agency is producing. The gift shop owner has submitted an illustration with candles and candies for the catalog. When complete, the gift shop catalog will consist of 48 pages with full color photos, illustrations, and descriptions of the various gifts sold by the company. One full page of the catalog measures 8 × 11 inches. This illustration, ultimately to be used with text describing the product, is to fill one-half of the page, approximately 8 × 5½ inches. The catalog will be mailed to a large population in time for the holiday season. Kevin has asked you to create a visually pleasing layout of these candles and candies, as a single image, which will appear in the catalog next to the description and pricing.

The copy editors will write the text description and price list around your finished image. With your basic knowledge of Photoshop, you decide to explore the selection tools to copy, transform, clone, and move the objects into an attractive display. Kevin suggests you try to straighten the tall candle in your final layout.

As you read through this chapter, you will learn how to use the marquee tools, the lasso tools, the Quick Selection and Magic Wand tools, and the Move tool in Photoshop to make selections and rearrange objects in a photo. You also will apply transformations to selected objects.

Using Selection Tools

Objectives

You will have mastered the material in this chapter when you can:

- Explain the terms perspective, layout, and storyboard
- Describe selection tools
- Open a file, select objects in a photo, and save a file
- Use the marquee tools
- Move a selection
- Make transformation edits

- View states in the History palette
- Employ the lasso tools
- Add and subtract from selections
- Create ruler guides
- Select objects using the Quick Selection and the Magic Wand tools
- Create new keyboard shortcuts

Introduction

In Chapter 1, you learned about the Photoshop interface as well as navigation and zooming techniques. You cropped and resized a photo, added a border, and saved the photo for both Web and print media. You learned about online Help, along with opening, saving, and printing photos. This chapter continues to emphasize those topics and presents some new ones.

Recall that specifying or isolating an area of your photo for editing is called making a selection. By selecting specific areas, you can edit and apply special effects to portions of your image while leaving the unselected areas untouched. The new topics covered in this chapter include the marquee tools to select rectangular or elliptical areas, the lasso tools to choose freeform segments or shapes, and the Quick Selection and Magic Wand tools to select consistently colored areas. Finally, you will learn how to use transformation tools and cut, copy, paste, drag, and drop those selections.

Chapter Two — Using Selection Tools

Chapter 2 illustrates the creation of an advertising piece used in a gift catalog. You will begin with the image in Figure 2-1a that shows candles and candies that are for sale by the owner of the gift shop. You then will manipulate the image by selecting, editing, and moving the objects to produce a more attractive layout, creating Figure 2-1b that will be displayed in the gift catalog.

(a) original photo

(b) edited photo

FIGURE 2-1

Figure 2-2 illustrates the design decisions made to create the final advertising piece. An attractive layout using multiple objects is a good marketing strategy, visually and subconsciously encouraging the viewer to purchase more than one item. **Layout** refers to placing visual elements into a pleasing and readable arrangement, suggestive of how the product or products might look in a buyer's home. Advertising or product designers try to determine how the target consumer will use the product and group objects accordingly.

From a design point of view, creating a visual diagonal line between the tall candles, along with the rule of thirds, creates perspective. **Perspective** is the technique photographers, designers, and artists use to create the illusion of three dimensions on a flat or two-dimensional surface. Perspective is a means of fooling the eye by making it appear as if there is depth or receding space in the image. Adjusting the sizes and juxtaposing the objects creates asymmetrical balance and visual tension between the featured products. The diagonal alignment of the tall candles leads the viewer to the background, as does the placement of candy in front of the short candle.

The horizon line in perspective drawing is a virtual horizontal line across the picture. The placement of the horizon line determines from where the viewer seems to be looking, such as from a high place, or from close to the ground. In the candle scene, the horizon line runs across the center of the drawing. The viewer is high enough to see the top of the short candles.

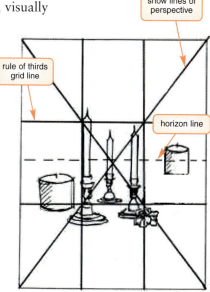

diagonals show lines of perspective

rule of thirds grid line

horizon line

FIGURE 2-2

Using white space, or non-image area, is effective in directing the viewer to see what is important. The products, grouped this way, are in a sense framed by the white space.

This product layout, using the rule of thirds grids, also helps other members of the design team when it is time to make decisions about type placement. The group of products can be shifted up or down, as one image, to accommodate the layout and text including the font sizes, placement, title, description, and price information. The rule of thirds offers a useful means to make effective layouts for image and text.

Designing a preliminary layout sketch, similar to Figure 2-2, to help you make choices about placement, size, perspective, and spacing is referred to as creating a **storyboard**, **thumbnail**, or **rough**.

Starting and Customizing Photoshop

To start and customize Photoshop, Windows must be running. If you are stepping through this project on a computer and you want your screen to match the figures in this book, then you should change your computer's resolution to 1024 × 768 and reset the tools and palettes. For more information about how to change the resolution on your computer, and other advanced Photoshop settings, read Appendix A.

The following steps describe how to start Photoshop and customize the Photoshop window. You may need to ask your instructor how to start Photoshop for your system.

To Start Photoshop

1 Click the Start button on the Windows taskbar, point to All Programs on the Start menu, and then click Adobe Photoshop CS3 on the All Programs submenu.

2 After a few moments, if Photoshop displays a Welcome screen, click the Close button on the Welcome Screen.

3 If the Adobe Photoshop window is not maximized, double-click its title bar to maximize it.

4 Click Window on the Photoshop menu bar, point to Workspace on the Window menu, and then click Default Workspace on the Workspace submenu.

5 Right-click the second button on the Tools palette and then click Rectangular Marquee Tool on the context menu.

6 Right-click the Rectangular Marquee Tool (M) button on the options bar and then click Reset All Tools. When Photoshop displays a confirmation dialog box, click the OK button.

Photoshop starts and, after a few moments, displays the palettes in the workspace. Photoshop resets the tools, palettes, and options.

Opening a File

To open a file in Photoshop, it must be stored as a digital file on your computer system. The photos and images used in this book are stored on a CD located in the back of the book. Your instructor may designate a different location for the photos.

The following steps illustrate how to open the file, Candles, from a CD located in drive E.

To Open a File

1 Insert the CD that accompanies this book into your CD drive. After a few seconds, if Windows displays a dialog box, click its Close button.

2 With the Photoshop Window open, click File on the menu bar and then click Open.

3 When the Open dialog box is displayed, click the Look in box arrow, and then click drive E or the drive associated with your CD.

4 Double-click the Chapter02 folder, and then click the file Candles to select it.

5 Click the Open button.

More About

Document Window Status Bar

The status bar of the document window in Figure 2-3 shows the current document size. If you would like to display the document dimensions, click the status bar menu button, point to Show, and then click Document Dimensions.

6 When Photoshop displays the image in the document window, if the magnification is not 25% as shown on the title bar, double-click the magnification box on the document window status bar, type 25, and then press the ENTER key.

Photoshop opens the file Candles from the CD in drive E. The image is displayed in the document window at 25% magnification (Figure 2-3).

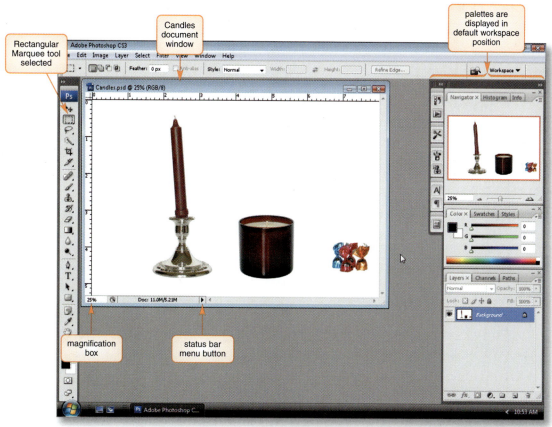

FIGURE 2-3

Table 2-1 displays information about the Candles photo. It was created as a Photoshop document and is stored as a PSD file. **Photoshop Document format** (**PSD**) is the default file format and the only format that supports all of the Photoshop features. Like most file formats, PSD can support files up to 2 GB in size. Adobe applications can directly import PSD files and preserve many Photoshop features, as can most page layout applications.

Table 2-1 Candles Image Characteristics	
File Name	Candles
File Type	PSD
Image Dimensions	8 × 5.333 inches
Color Mode	RGB
Resolution	300 pixels/inch
File Size	1, 574 KB

Saving a File

Even though you have yet to edit the photo, it is a good practice to save the file on your personal storage device early in the process. The next step is to save the photo with the name Candles Edited, as the steps on the next page illustrate.

To Save a Photo

1 With your USB flash drive connected to one of the computer's USB ports, click File on the menu bar and then click Save As.

2 When the Save As dialog box is displayed, type `Candles Edited` in the File name text box. Do not press the ENTER key after typing the file name.

3 Click the Save in box arrow and then click USB (F:), or the location associated with your USB flash drive, in the list.

The Save As dialog box is displayed (Figure 2-4). Other files on your storage device may not be listed because the Save As dialog box is displaying only PSD files.

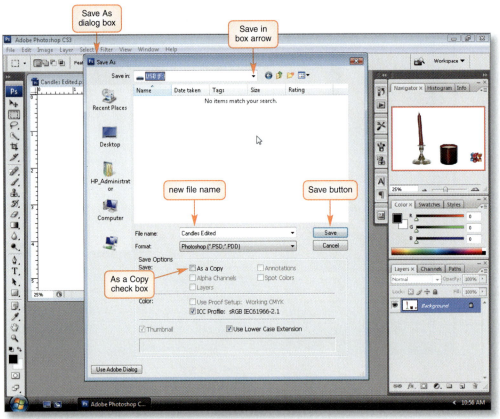

FIGURE 2-4

4 Click the Save button in the Save As dialog box.

Photoshop saves the file on the USB flash drive with the file name Candles Edited, and displays the new name on the document window title bar. Although the image is saved on a storage device, it also remains in main memory and is displayed on the screen.

The Save As dialog box (Figure 2-4) also contains the **As a Copy check box**. When checked, Photoshop automatically appends the word, copy, to the file name, thus allowing you to save a second copy of the file in the same location. A copy file has the same attributes and can be edited in the same manner as the original file. Making multiple copies of an original file also is useful if you want to make and save several different versions of a layout.

In the following sections, you will learn about the various selection tools available in Photoshop, including the marquee tools, the lasso tools, the Quick Selection tool, and the Magic Wand tool, as you make changes to the Candles Edited file.

More About

Saving

Working off your USB drive is convenient if you are in a public lab. At home, it is recommended that you work off your hard drive, in a folder such as My Documents, as a hard drive is more reliable and faster when saving files.

The Marquee Tools

The **marquee tools** let you draw a marquee that selects a portion of the document window. A **marquee** is a selection that displays with a flashing or pulsating selection border sometimes described as marching ants. Marquees are useful when the part of an image or photo that you wish to select fits into rectangular or elliptical shapes. Photoshop has four marquee tools (Figure 2-5) that display in a context menu when you click the tool and hold down the mouse button, or right-click the tool. You can select any of the marquee tools from this context menu.

The **Rectangle Marquee tool** is the default marquee tool that selects a rectangular or square portion of the image or photo. The **Elliptical Marquee tool** allows you to select an ellipsis, oval, or circular area.

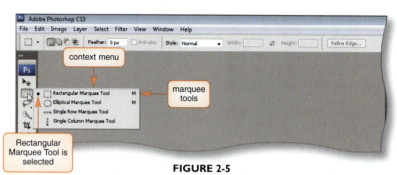

FIGURE 2-5

Dragging with the Rectangular or Elliptical Marquee tools creates a marquee drawn from a corner. If you press the SHIFT key while dragging a marquee, Photoshop **constrains** the proportions of the shape creating a perfect square or circle. If you press the ALT key while drawing a selection, the marquee is created from the center. Pressing SHIFT+ALT starts from the center and constrains the proportions.

The **Single Row Marquee tool** allows you to select a single row of pixels. The **Single Column Marquee tool** allows you to select a single column of pixels. You must choose the row and column marquees from the context menu — there is no keyboard shortcut. A single click in the document window creates the selection. Because a single row or column of pixels is so small, it is easier to use these two marquee tools at higher magnifications.

Table 2-2 describes the four marquee tools.

Table 2-2   The Marquee Tools

TOOL	PURPOSE	SHORTCUT	BUTTON
Rectangular Marquee	selects a rectangular or square portion of the document window	M SHIFT+M toggles to Elliptical Marquee	
Elliptical Marquee	selects an elliptical or oval portion of the document window	M SHIFT+M toggles to Rectangular Marquee	
Single Row Marquee	selects a single row of pixels in the document window	(none)	
Single Column Marquee	selects a single column of pixels in the document window	(none)	

The Marquee Options Bar

The options bar associated with each of the marquee tools displays many buttons and settings to draw effective marquees (Figure 2-6 on the next page). The options bar displays the chosen marquee on the left followed by the Tool Preset picker. The **Tool Preset picker** allows you to save and reuse toolbar settings. You will learn how to save toolbar settings in a later chapter.

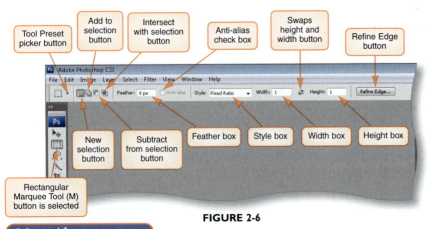

Tool Preset picker button

Add to selection button

Intersect with selection button

Anti-alias check box

Swaps height and width button

Refine Edge button

New selection button

Subtract from selection button

Feather box

Style box

Width box

Height box

Rectangular Marquee Tool (M) button is selected

FIGURE 2-6

The options bar associated with each of the marquee tools displays four buttons to adjust the selection (Figure 2-6). The **New selection button** allows you to draw a new marquee.

The **Add to selection button** allows you to draw an adjacent rectangle or ellipsis to expand the selection. The Add to selection button is useful for selecting the extra corners of an L-shaped object or for shapes that do not fit within a single rectangle or ellipsis. To activate the Add to selection button, you can click it on the options bar or hold down the SHIFT key while dragging a second selection. When adding to a selection, the mouse pointer changes to a crosshair with a plus sign.

The **Subtract from selection button** allows you to deselect or remove a portion of an existing selection. The new rectangle or ellipsis is removed from the original selection. It is useful for removing block portions of the background around oddly shaped images or for deselecting ornamentation in an object. To activate the Subtract from selection button, you can click it on the options bar, or hold down the ALT key while dragging. When subtracting from a selection, the mouse pointer changes to a crosshair with a minus sign.

The **Intersect with selection button** allows you to draw a second rectangle or ellipsis across a portion of the previously selected area, resulting in a selection border only around the area in which the two selections intersect. When creating an intersection, the mouse pointer changes to a crosshair with an x.

Once an area has been selected, there are options for further manipulating the selected area. Right-clicking a selection provides access to many other useful commands such as deselecting, or selecting the **inverse**, which means selecting everything in the image except the previous selection. Right-clicking a selection also enables you to create layers, apply color fills and strokes, and make other changes to a selection, which you will learn about in future chapters.

To the right of the selection buttons, the options bar displays a Feather box. **Feathering** softens the edges of the selection for blending into backgrounds. The width of the feather is measured in pixels. When using the Elliptical Marquee tool, you can further specify blending by selecting the **Anti-alias check box** to adjust the blocklike, staircase look of rounded corners. Figure 2-7 shows a rectangle with no feathering and one with 5 pixels of feathering. Figure 2-7 also shows an ellipsis with no anti-aliasing and one created with a check mark in the Anti-alias check box.

When using the Rectangle Marquee tool or the Elliptical Marquee tool, you can click the **Style box arrow** to choose how the size of the marquee selection is determined. A **Normal** style sets the selection marquee proportions by dragging. A **Fixed Aspect Ratio** style sets a height-to-width ratio using decimal values. For example, to draw a marquee twice as wide as it

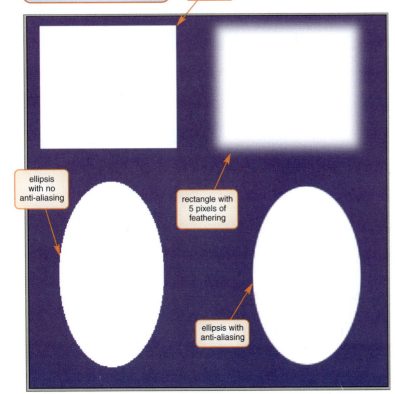

rectangle with no feathering

ellipsis with no anti-aliasing

rectangle with 5 pixels of feathering

ellipsis with anti-aliasing

FIGURE 2-7

is high, type 2 for the width and 1 for the height. **Fixed Size** allows you to specify exact pixel values for the marquee's height and width. The **Refine Edge button** is new to Photoshop CS3. When clicked, it opens a dialog box where you can make choices about improving selections with jagged edges, soft transitions, hazy borders, or fine details.

Using the Rectangular Marquee Tool

The following step illustrates how to select the short candle in the Candles Edited image, using the Rectangular Marquee tool.

To Use the Rectangular Marquee Tool

1

• **Right-click the Rectangular Marquee Tool (M) button on the Tools palette and then click Rectangular Marquee Tool. If necessary, on the options bar, click the New selection button.**

• **In the photo, use the mouse to draw a rectangle as close as possible around the short candle.**

The selection border, or marquee, pulsates around the short candle (Figure 2-8). The mouse pointer displays an arrow with a selection rectangle.

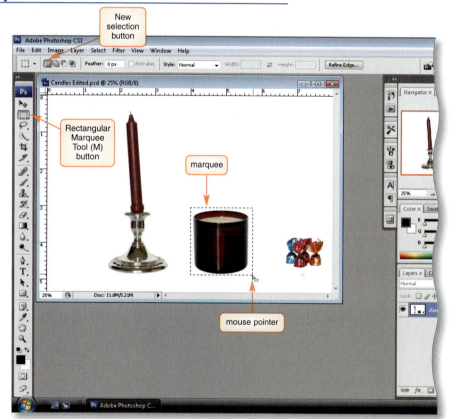

FIGURE 2-8

If you make a mistake or change your mind when drawing a marquee, you can do one of three things. 1) If you want to start over, you can click somewhere else in the document window to deselect the marquee; then, simply draw a new marquee. 2) If you have already drawn the marquee, but wish to move or reposition it, you can drag the selection to the new location. 3) If you want to reposition while you are creating the marquee, do not release the mouse button. Press and hold the SPACEBAR, drag the marquee to the new location, and then release the SPACEBAR. At that point, you can continue dragging to finish drawing the marquee.

If you were to drag a newly defined marquee, the image inside the marquee would not move. Dragging a marquee only moves the selection border to outline a new portion of the image. To move the selection border and its contents, you use the Move tool.

The Move Tool

The **Move tool** on the Photoshop Tools palette is used to move or make other changes to selections. Activating the Move tool by clicking the Move Tool (V) button or pressing the V key on the keyboard allows you to move the selection border and its contents by dragging them in the document window. When you first begin to drag with the Move tool, the mouse pointer changes to an arrow with scissors indicating a cut from the original position. To move the selection in a straight line, press and hold the SHIFT key before dragging. If you press and hold the ALT key before dragging, you **duplicate** or move only a copy of the selected area, effectively copying and pasting the selection. While moving a copy, the mouse pointer changes to a black arrow with a white arrow behind it.

When you move selections, you need to be careful about overlapping images. As you will learn in Chapter 3, Photoshop layers or overlaps portions of images when you move them. While that sometimes is preferred when creating collages or composite images, it is undesirable if an important object is obscured. Close tracing while creating selections, and careful placement of moved selections, will prevent unwanted layering.

The Move Options Bar

The Move options bar displays tools to help define the scope of the move (Figure 2-9). Later, as you learn about layers, you will use the **Auto-Select check box** to select layer groupings or single layers, designated in the Groups box. When selected, the **Show Transform Controls check box** causes Photoshop to display sizing handles on the selection border and adds a center reference point indicator to the selection. The align and distribute buttons help position selections when more than one layer is selected. The **Auto-Align Layers button** can align layers automatically, based on similar content such as corners and edges.

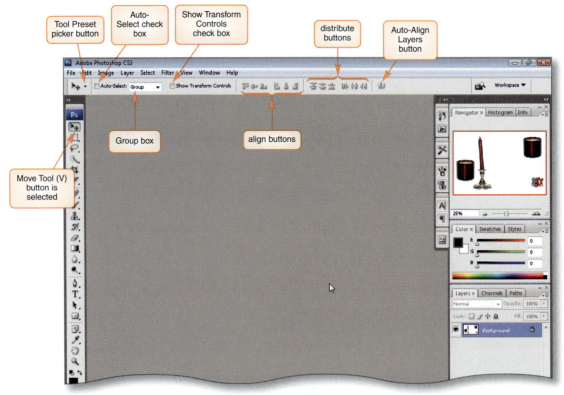

FIGURE 2-9

Using the Move Tool

The next step in preparing the layout for the catalog involves rearranging the components of the original image. Using the Move tool, the short candle is moved to the left of the tall candle and slightly higher in the image. Then a copy of the candle is moved to a location above the single piece of candy. The following steps show how to use the Move tool.

To Use the Move Tool

1

• **With the short candle still selected, click the Move Tool (V) button on the Tools palette. If necessary, on the options bar, click the Auto-Select check box so it does not display a check mark. If necessary, click the Show Transform Controls check box so it does not display its check mark.**

The Move Tool (V) button is selected (Figure 2-10).

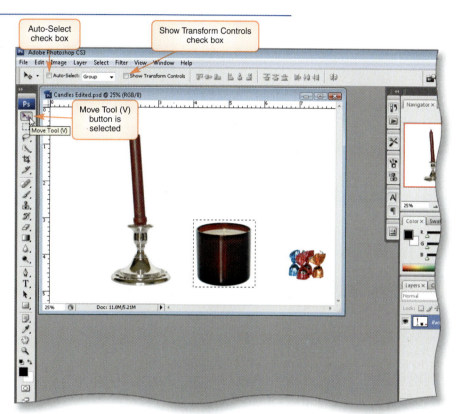

FIGURE 2-10

2

• **Drag the candle to a position left of the tall candle and slightly higher. Do not allow the moved selection to overlap any portion of the tall candle.**

Photoshop moves the selection and displays the short candle to the left of the tall candle (Figure 2-11).

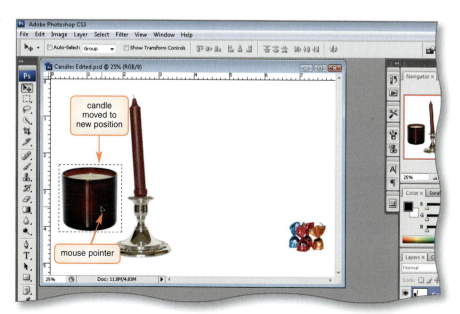

FIGURE 2-11

3

• **With the short candle still selected, press and hold the ALT key and then drag the selection to a location above the candy.**

Photoshop copies the selection to the new location (Figure 2-12).

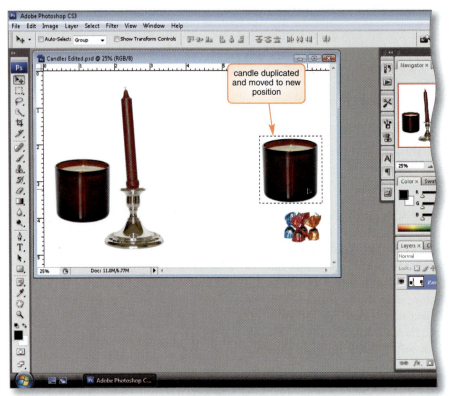

candle duplicated and moved to new position

FIGURE 2-12

Just as you do in other applications, you can use the Cut, Copy, and Paste commands from the Edit menu or shortcut keys to make changes to selections. Unless you predefine a selection area by dragging a marquee, the Paste command pastes to the center of the document window.

The copy of the short candle now will be resized using a transformation command as described in the next section.

The Transformation Commands

In Photoshop, the word **transform** refers to making physical changes to a selection. To choose a transformation command, click the Edit menu, point to Transform, and then click the desired transformation. Or, you can click Transform Selection on the shortcut menu that is displayed when you right-click the selection.

When you choose a transformation or when you click the Show Transform Controls check box on the Move options bar, Photoshop displays a **bounding box** or border with six sizing handles around the selection (Figure 2-13). A small **reference point** or fixed pivot point is displayed in the center of the selection.

If you click a sizing handle or the reference point of the bounding box, you enter transformation mode. In **transformation mode**, the Transform options bar

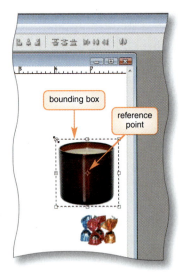

bounding box

reference point

FIGURE 2-13

(Figure 2-14 on the next page) is displayed and the associated shortcut menu displays the transformation commands. In transformation mode, the bounding box displays a solid line on the top and left, and a pulsating line on the bottom and right.

Table 2-3 lists the types of transformations you can perform on a selection, the techniques used to perform the transformation, and the result of the transformation. If you choose **Free Transform**, you must use the mouse techniques to perform the transformation.

Table 2-3 Transformation Commands			
CHOOSE A TRANSFORMATION FROM THE MENU	USING THE MOUSE (FREE TRANSFORM)	USING THE OPTIONS BAR	RESULT
Scale	Drag a sizing handle on the bounding box; SHIFT+drag to scale proportionately.	To scale numerically, enter percentages in the Width and Height boxes, shown as W and H, on the options bar. Click the Link icon to maintain the aspect ratio.	Selection is displayed at a different size.
Rotate Rotate 180° Rotate 90° CW Rotate 90° CCW	Move the mouse pointer outside the bounding box border. It becomes a curved, two-headed arrow. Drag in the direction you wish to rotate. SHIFT+drag to constrain the rotation to 15° increments.	In the Rotate box, type a positive number for clockwise rotation or a negative number for counter-clockwise rotation.	Selection is rotated or revolved around a reference point.
Skew	Drag a side of the bounding box. ALT+drag to skew both vertically and horizontally.	To skew numerically, enter decimal values in the horizontal skew and vertical skew boxes on the options bar.	Selection is slanted or tilted, either vertically or horizontally.
Distort	Drag a corner sizing handle to stretch the bounding box.	Enter new numbers in the location, size, rotation, and skew boxes.	Selection is larger on one edge of the selection than the others.
Perspective	Drag a corner sizing handle to apply perspective to the bounding box.	Enter new numbers in the size, rotation, and skew boxes.	A portion of the selection appears closer on one edge than the others.
Warp	When the warp mesh is displayed, drag any line or point.	Click the Custom box arrow. Click a custom warp.	Selection is displayed reshaped with bulge, arch, wrapped corner, or twist.
Flip Horizontal Flip Vertical	Flipping is available only on the menu.	Flipping is available only on the menu.	Selection is displayed upside down or rotated 90 degrees.

After you are finished making transformations, you **commit changes** or apply the transformations by pressing the ENTER key or by clicking the Commit transform (Return) button on the Transform options bar. If you change your mind and do not wish to make the transformation, selecting another tool will cause a dialog box to display. Click the Don't Apply button in the dialog box.

The Transform Options Bar

To display the Transform options bar, create a selection and then press CTRL+T. Photoshop displays a Transform options bar (Figure 2-14a) or a Warp options bar (Figure 2-14b) that contain boxes and buttons to help you with your transformation.

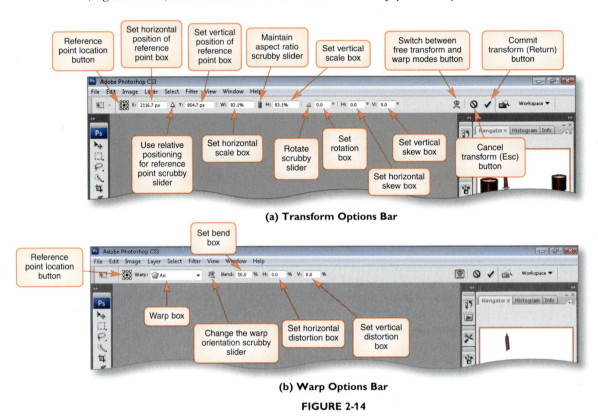

(a) Transform Options Bar

(b) Warp Options Bar

FIGURE 2-14

On the left side of the Transform options bar, Photoshop displays the **Reference point location button**. Each of the nine squares on the button corresponds to a point on the bounding box. Any transformations applied to the selection will be made in relation to the selected reference point. The middle square is selected by default. To select a different reference point, click a different square on the Reference point location button. The other boxes on the Transform options bar display information about the selected square's location in the document.

The X and Y boxes allow you to enter a horizontal and vertical location for the selected reference point, thus altering the location of the selection in the document. The new location is based on the actual pixel measurements entered. When you click the **Use relative positioning for reference point button** in between the X and Y boxes, the movement of the selection is relative to the current location of the selected reference point.

The W and H boxes allow you to scale the width and height of the selection. When you click the **Maintain aspect ratio button** between the W and H boxes, the aspect ratio of the selection is maintained.

To the right of the scale boxes is a Rotate box. Entering a positive number rotates the selection clockwise; a negative number rotates the selection counter-clockwise.

The H and V boxes, to the right of the Rotate box, set the horizontal and vertical skews of the selection, measured in degrees. A positive number skews the selection to the right; a negative number skews to the left.

A unique feature is the ability to drag the labels, called **scrubby sliders**, located left of the text boxes. For example, if you drag the H, Y, W, or other labels, the values in the text boxes change. Dragging to the right increases the value; dragging to the left decreases the value. When you point to any of the scrubby sliders on the Transform options bar, the mouse pointer changes to a hand with a double-headed arrow indicating its ability to drag.

On the far right of the Transform options bar are three special buttons. The first one switches between the Transform options bar and the Warp options bar. The second button cancels the transformation. The third button commits the transformation. After transforming a selection, you must cancel or commit the transformation before Photoshop will let you perform another action.

Scaling a Selection

As described in Table 2-3 on page PS 77, when you scale a selection, you resize it by changing its width, height, or both. The following steps illustrate how to use the Show Transform Controls check box to display the bounding box. Then, to reduce the size of the candle proportionally, the steps show how to transform freely by SHIFT+dragging a corner sizing handle.

To Scale a Selection

1

• **With the Move Tool (V) button still selected, click the Show Transform Controls check box on the options bar.**

• **Point to the upper-left sizing handle of the selection border.**

The mouse pointer changes to a two-headed arrow when positioned over a sizing handle (Figure 2-15).

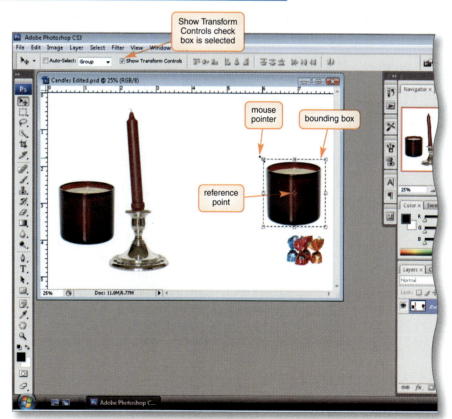

FIGURE 2-15

• SHIFT+drag the upper-left sizing handle toward the center of the candle until it is resized to approximately 75% of its original size.

The candle is resized. The W: and H: boxes on the options bar display 75% (Figure 2-16).

3

• Press the ENTER key to commit the change.

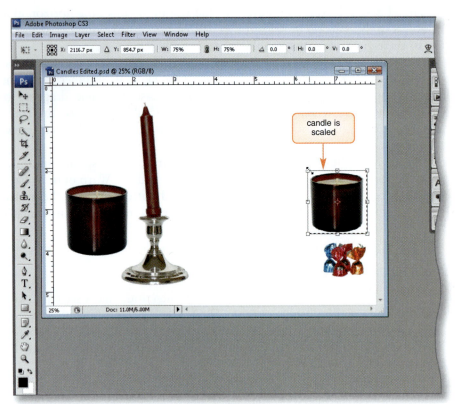

FIGURE 2-16

Photoshop allows you to apply some transformations to entire images or photos, rather than just selections. For example, you can change the size of the photo or rotate the image using the Image menu. You then can enter dimensions or rotation percentages on the submenu and subsequent dialog boxes.

The History Palette

The **History palette** is displayed by clicking the first button in the dock of collapsed palettes on the right side of the workspace. The History palette records each step, called a **state**, as you edit a photo. The initial state of the document is displayed at the top of the palette. Each time you apply a change to an image, the new state of that image is added to the bottom of the palette. Each state change is listed with the name of the tool or command used to change the image. For example, when you performed the scale transformation on the short candle, the words Free Transform were displayed as a step in the history of the file (Figure 2-17). The step just above Free Transform in the History palette denotes the duplication of the candle when you dragged a new copy to its current location.

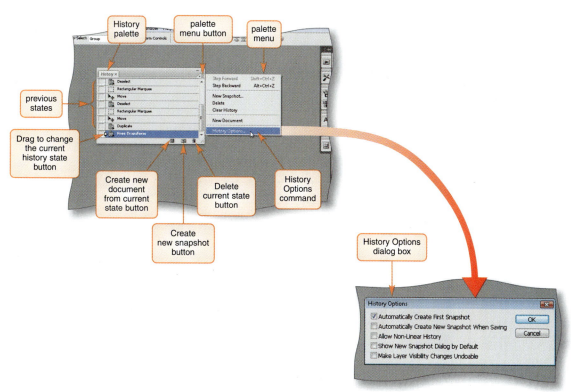

FIGURE 2-17

The History palette is used in several different ways. When you select one of the states, the image reverts to how it looked when that change first was applied. You can view the state temporarily, or start working again from that point. Selecting a state and then changing the image eliminates all the states in the History palette that came after it. If you select a state and change the image by accident, you can use the Undo command on the Edit menu to restore the eliminated states. By default, deleting a state deletes that state and those that came after it. If you select the Allow Non-Linear History box in the History Options dialog box, deleting a state deletes only that state.

You can use the History palette to jump to any recent state of the image created during the current working session by clicking the state. Alternately, you also can give a state a new name called a **snapshot**. Naming a snapshot makes it easy to identify. Snapshots are stored at the top of the history palette and make it easy to compare effects. For example you can take a snapshot before and after a series of transformations. Then, by clicking between the two snapshots in the History palette you can see the total effect or choose the before snapshot and start over. Snapshots are not saved with the image — closing an image deletes its snapshots. To create a snapshot, right-click the step and then click New Snapshot on the shortcut menu, or click the Create new snapshot button on the History palette status bar.

Not all steps are recorded in the History palette. For instance, changes to palettes, color settings, actions, and preferences, are not reflected in the History palette, because they are not changes to a particular image.

By default, the History palette lists the previous 20 states. You can change the number of remembered states by changing a preference setting (see Appendix A). Older states are automatically deleted to free more memory for Photoshop. Once you close and reopen the document, all states and snapshots from the last working session are cleared from the palette.

Using the History Palette

The following steps show how to use the History palette to view a previous state.

To Use the History Palette

1

• **Click the History button in the dock of collapsed palettes.**

• **When Photoshop displays the History palette, scroll as necessary and then click the Move state above the Free Transform and Duplicate states. Do not click anywhere else.**

The document window displays the candle before you created a second copy (Figure 2-18).

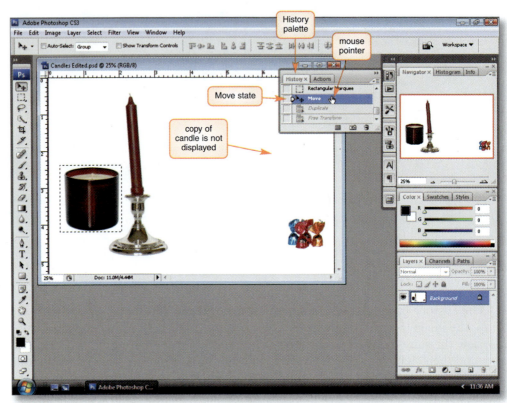

FIGURE 2-18

2

• **In the History palette, click the Free Transform state at the bottom of the list.**

The document window again displays the second candle, scaled to 75% (Figure 2-19).

3

• **Click the History button again, to collapse the palette.**

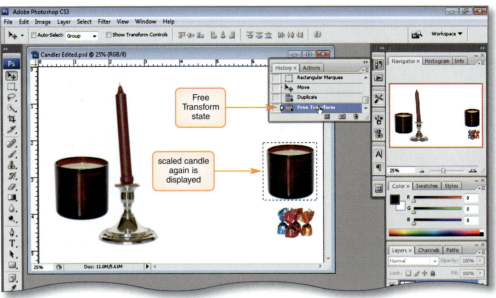

FIGURE 2-19

Like the Navigator palette that you learned about in Chapter 1, the History palette also has a palette menu where you can clear all states, change the history settings, or dock the palette (Figure 2-17 on page PS 81). To display the palette menu, click the History palette menu button. To move the palette, drag its title bar. To change the size of the palette, drag its border. Buttons on the History palette status bar allow you to create a new document, a new snapshot, or delete the selected state.

The Lasso Tools

The lasso tools are used to draw a freehand selection border around objects, which provides more flexibility than the marquee tools with their standardized shapes. There are three kinds of lasso tools. The first is the default **Lasso tool** that allows you to create a selection by using the mouse to drag around any object in the document window. You select the Lasso Tool (L) button on the Tools palette. You then begin to drag around the desired area. When you release the mouse, Photoshop connects the selection border to the point where you began dragging, finishing the loop. The Lasso tool is useful for a quick, rough selection.

The **Polygonal Lasso tool** is chosen from the Lasso tool context menu. It is similar to the Lasso tool in that it draws irregular shapes in the image; however, the Polygonal Lasso tool uses straight line segments. To use the Polygonal Lasso tool, choose the tool, click in the document window, release the mouse button, and then move the mouse in straight lines, clicking each time you turn a corner. When you get back to the beginning of the polygon, double-click to complete the selection.

The **Magnetic Lasso tool** also can be chosen from the context menu. You then click close to the edge of the object you wish to select. The Magnetic Lasso tool tries to find the edge of the object by looking for the closest color change and attaches the selection to the pixel on the edge of the color change. As you move the mouse, the Magnetic Lasso tool follows that change with a magnetic attraction. The magnetic lasso displays **fastening points** on the edge of the object. You can click points as you drag to force a change in direction or adjust the magnetic attraction. When you get all the way around the object, you click at the connection point to complete the loop, or double-click to have Photoshop connect the loop for you. Because the magnetic lasso looks for changes in color to define the edges of an object, it may not be very effective for making selections on images with a busy background or images with low contrast.

Table 2-4 describes the three lasso tools.

Table 2-4 The Lasso Tools

TOOL	PURPOSE	SHORTCUT	BUTTON
Lasso	Used to draw freeform segments of a selection border	L SHIFT+L toggles through all three lasso tools	
Polygonal Lasso	Used to draw straight-edged segments of a selection border	L SHIFT+L toggles through all three lasso tools	
Magnetic Lasso	Used to draw a selection border that snaps to the edges of defined areas in the image	L SHIFT+L toggles through all three lasso tools	

The Lasso Options Bar

Each of the lasso tools displays an options bar similar to the Marquee options bar, with buttons to add to, subtract from, and intersect with the selection, as well as the ability to feather the border. The Magnetic Lasso options bar (Figure 2-20) also includes an Anti-alias check box to smooth the borders of a selection. Unique to the Magnetic Lasso options bar, however, is a text box to enter the **contrast** or sensitivity of color that Photoshop will consider in making the path selection. A higher value detects only edges that contrast sharply with their surroundings; a lower value detects lower-contrast edges. The Width box causes the Magnetic Lasso tool to detect edges only within the specified distance from the mouse pointer. A **Frequency** box allows you to specify the rate at which the lasso sets fastening points. A higher value anchors the selection border in place more quickly. A **Use tablet pressure to change pen width button** on the right is used to change the pen width when using graphic drawing tablets instead of a mouse.

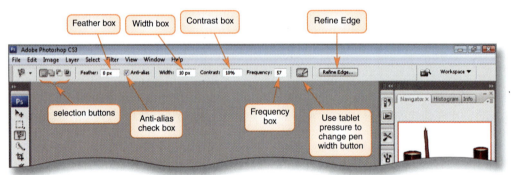

FIGURE 2-20

Using the Magnetic Lasso Tool

You will use the Magnetic Lasso tool to select the tall candle on top of the candle holder. You then will rotate and move the candle to straighten it. As you work with the Magnetic Lasso tool, remember that you can undo errors by clicking Undo on the Edit menu, and undo state changes by clicking the Delete button on the History palette status bar. Clicking as you turn corners with the Magnetic Lasso tool helps set the fastening points.

The following steps illustrate how to zoom to 50% magnification and resize the document window to facilitate selecting the candle.

To Zoom and Resize the Document Window

1 On the Navigator palette status bar, click the Zoom In button twice to display the document window at 50%.

2 Drag the lower-right corner of the document window to enlarge the display area.

3 Scroll the document window to display the entire tall candle.

The magnification increases, making the candle appear larger (Figure 2-21).

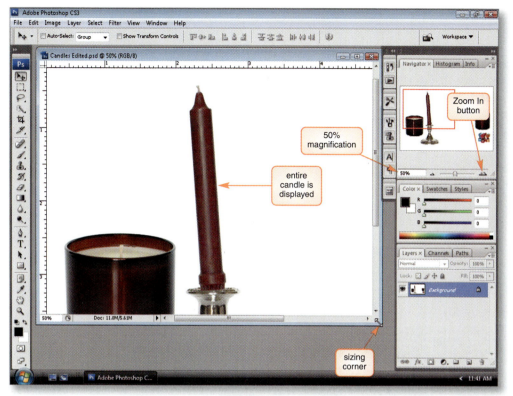

FIGURE 2-21

With the magnification increased, it now is easier to use the magnetic lasso to select the candle on top of the candle holder. In the following steps, the Magnetic Lasso Tool (L) button is selected and then the contrast is changed to 75 to detect only edges that contrast sharply with their surroundings, increasing the magnetism of the edge of the red candle on a white background.

As you use the Magnetic Lasso tool, if you make a mistake and want to start over, double-click to complete the lasso and then press CTRL+Z, click Undo on the Edit menu, or delete the state in the History palette. The following steps show how to use the Magnetic Lasso tool.

To Use the Magnetic Lasso Tool

1

• **Right-click the Lasso Tool (L) button on the Tools palette.**

The context menu is displayed (Figure 2-22).

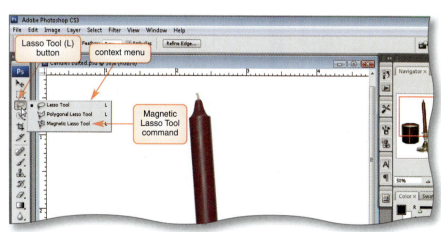

FIGURE 2-22

2

• **Click Magnetic Lasso Tool.**

• **If necessary, on the options bar, click the New selection button. Double-click the Contrast box and type** 75 **to replace the value.**

• **Move the mouse pointer close to the edge of the tall candle.**

The mouse pointer changes to a magnetic lasso (Figure 2-23). The end of the lasso's rope is the actual location when clicked.

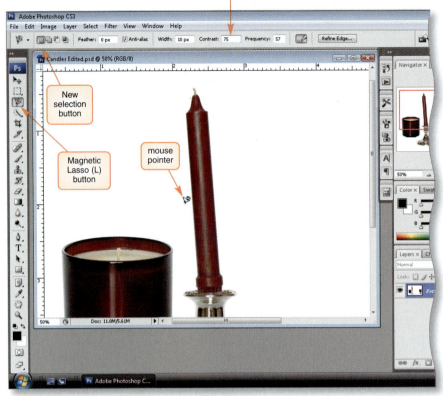

FIGURE 2-23

3

• **Click the white space close to the left edge of the candle.**

• **Release the mouse button.**

A gray fastening point is displayed (Figure 2-24).

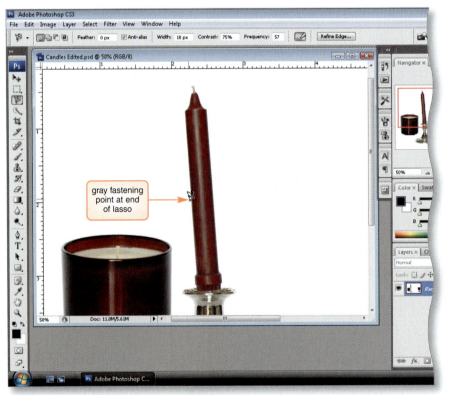

FIGURE 2-24

4

• **Move the mouse up, staying close to the edge of the candle.**

As you move the mouse, the fastening points move to the edge of the candle's red color on the white background (Figure 2-25).

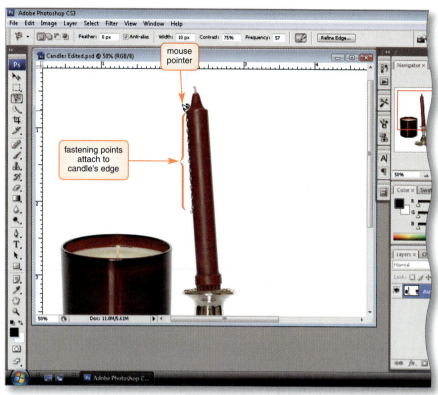

FIGURE 2-25

5

• **Continue moving the mouse slowly to the top of the candle. Stay close to the edge of the candle and click whenever you want to change direction, for example when the candle tapers toward the wick. As you encounter corners in the candle, click the white space slightly away from the candle, so the lasso includes the entire corner.**

• **When you get to the top of the wick, click before moving to the right.**

• **Click again to turn the corner and come down the right side of the candle.**

The fastening points adhere to the edge of the candle and the wick (Figure 2-26). Your selection may be slightly different. Do not worry if you have included some extra white space around the candle or wick.

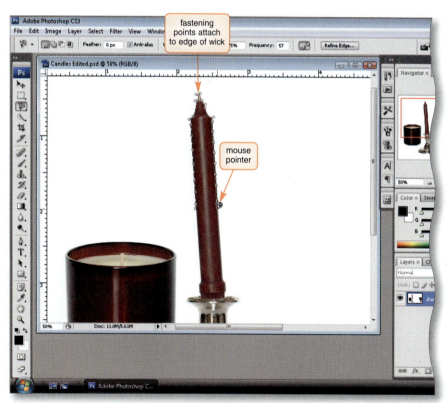

FIGURE 2-26

6

• **When you get to the lower-right corner, click again, and then drag across the bottom of the candle. The magnetic lasso will not closely align with the red color in the candle, but may include some of the candle holder in the selection.**

• **Click to turn the corner and move the mouse up toward the beginning point.**

The magnetic lasso includes some of the candle holder in the selection (Figure 2-27).

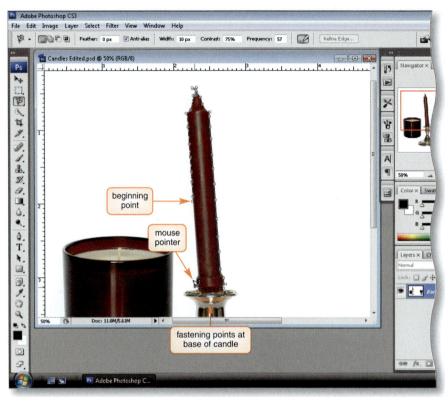

FIGURE 2-27

7

• **When you get back to the beginning point, click to finish the loop. If the selection border does not begin to pulsate, move the mouse closer to the beginning point and click again.**

The selection border flashes or pulsates around the candle (Figure 2-28).

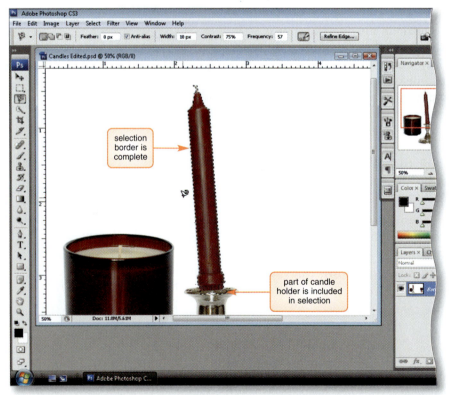

FIGURE 2-28

Other Ways

1. Press SHIFT+L twice, click image, move mouse

The Lasso Tools • **PS 89**

Photoshop Chapter 2

Subtracting from the Selection Using the Polygonal Lasso Tool

The following steps show how to select the Polygonal Lasso tool and then use it to subtract the candle holder from the selection. You also may use the tool to subtract other portions of the image you may have selected inadvertently.

To Select the Polygonal Lasso Tool

1

• **Right-click the Magnetic Lasso Tool (L) button on the Tools palette.**

The context menu is displayed (Figure 2-29).

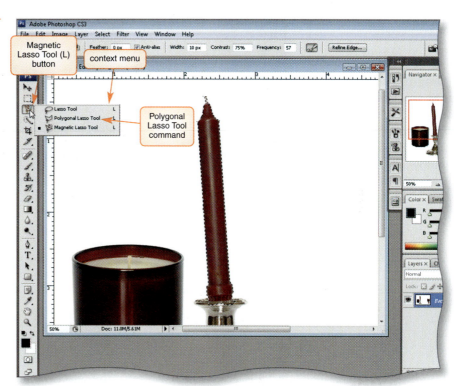

FIGURE 2-29

2

• **Click Polygonal Lasso Tool in the list.**

The tool button icon changes to reflect the polygonal lasso (Figure 2-30).

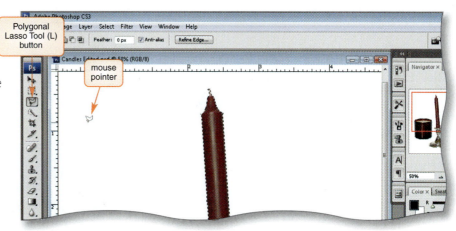

FIGURE 2-30

Other Ways

1. From Magnetic Lasso tool, press SHIFT+L twice

When subtracting from small portions of the document window, it often is necessary to zoom the magnification greater than 100% and then scroll the document window as shown in the steps on the next page.

To Zoom and Reposition the Document Window

1

• **On the Navigator palette status bar, click the Zoom In button several times to display the document window at 200%.**

2

• **Drag the scroll bars until the lower part of the selected area is displayed in the center of the document window.**

The selection border is displayed around the candle and a portion of the candle holder (Figure 2-31).

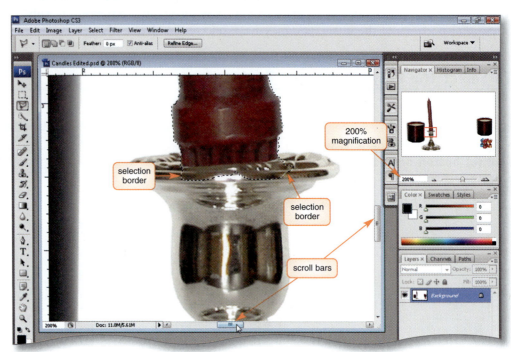

FIGURE 2-31

In the next section, you will use the Subtract from selection button and the Polygonal Lasso tool to subtract from the selection so only the candle is selected as the following steps illustrate. While you are drawing the selection, if you make a mistake, double-click to finish the selection and then click Undo on the Edit menu.

To Subtract from a Selection

1

• **Click the Subtract from selection button on the options bar.**

• **Move the mouse pointer into the document window.**

The mouse pointer changes to a polygonal lasso with a minus sign (Figure 2-32).

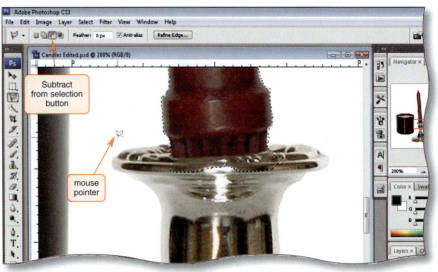

FIGURE 2-32

2

• **Click to the left of the candle holder level with the bottom of the candle.**

The beginning point of the lasso selection is set (Figure 2-33).

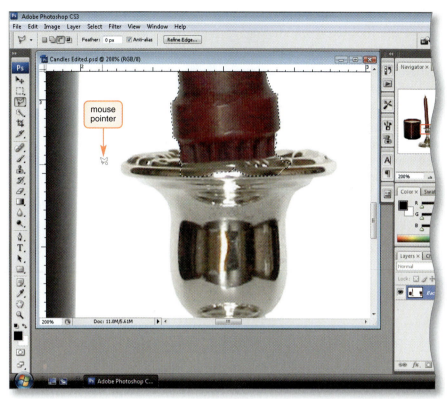

FIGURE 2-33

3

• **Move the mouse across the selection border, along the bottom of the candle, clicking at any curve you see in the bottom of the candle.**

• **Move the mouse pointer to the right side of the candle holder and then click.**

The lasso tool draws a line across the bottom of the candle (Figure 2-34).

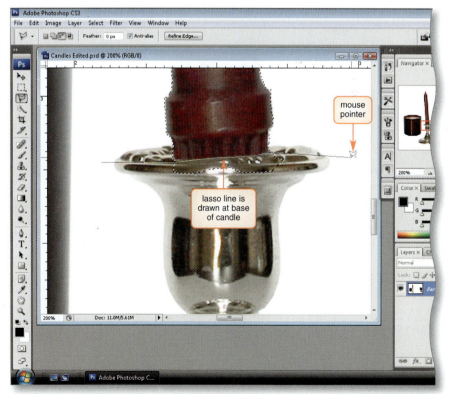

FIGURE 2-34

4

• **Move the mouse down, staying outside the selection border.**

• **When you are completely below the selection border, click and then move left.**

• **When you get to the lower-left corner of the selection, click and then move up toward the beginning point.**

The lasso tool draws a box around the portion of the selection containing the candle holder across the bottom of the candle (Figure 2-35).

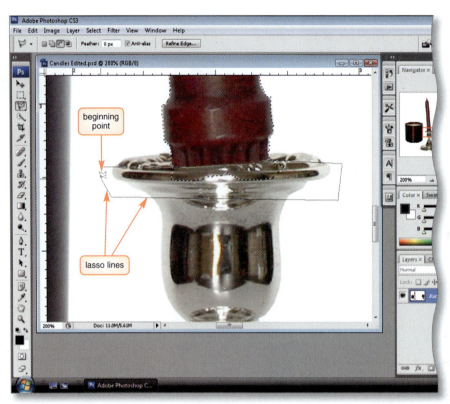

FIGURE 2-35

5

• **Position the mouse as closely as possible to the beginning point fastener and then click.**

The polygonal lasso selection is subtracted from the previous selection (Figure 2-36).

6

• **If you have other portions of the selection that do not include the candle itself, repeat Steps 2 through 5 to subtract them.**

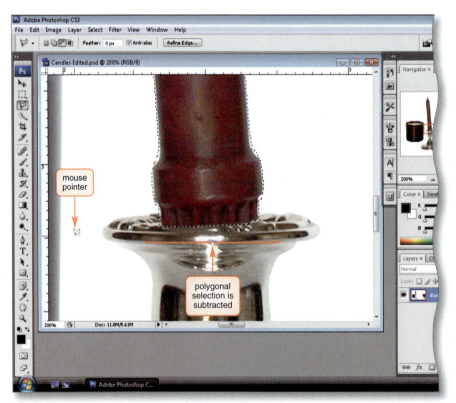

FIGURE 2-36

Other Ways

1. To subtract from selection, ALT+drag

If you make errors using the Polygonal Lasso tool, and want to go back to the original selection, in the History palette, scroll if necessary to display the state labeled Magnetic Lasso. Click the state and begin again.

If you notice a corner or edge of the candle not included in the selection, click the Add to selection button on the options bar and then draw a lasso encompassing the corner or edge.

Rotating a Selection

Finally, you will use the Move tool to straighten the candle. Recall that the Move tool can be used to make several kinds of transformations other than simple moves. The following steps illustrate how to rotate the candle to a straighter position on the candle holder. The arrow keys are used to **nudge**, or move, the selection in small increments.

To Rotate a Selection

1

• **Click the Zoom Out button in the Navigator palette until the magnification is 33.33%.**

• **Click the Move Tool (V) button on the Tools palette.**

• **If necessary, click the Show Transform Controls box to select it.**

• **Move the mouse pointer to a location slightly above and to the right of the selection, until the mouse pointer displays a rotation icon.**

Photoshop displays the bounding box, and the mouse pointer displays a rotation icon (Figure 2-37).

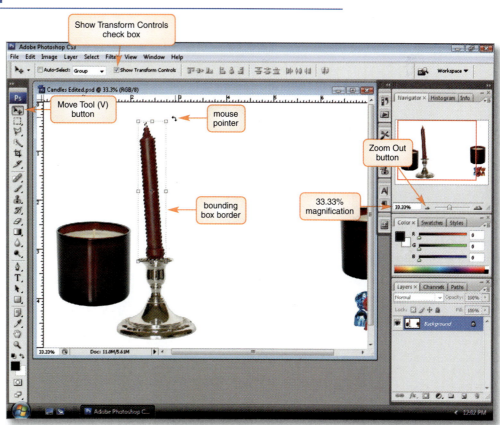

FIGURE 2-37

2

• **Drag down slightly to straighten the candle.**

Photoshop moves the selection clockwise (Figure 2-38).

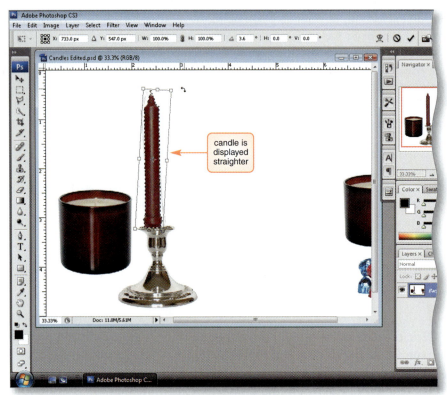

FIGURE 2-38

3

• **On the keyboard, press the RIGHT ARROW key several times to nudge the selection to the right, centering the candle over the candle holder.**

Photoshop moves the selection to the right (Figure 2-39).

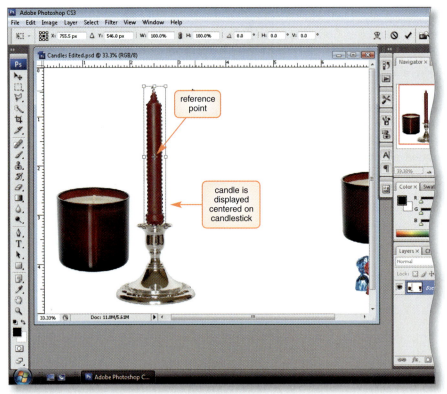

FIGURE 2-39

4

• **Press the ENTER key to commit the changes.**

• **Click Select on the menu bar and then click Deselect on the Select menu.**

Photoshop deselects the candle (Figure 2-40).

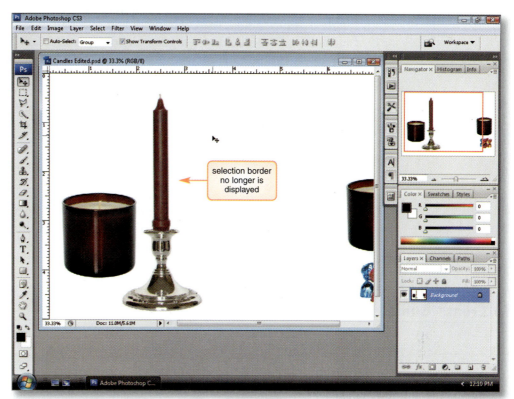

FIGURE 2-40

Other Ways

1. To rotate, on options bar enter degree rotation in Rotate box
2. To nudge, on options bar enter new horizontal or vertical placement value
3. To deselect, press CTRL+D

The reference point, the small circle at the center of a selection, serves as the pivot point during rotation (Figure 2-39). The default placement is in the center of the selection. If you drag the reference point to another location, any rotation performed on the selection will pivot around that new location.

Now that the candle is straight, it is time to use the lasso tools to select the candle and its holder, make two copies, and then move and resize them. To help position the candles, you first will learn about creating guides.

Creating Guides

A **guide** is a nonprinting ruler line that graphic designers use to align objects or mark key measurements. To create a guide, you turn on the ruler display and then drag from the horizontal ruler at the top of the document window or from the vertical ruler at the left side of the document window. When you release the mouse, a light, blue-green line is displayed across the image.

Photoshop also has a **grid** of lines that can be displayed over the top of the image. To display the grid, click Show on the View menu and then click Grid. The grid is useful for laying out elements symmetrically. The grid can display as nonprinting lines or as dots. Guides and grids help position images or elements precisely.

More About

Guides and Grids

You can change the color or style of guides and grids. On the Edit menu, point to Preferences, and then click Guides, Grid, & Slices or Guides, Grid, Slices & Convert.

The term **snapping** refers to the ability of objects to attach, or automatically align with, a grid or guide. For example, if you select an object in your image and begin to move it, as you get close to a guide the object's selection border will attach itself to the guide. It is not a permanent magnetic hold. If you do not wish to leave the object there, simply keep dragging. To turn off snapping, click Snap on the View menu.

In a later chapter, you will learn about **smart guides** that are displayed automatically when you draw a shape or move a layer. Smart guides further help align shapes, slices, selections, and layers. Appendix A describes how to set guides and grid preferences using the Edit menu.

Creating Guides

To copy and place the tall candles, guides will be placed in the image to create nine areas. Figure 2-2 on page PS 67 uses the rule of thirds to draw the reader's eye to the important aspects of this advertising image. The following steps show how to create guides.

To Create Guides

1

• **If the rulers do not display in the document window, click Rulers on the View menu.**

• **Click the horizontal ruler at the top of the document window and then drag down into the image.**

• **Do not release the mouse button.**

A ruler guide is displayed across the image (Figure 2-41).

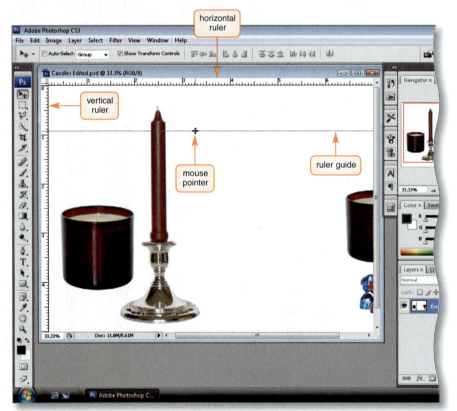

FIGURE 2-41

2

- **Drag until the ruler guide is approximately even with the 1¾ inch mark on the vertical ruler.**
- **Release the mouse button.**
- **If Photoshop does not display the guide, click View on the menu bar, point to Show, and then click Guides on the Show submenu.**

Photoshop displays a light, blue-green horizontal ruler guide at 1¾ inches (Figure 2-42).

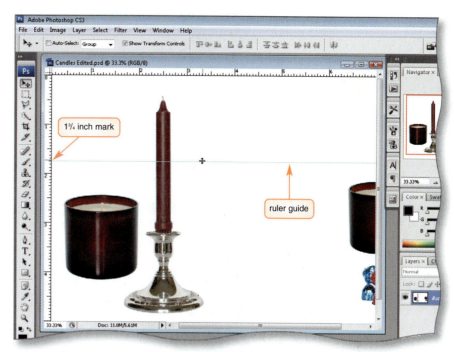

FIGURE 2-42

3

- **Using the same technique, drag another guide from the horizontal ruler and release the mouse button at 3½ inches as measured on the vertical ruler.**
- **Drag from the vertical ruler to create guides at 2¾ inches and 5¼ inches as measured on the horizontal ruler.**

Photoshop displays ruler guides splitting the image into thirds both vertically and horizontally (Figure 2-43).

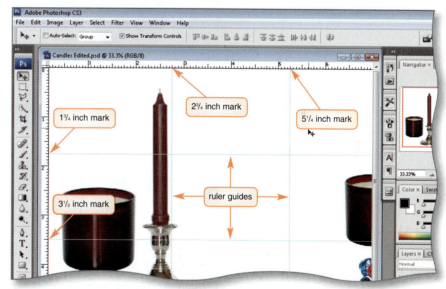

FIGURE 2-43

To move a guide, drag it. To remove a guide, drag it back to the ruler. To clear all guides, click Clear Guides on the View menu. To turn the display of the guides on and off, you can point to Show on the View menu and then click Guides on the Show submenu. Pressing CTRL+; also toggles the guides on and off. To lock the guides in place, click Lock Guides on the View menu.

Now that the guides are in place, the steps on the next page describe how to use the lasso tools to select the large candle in order to create copies.

Other Ways

1. To display or turn off guides, press CTRL+;
2. To create guide, on View menu click New Guide

Using the Lasso Tools

Recall that the lasso tools allow you to drag around any object in the document window to select it. The following steps illustrate how to draw around the tall candle and the candleholder freehand to select it.

To Use the Lasso Tools

1

• **Right-click the Polygonal Lasso Tool (L) button on the Tools palette and then click Lasso Tool in the list. Move the mouse pointer to the document window.**

The Lasso tool is displayed on the button and as the mouse pointer (Figure 2-44).

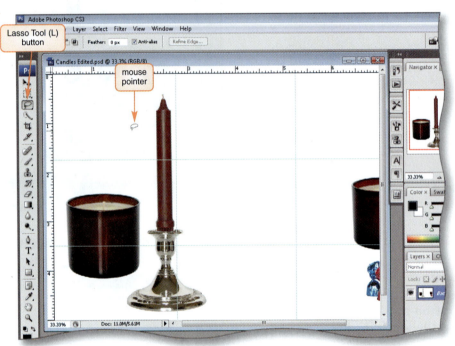

FIGURE 2-44

2

• **Drag around the candle and the candle holder. Be careful not to include any other object in the image. If you make a mistake, release the mouse, press CTRL+D, and begin dragging again. When you get all the way around the image, release the mouse button close to the beginning of the lasso.**

Photoshop displays the selection border around the candle (Figure 2-45)

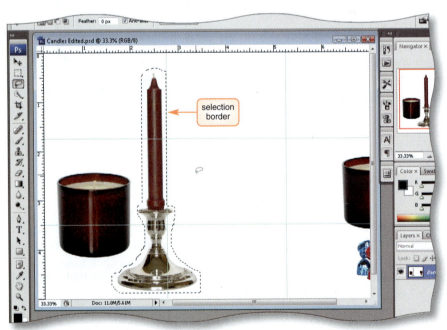

FIGURE 2-45

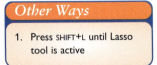

Other Ways

1. Press SHIFT+L until Lasso tool is active

The following steps show how to duplicate the candle by pressing the ALT key while dragging. The candle then is scaled proportionately.

To Duplicate and Scale the Candle

1

• **With the candle and candle holder selected, click the Move Tool (V) button on the Tools palette.**

• **ALT+drag the selection to the right and slightly up, to a location at or near the rightmost vertical ruler guide.**

A second copy of the candle is displayed with bounding box borders (Figure 2-46).

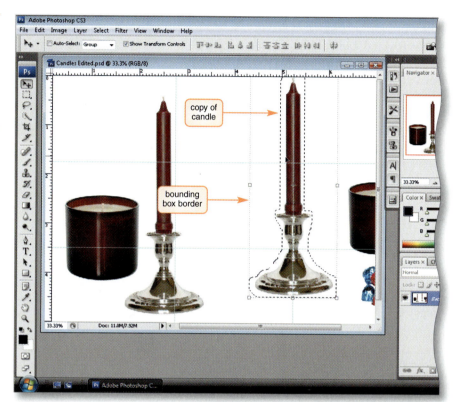

FIGURE 2-46

2

• **SHIFT+drag the lower-left sizing handle toward the middle of the candle, until it is displayed approximately 15% smaller than it was before.**

Photoshop scales the selection (Figure 2-47). Recall that shift-dragging maintains the height to width ratio.

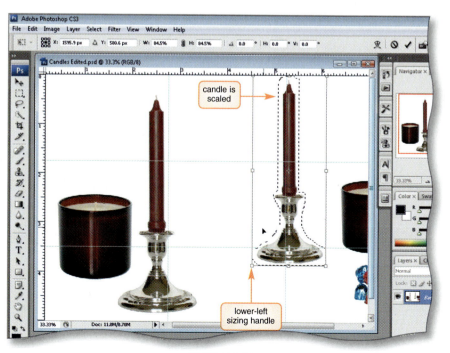

FIGURE 2-47

3

• Press the ENTER key to commit the transformation.

• ALT+drag the selection slightly down and to the left to create another copy.

• SHIFT+drag the lower-left sizing handle toward the middle of the candle, until it is displayed approximately 25% smaller than it was before. The bottom of the candle holder will be approximately even with the lower ruler guide. Drag the selection to reposition it, if necessary.

A third candle is displayed (Figure 2-48).

4

• Press the ENTER key to commit the transformation.

• Press CTRL+D to deselect.

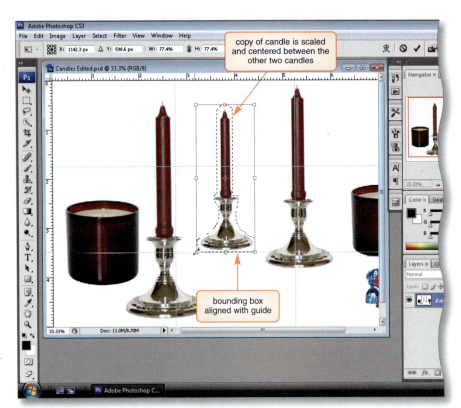

FIGURE 2-48

The Quick Selection Tool

Recall that creating a selection in Photoshop allows you to edit that portion of the image. In Chapter 1 you used the menu to select all of the image and then create a border. A selection is identified by the dotted, pulsating border visible on the screen. The **Quick Selection tool**, which is new to Photoshop CS3, is used to draw a selection quickly using the mouse. As you drag, a selection is created automatically, expanding outward to find and follow the defined edges in the image.

When you click the **Quick Selection Tool (W) button** on the Tools palette, the mouse pointer changes to a brush tip that displays a circle with a centered cross inside. You can increase or decrease the size of the brush tip using the [or] keys, or by using the options bar. The Quick Selection options bar (Figure 2-49) displays the size of the brush and contains some of the same selection buttons as other selection tools. It also contains an Auto-Enhance check box which reduces roughness in the selection boundary when the box is checked. Auto-Enhance applies some of the same the effects found in the Refine Edge dialog box.

Using the Quick Selection Tool

The following steps illustrate how to use the Quick Selection tool to select the small candle on the right side of the image. Then, the selection is expanded using the Modify command on the Select menu. Recall that the Modify commands help you change selection borders.

To Use the Quick Selection Tool

1

• Scroll to display the right side of the image. Click the Quick Selection Tool (W) button on the Tools palette.

• On the options bar, click the New selection button, if necessary. Move the mouse pointer to the upper-left corner of the copy of the short candle. If necessary press the] key several times to increase the size of the mouse pointer, until it is approximately the size shown in Figure 2-49.

Photoshop changes the mouse pointer to the Quick Selection tool shape (Figure 2-49).

FIGURE 2-49

2

• Keeping the mouse pointer over the candle rather than over the white area around the candle, drag diagonally from the upper left to the lower right, so the selection border is displayed around the candle.

The candle is selected (Figure 2-50).

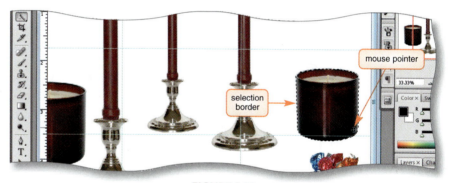

FIGURE 2-50

3

• Click Select on the menu bar, point to Modify, and then click Expand. When Photoshop displays the Expand Selection dialog box, type 5 in the Expand By box.

Expanding the border ensures that all of the color around the edges is included in the selection (Figure 2-51).

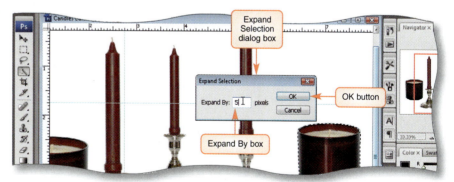

FIGURE 2-51

4

• Click the OK button. Press the V key to activate the Move tool and then drag the candle upward, approximately one inch as shown in Figure 2-53 on page PS103.

More About

The History Palette

The history palette will list a Duplicate state when the ALT key is used to copy a selection. The word Paste will display when the Copy and Paste commands are used from the keyboard or menu. The Copy command alone does not affect how the image looks, it merely sends a copy to the system clipboard. Therefore it is not saved as a state.

The Magic Wand Tool

Another selection tool useful in situations where you want to select an entire object is the Magic Wand tool. Some objects, like a flower with many curves and corners, would be difficult to trace with the lasso tools. The **Magic Wand tool** lets you select a consistently colored area without having to trace its outline. To use the Magic Wand tool, you click the Magic Wand Tool (W) button on the Tools palette or press the W key on the keyboard. When you use the Magic Wand tool and click in the image, Photoshop selects every pixel that contains the same or similar colors as the location you clicked. The default setting is to select contiguous pixels only; but Photoshop allows you to change that setting in order to select all pixels of the same color. You also can set the color range or tolerance, and specify a smoothed edge.

The Magic Wand Options Bar

The Magic Wand options bar (Figure 2-52) contains the same selection buttons as other selection tools, to create a new selection, add to or subtract from a selection, and intersect with selections. The Magic Wand options bar also has a **Tolerance** box that allows you to enter a value that determines the similarity or difference of the pixels selected. A low value selects the few colors very similar to the pixel you click. A higher value selects a broader range of colors. The Anti-alias check box smoothes the jagged edges of a selection by softening the color transition between edge pixels and background pixels. While anti-aliasing is useful when cutting, copying, and pasting selections to create composite images, it may leave behind a trace shadow when the selection is cut or moved. When checked, the **Contiguous** check box selects only adjacent areas using the same colors. Otherwise, all pixels in the entire image using the same colors are selected. Finally, the **Sample All Layers** check box selects colors using data from all visible layers. You will learn about layers in Chapter 3. Otherwise, the Magic Wand tool selects colors from the active layer only.

More About

The Magic Wand

The Magic Wand tool especially is effective for solid colored objects. When used in conjunction with the Subtract from selection button, the Magic Wand tool can remove background colors in land-locked openings to create a selection that appears three-dimensional and floating when moved around. When used in conjunction with the Select inverse command, the Magic Wand tool is useful for selecting only the objects on a solid background.

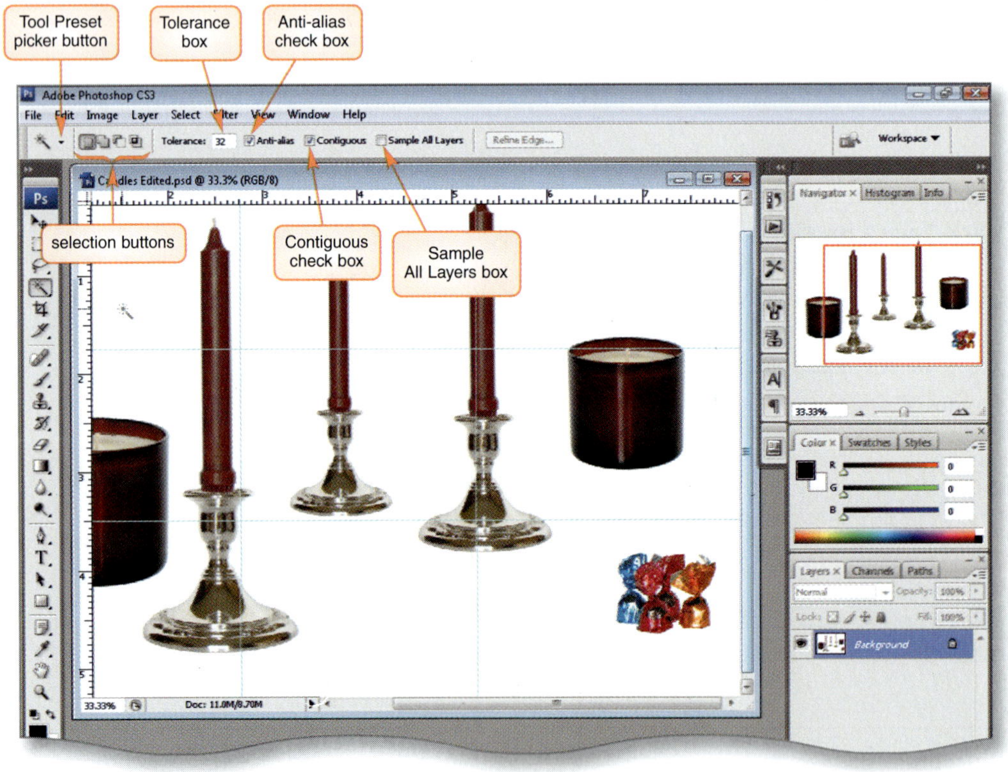

FIGURE 2-52

Using the Magic Wand Tool

You will use the Magic Wand tool to eliminate background around and in between the pieces of candy that are grouped together. First you will use the Rectangular Marquee tool to select the candies; then, you will remove the white background with the Magic Wand tool as the following steps illustrate.

To Select the Candies with the Rectangular Marquee Tool

1 Click the Rectangular Marquee Tool (M) button on the Tools palette.

2 Draw a rectangle around the group of candies leaving a small amount of white space on all four sides.

The selection border pulsates around the candy (Figure 2-53).

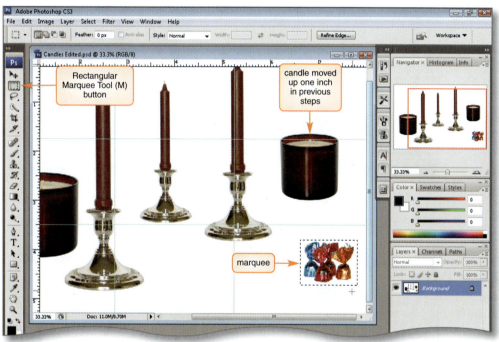

FIGURE 2-53

As you use the Magic Wand tool, remember that if you make a mistake while selecting, you can cancel the previous step by clicking Undo on the Edit menu or go back several steps by clicking a previous state in the History palette.

To Use the Magic Wand Tool

1

• **Zoom to 66.67% and scroll as necessary to display the selection.**

• **Right-click the Quick Selection Tool (W) button on the Tools palette.**

Photoshop displays the context menu (Figure 2-54).

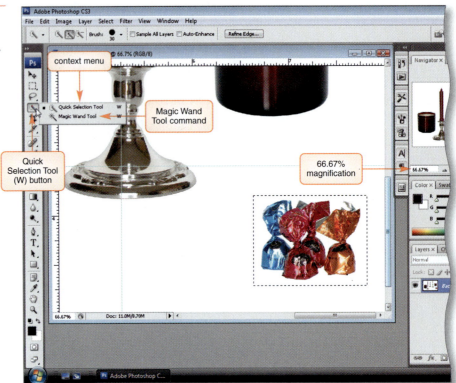

FIGURE 2-54

2

• **Click Magic Wand Tool in the context menu.**

• **On the options bar, click the Subtract from selection button. Click the Anti-alias check box so it does not display a check mark.**

• **Using the tip of the Magic Wand mouse pointer, click each of the white spaces between the candies.**

Photoshop removes the white space from the selection. The pulsating border is displayed around the inner edges of the candy (Figure 2-55).

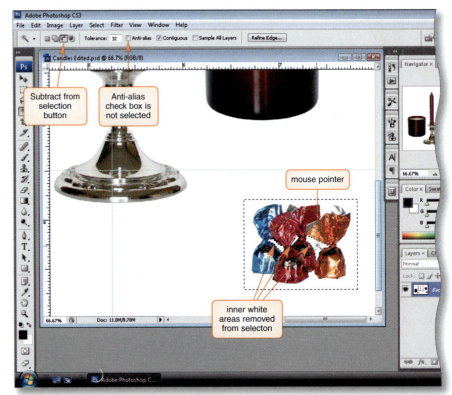

FIGURE 2-55

3

• **Click the white area around the candy but still inside the selection border.**

Photoshop removes the white space around the outside of the candies (Figure 2-56). Now the candies only are selected — without any white background around or between the images.

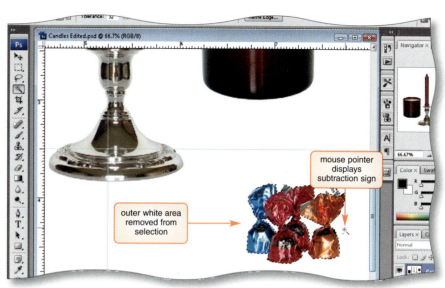

outer white area removed from selection

mouse pointer displays subtraction sign

FIGURE 2-56

Other Ways

1. Press W key, then click image

The next step is to move the candies in front of the short candle and then deselect them as shown in the following steps.

To Move the Candies and Deselect

1 **Click the Move Tool (V) button on the Tools palette.**

2 **Drag the candies to a location on the lower-right corner of the nearest tall candle, as shown in Figure 2-57.**

3 **Press CTRL+D to deselect the candies.**

The candies display in front of the candlestick. Part of the candlestick can be seen between the pieces of candy.

Other Ways

1. To deselect, press CTRL+D
2. To move, press V key, then drag selection

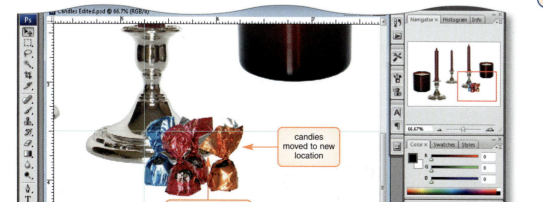

candies moved to new location

candlestick displays behind candies

FIGURE 2-57

Saving an Image with the Same File Name

You will save the image with the same file name, Candles Edited, to the same location as you used at the beginning of the chapter.

To Save an Image with the Same File Name

1 **Click File on the menu bar.**

2 **Click Save on the File menu.**

Photoshop saves the image on a USB flash drive using the currently assigned file name, Candles Edited.

Printing an Image

The final step is to print a hard copy of the advertising image. The following steps show how to print the photo created in this chapter.

To Print an Image

1 **Ready the printer according to the printer instructions.**

2 **Click File on the menu bar. Click Print One Copy on the File menu.**

3 **When the printer stops printing the photo, retrieve the printout, which should look like Figure 2-1b on page PS 67.**

Other Ways

1. To print one copy, press
   ALT+SHIFT+CTRL+P
2. To display the Print dialog box, press CTRL+P

Closing a Photo

Recall that when you are finished editing a photo, you should close it. Closing a photo helps save system resources. You can close a photo after you have saved it and continue working in Photoshop, as the following steps illustrate.

To Close a Photo

1 **With the Candles Edited document window selected, click the Close button on the document window title bar.**

2 **If Photoshop displays a dialog box, click the No button to ignore the changes since the last time you saved the photo.**

Other Ways

1. On File menu, click Close
2. Press CTRL+W

Photoshop closes the Candles Edited document window.

Keyboard Shortcuts

As you have learned, a keyboard shortcut is a way to activate menu or tool commands using the keyboard rather than the mouse. For example, pressing the w key on the keyboard immediately selects the Magic Wand tool without having to move your mouse away from working in the image. Shortcuts with two keystrokes are common as well, such as the use of CTRL+A to select an entire image. Shortcuts are useful when you do not want to take the time to traverse the menu system, or when you are making precise edits and selections with the mouse and do not want to go back to any of the palettes to change tools. A Quick Reference Summary describing Photoshop's keyboard shortcuts is included in the back of the book.

While many keyboard shortcuts already exist in Photoshop, there may be times when additional shortcuts would be useful. For instance, the Single Row and Single Column Marquee tools have no shortcut key. If those are tools that you use frequently, a keyboard shortcut might be helpful. Photoshop allows users to create, customize, and save keyboard shortcuts in one of three areas: menus, palettes, and tools. When you create keyboard shortcuts, you can add them to Photoshop's default settings, save them in a personalized set for retrieval in future editing sessions, or delete them from your system.

Creating a Keyboard Shortcut

To create a new keyboard shortcut, Photoshop provides a dialog box interface accessible from the Edit menu. Using that dialog box, you can choose one of the three shortcut areas and then choose a shortcut key or combination of keys. Photoshop immediately warns you if you have chosen a keyboard shortcut used somewhere else in the program.

In the following steps, you will learn how to create a shortcut for the Default Workspace command. While that command is accessible via the Window menu and the Workspace submenu, a one keystroke shortcut would save time when you need to restore the workspace palettes to their original locations.

To Create a New Keyboard Shortcut

1

• **Click Edit on the menu bar and then point to Keyboard Shortcuts.**

Photoshop displays the Edit menu (Figure 2-58).

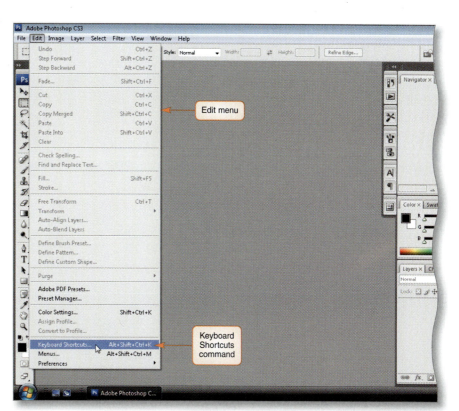

FIGURE 2-58

2

• **Click Keyboard Shortcuts.**

• **When the Keyboard Shortcuts and Menus dialog box is displayed, if necessary, click the Keyboard Shortcuts tab.**

• **If the Set box does not display Photoshop Defaults, click the Set box arrow and then click Photoshop Defaults in the list.**

• **If the Shortcuts For box does not display Application Menus, click the Shortcuts For box arrow and then click Application Menus in the list.**

Photoshop displays the Keyboard Shortcuts and Menus dialog box (Figure 2-59). Photoshop Defaults is the chosen set on the Keyboard Shortcuts tab.

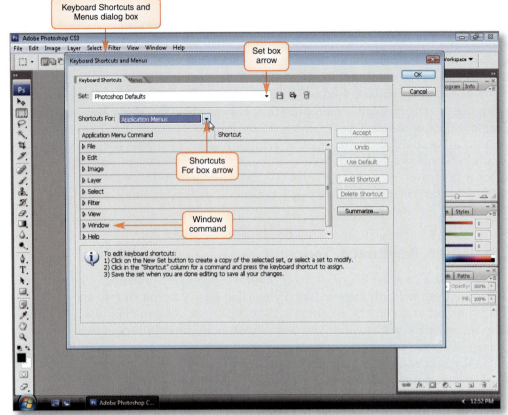

FIGURE 2-59

3

• **Double-click the Window command in the Application Menu Command list.**

• **Scroll down to display Workspace under the Windows menu and Default Workspace under the Workspace submenu.**

• **Click Default Workspace.**

Photoshop displays a blank shortcut key box next to Default Workspace (Figure 2-60).

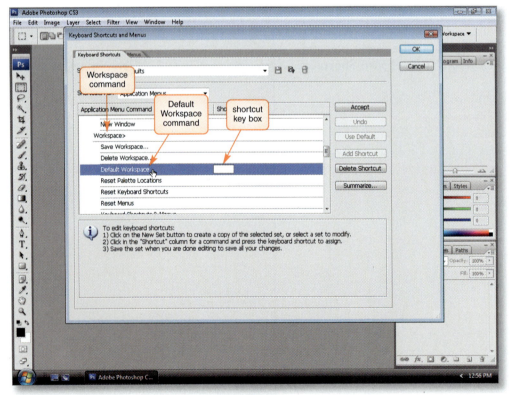

FIGURE 2-60

4

• **Press the F12 key.**

Photoshop warns you that F12 is being used as a shortcut for a different command (Figure 2-61).

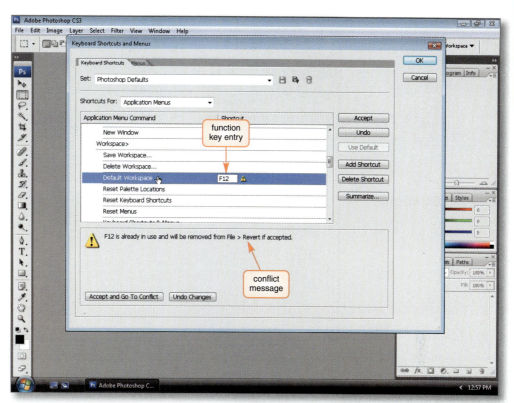

FIGURE 2-61

5

• **Press the F11 key.**

Photoshop displays a message indicating the F11 key is available to use (Figure 2-62).

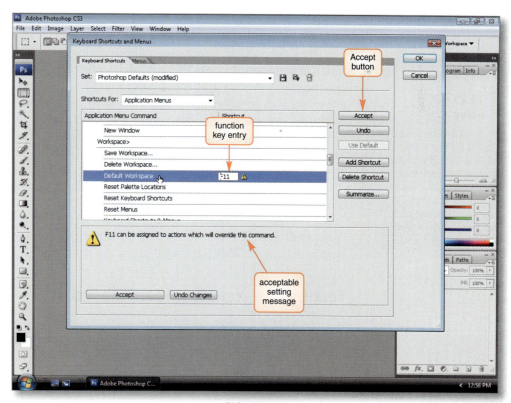

FIGURE 2-62

6

• **Click either of the Accept buttons.**

Photoshop displays the shortcut, and the word modified has been added in the Set box (Figure 2-63).

7

• **Click the OK button.**

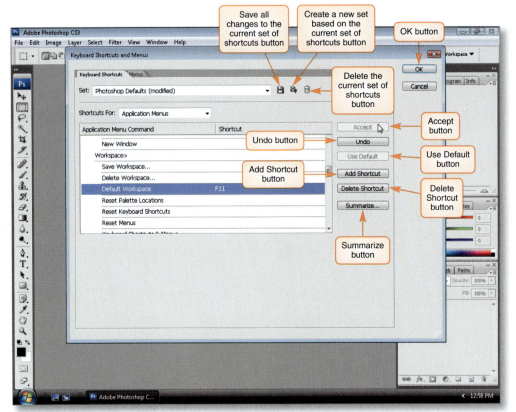

FIGURE 2-63

The Keyboard Shortcuts and Menus dialog box displays three buttons to use when saving the shortcuts (Figure 2-63). When clicked, the Save all changes to the current set of shortcuts button allows you to name the set for retrieval in future sessions. Photoshop stores the set in a file with the extension .kys in the Presets folder on the current computer. The Create a new set based on the current set of shortcuts button allows you to create a copy of the current keyboard shortcut settings. Finally, the Delete the current set of shortcuts button deletes the set. If you do not save the new keyboard shortcuts, they last for the current Photoshop session only.

The Undo button cancels the most recent setting and after it is clicked the button changes to the Redo button. The Use Default button restores a deleted Photoshop shortcut. The Add Shortcut button allows you to add a second shortcut to the same command. The Delete Shortcut button deletes the selected shortcut. The Summarize button displays a Web page with all of the keyboard shortcuts in the set.

Testing the New Keyboard Shortcut

The next steps demonstrate how to test the new keyboard shortcut.

To Test the New Keyboard Shortcut

1

• **Drag the Navigator palette tab toward the center of the document window.**

• **Drag the gripper bar on the Tools palette toward the center of the document window.**

• **Click the button that displays a small double arrow on the Tool palette's gripper bar, to display the palette in two columns (Figure 2-64).**

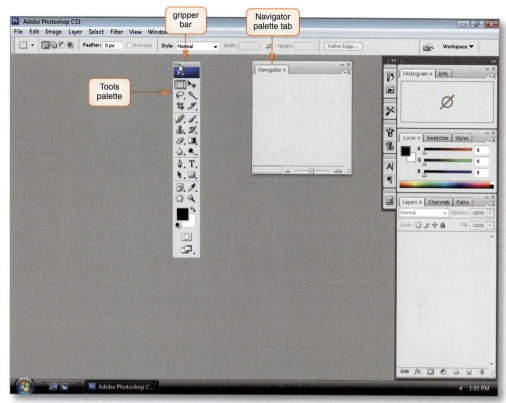

FIGURE 2-64

2

• **Press the F11 key. Do not press the ENTER key. If Photoshop displays a message about saving the shortcut file, click the No button.**

Photoshop restores the Navigator palette and the Tools palette to their original locations (Figure 2-65).

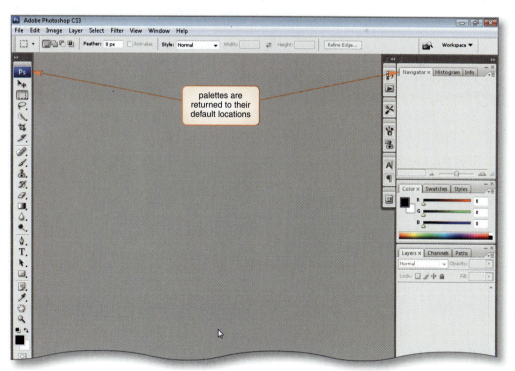

FIGURE 2-65

Keyboard shortcuts assigned to menu commands will display on the right of the command in the menu system.

Quitting Photoshop

The following steps show how to quit Photoshop and return control to Windows.

To Quit Photoshop

1 **Click the Close button on the right side of the title bar. If Photoshop displays a dialog box asking you to save changes, click the No button.**

The Photoshop window closes.

Chapter Summary

Chapter 2 introduced you to several new selection tools. You learned how to use the Rectangular Marquee tool, the Move tool, the lasso tools, and the Magic Wand tool. Once you drew a selection, you then learned many of the transformation commands including scaling and rotating. Each of the tools and commands had its own options bar with settings to control how the tool or command worked. You learned about the History palette and its states. You used the Magic Wand tool to subtract from selected portions of the image with the same color. Finally, you learned how to create and test a new keyboard shortcut.

What You Should Know

Having completed this chapter you should be able to perform the tasks below. The tasks are listed in the same order they were presented in this chapter. For a list of the buttons, menus, tools, and other commands introduced in this chapter, see the Quick Reference Summary at the back of this book and refer to the Page Number column.

1. Start Photoshop (PS 68)
2. Open a File (PS 68)
3. Save a Photo (PS 70)
4. Use the Rectangular Marquee Tool (PS 73)
5. Use the Move Tool (PS 75)
6. Scale a Selection (PS 79)
7. Use the History Palette (PS 82)
8. Zoom and Resize the Document Window (PS 84)
9. Use the Magnetic Lasso Tool (PS 85)
10. Select the Polygonal Lasso Tool (PS 89)
11. Zoom and Reposition the Document Window (PS 90)
12. Subtract from a Selection (PS 90)
13. Rotate a Selection (PS 93)
14. Create Guides (PS 96)
15. Use the Lasso Tools (PS 98)
16. Duplicate and Scale the Candle (PS 99)
17. Use the Quick Selection Tool (PS 101)
18. Select the Candies with the Rectangular Marquee Tool (PS 102)
19. Use the Magic Wand Tool (PS 103)
20. Move the Candies and Deselect (PS 105)
21. Save an Image with the Same File Name (PS 106)
22. Print an Image (PS 106)
23. Close a Photo (PS 106)
24. Create a New Keyboard Shortcut (PS 107)
25. Test the New Keyboard Shortcut (PS 111)
26. Quit Photoshop (PS 112)

Learn It Online

Instructions: To complete the Learn It Online exercises, start your browser, click the Address bar, and then enter the Web address scsite.com/pscs3/learn. When the Photoshop CS3 Learn It Online page is displayed, follow the instructions in the exercises below. Each exercise has instructions for printing your results, either for your own records or for submission to your instructor.

1 Chapter Reinforcement TF, MC, and SA

Below Photoshop Chapter 2, click the Chapter Reinforcement link. Print the quiz by clicking Print on the File menu for each page. Answer each question.

2 Flash Cards

Below Photoshop Chapter 2, click the Flash Cards link and read the instructions. Type 20 (or a number specified by your instructor) in the Number of playing cards text box, type your name in the Enter your Name text box, and then click the Flip Card button. When the flash card is displayed, read the question and then click the ANSWER box arrow to select an answer. Flip through Flash Cards. If your score is 15 (75%) correct or greater, click Print on the File menu to print your results. If your score is less than 15 (75%) correct, then redo this exercise by clicking the Replay button.

3 Practice Test

Below Photoshop Chapter 2, click the Practice Test link. Answer each question, enter your first and last name at the bottom of the page, and then click the Grade Test button. When the graded practice test is displayed on your screen, click Print on the File menu to print a hard copy. Continue to take practice tests until you score 80% or better.

4 Who Wants to Be a Computer Genius?

Below Photoshop Chapter 2, click the Computer Genius link. Read the instructions, enter your first and last name at the bottom of the page, and then click the PLAY button. When your score is displayed, click the PRINT RESULTS link to print a hard copy.

5 Wheel of Terms

Below Photoshop Chapter 2, click the Wheel of Terms link. Read the instructions, and then enter your first and last name and your school name. Click the PLAY button. When your score is displayed, right-click the score and then click Print on the shortcut menu to print a hard copy.

6 Crossword Puzzle Challenge

Below Photoshop Chapter 2, click the Crossword Puzzle Challenge link. Read the instructions, and then enter your first and last name. Click the SUBMIT button. Work the crossword puzzle. When you are finished, click the Submit button. When the crossword puzzle is redisplayed, click the Print Puzzle button to print a hard copy.

7 Tips and Tricks

Below Photoshop Chapter 2, click the Tips and Tricks link. Click a topic that pertains to Chapter 2. Right-click the information and then click Print on the shortcut menu. Construct a brief example of what the information relates to in Photoshop to confirm you understand how to use the tip or trick.

8 Expanding Your Horizons

Below Photoshop Chapter 2, click the Expanding Your Horizons link. Click a topic that pertains to Chapter 2. Print the information. Construct a brief example of what the information relates to in Photoshop to confirm you understand the contents of the article.

9 Search Sleuth

Below Photoshop Chapter 2, click the Search Sleuth link. To search for a term that pertains to this chapter, select a term below the Chapter 2 title and then use the Google search engine at google.com (or any major search engine) to display and print two Web pages that present information on the term.

10 Photoshop Online Training

Below Photoshop Chapter 2, click the Photoshop Online Training link. When your browser displays the Web page, click one of the Photoshop tutorials that covers one or more of the objectives listed at the beginning of the chapter on page PS 66. Print the first page of the tutorial before stepping through it.

Apply Your Knowledge

1 Transforming Selections

Problem: Your older sister teaches grade school and is planning a science unit on outer space. To elicit enthusi-asm among her students, she is planning a bulletin board with the theme, "Blast off with Science!" She knows you have been studying Photoshop and has found a picture that she wants you to edit. She hopes you can add a sense of motion to the photo. You decide to angle the rocket ship, apply perspective, and warp the trail of flames.

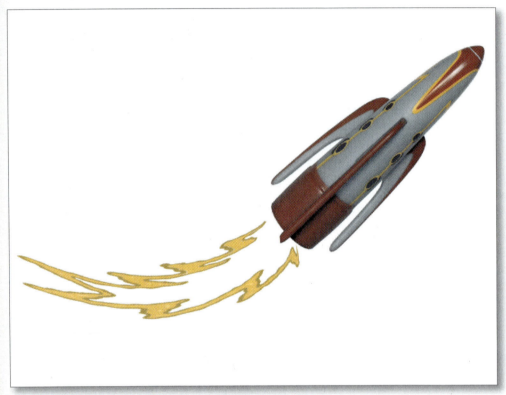

FIGURE 2-66

Instructions: Start Photoshop and set the workspace and tools to default settings. Open the Toy Rocket file from the Chapter02 student data files, located either on the CD that came with this book, or in a location speci-fied by your instructor. The purpose of this exercise is to apply a series of transformations to add a sense of motion to a photograph. The edited photo is displayed in Figure 2-66.

1. Use the Save As command on the File menu to save the file on your storage device with the name, Toy Rocket Edited. If Photoshop displays a JPEG Options dialog box, click the OK button.
2. Zoom in to approximately 25% and enlarge the document window to focus on the rocket ship.
3. Use the Magnetic Lasso tool to draw carefully around the rocket ship only. Do not include the trail of flames. Use the Polygonal Lasso tool to add or subtract from the selection as necessary to include only the rocket ship.
4. Zoom out to 16.67% and then click the Move Tool (V) button.

Apply Your Knowledge

5. To rotate the rocket ship:
   a. When Photoshop displays the bounding box, point to a location outside the upper-right corner of the rocket ship. The mouse pointer will change to the rotate icon.
   b. Drag down or clockwise until the rocket ship displays at approximately a 50 degree angle. *Hint*: Use the Rotate box on the options bar to view the angle as you drag.
6. To add perspective to the rocket ship:
   a. Right-click the selection and then click Perspective on the shortcut menu.
   b. Locate the upper-right sizing handle in relation to the rocket ship. Drag the sizing handle toward the nose of the rocket. Recall that perspective is different than a slant created by skewing. It makes part of the image look farther away.
   c. Press the ENTER key to commit the transformation.
7. Use the Rectangular Marquee tool to select the trail of flames.
8. To rotate and scale the trail of flames:
   a. Press CTRL+T to freely transform the marquee. Photoshop displays the bounding box.
   b. Rotate the selection clockwise 50 degrees as you did with the rocket ship.
   c. Right-click the selection and then click Scale on the shortcut menu.
   d. Locate the top-center sizing handle in relation to the trail of flames. Drag the sizing handle to scale the selection vertically to approximately 250% as shown in the H: box on the options bar.
   e. Press the ENTER key to commit the transformation.
9. To move and warp the trail of flames:
   a. Drag the selection to a position behind the rocket ship.
   b. Press CTRL+T to freely transform.
   c. Right-click the selection and then click Warp on the shortcut menu.
   d. When the Warp options bar is displayed, click the Custom box arrow and then click Arc. The selection will display a grid with one sizing handle.
   e. Drag the sizing handle down until the trail of flames curves as shown in Figure 2-66. Reposition the trail of flames as necessary.
   f. Press the ENTER key to commit the transformation.
10. Deselect the trail of flames.
11. Save the image again.
12. Print the image.
13. Close the document window.
14. Quit Photoshop.

Adobe Photoshop CS3

In the Lab

1 Using the Keyboard with the Magic Wand

Problem: As e-cards gain popularity, the need for good graphics also has increased. A small e-commerce site has hired you as its photo specialist to assist with images and photos used in the greeting cards provided online. Your first assignment is to provide a clean image for a card whose greeting will read, "Happy birthday! My how you've grown!" A photographer has submitted a photo of a giraffe, but the layout artist wants the giraffe to face the other way to fit in with the greeting he has designed. He also needs the background sky removed. You decide to practice using the function keys to perform most of the editing tasks. The edited photo displays in Figure 2-67. (*Hint*: In future chapters, you will learn how to feather and smooth edges for a more natural appearance. For the purposes of this assignment, be as careful as you can when removing portions of the background sky.)

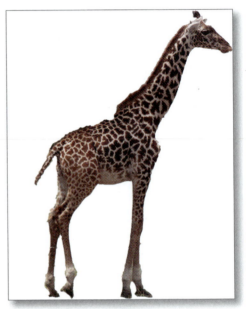

FIGURE 2-67

Instructions:

1. Start Photoshop. Set the default workspace and reset all tools.
2. Press CTRL+O to open the Giraffe file from the Chapter02 folder on the CD that accompanies this book, or from a location specified by your instructor.
3. Press SHIFT+CTRL+S to use the Save As command to save the file on your storage device with the name, Giraffe Edited. If Photoshop displays a JPEG Options dialog box, click the OK button.
4. If the photo does not display at 100% magnification, press CTRL++ or CTRL+- to zoom in or out as necessary.
5. If necessary, resize the document window to display the entire photo.
6. Press the W key to choose the Magic Wand tool.
7. Click the area of blue sky to the left of the giraffe.
8. SHIFT+CLICK the area of blue sky to the right of the giraffe.
9. Click any other portions of the sky that are not already selected.
10. Press CTRL+X to delete the selected areas.
11. Press CTRL+D to remove any selection border, if necessary.
12. If some area of blue still is displayed, repeat Steps 8 through 11. If you make an error or some areas are deleted by mistake, click the first state in the History palette and begin again with Step 6.
13. On the Magic Wand options bar, double-click the Tolerance box and type 0 to replace the value. Click the Anti-alias check box so it does not display its check mark. Click the Sample All Layers check box so it displays its check mark.
14. With the Add to selection button selected, use the Magic Wand tool to select all the white areas of the photo.
15. Press SHIFT+CTRL+I to select the inverse. The giraffe now should be selected.
16. Press CTRL+T to freely transform the giraffe selection. Right-click the selection and then click Flip Horizontal on the shortcut menu.
17. Press the ENTER key to commit the transformations.
18. Press CTRL+D to deselect, if necessary.
19. Press CTRL+S to save the file with the same name.
20. Press ALT+SHIFT+CTRL+P to use the Print One Copy command on the File menu to print a copy of the photo.

In the Lab

21. Close the document window by pressing CTRL+W.
22. Quit Photoshop by pressing CTRL+Q.
23. Send the photo as an e-mail attachment to your instructor, or follow your instructor's directions for submitting the lab assignment.

2 Skew, Perspective, and Warp

Problem: Hobby Express, a store that specializes in model trains and remote control toys wants a new logo. They would like to illustrate the concept of a train engine that looks like it is racing to the store. The picture will display on their letterhead, business cards, and advertising pieces. They would like a digital file so they can use the logo for other graphic purposes. The edited photo is shown in Figure 2-68.

FIGURE 2-68

Instructions:

1. Start Photoshop. Set the default workspace and reset all tools.
2. Open the file, Engine, from the CD that accompanies this book, or from a location specified by your instructor.
3. Use the Save As command to save the file on your storage device with the name `Engine Edited`. When Photoshop displays a JPEG Options dialog box, type 8 in the Quality box, and then click the OK button.
4. Click the Magic Wand Tool (W) button on the Tools palette and deselect the Contiguous check box on the options bar. Type 32 in the Tolerance box. Select all of the blue background.
5. To add the green grass in the lower-right corner of the photo to the selection, on the Magic Wand options bar, click the Add to selection button. Type 50 in the Tolerance box, click the Contiguous check box so it displays its check mark, and then click the grass.
6. Press the DELETE key to delete the selected areas.
7. On the Select menu, click Inverse.

(continued)

In the Lab

Skew, Perspective, and Warp *(continued)*

8. On the Edit menu, point to Transform, and then click Warp. When Photoshop displays the warp grid, locate the upper-left warp point that displays as a gray circle on the grid. Drag the warp point to the right until the smokestack bends slightly.

9. Right-click the selection and then click Skew on the shortcut menu. Drag the upper-left sizing handle to the left.

10. Experiment with the Perspective and Distort commands to make the engine look as if it were moving. The front of the engine should appear closer than the rear. The smokestack should curve backward to simulate motion. Apply any transformations.

11. Save the photo again and print a copy for your instructor.

3 Creating Shortcuts, Saving Sets, and Viewing the Shortcut Summary

Problem: You have decided that many times, while you are working with tools in Photoshop, it would be beneficial to reset the options bar settings back to their defaults as you change tools. You decided to create a new keyboard shortcut to reset all tools, rather than having to move the mouse to the options bar, right-click, and then choose to reset all tools. Because other family members work on your computer system, you would like to save the new shortcuts in a separate set for your personal use. You also would like to see a complete listing of the Photoshop shortcuts for your system.

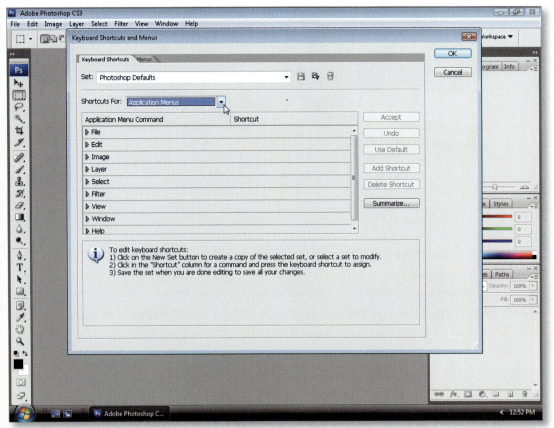

FIGURE 2-69

Instructions:

1. Start Photoshop. Set the default workspace and reset all tools.
2. On the Edit menu, click Keyboard Shortcuts.
3. When the Keyboard Shortcuts and Menus dialog box is displayed (Figure 2-69), if necessary click the Keyboard Shortcuts tab. If necessary, click the Set box arrow and then click Photoshop Defaults in the list.
4. Click the Shortcuts For box arrow and then click Palette Menus in the list.
5. Double-click Tool Presets in the list.
6. Click Reset All Tools in the list and then press the F10 key to choose it as the shortcut.
7. Click either Accept button.
8. Click the Create a new set based on the current set of shortcuts button. When the Save dialog box is displayed, type your name in the File name box. Click the Save button.
9. When the Keyboard Shortcuts and Menus dialog box again is displayed, click the Summarize button. When the Save dialog box is displayed, type My Shortcut Summary in the File name box. Click the Save in box arrow and choose your USB flash drive location. Click the Save button.
10. The Shortcut Summary should open automatically in your browser (Figure 2-70). If it does not, use a Computer window or an Explore window to navigate to your USB flash drive. Double-click the My Shortcut Summary HTML file. When the summary displays, print the page and turn it in to your instructor.
11. Close the browser. Click the OK button to close the Keyboard Shortcuts and Menus dialog box. Quit Photoshop.

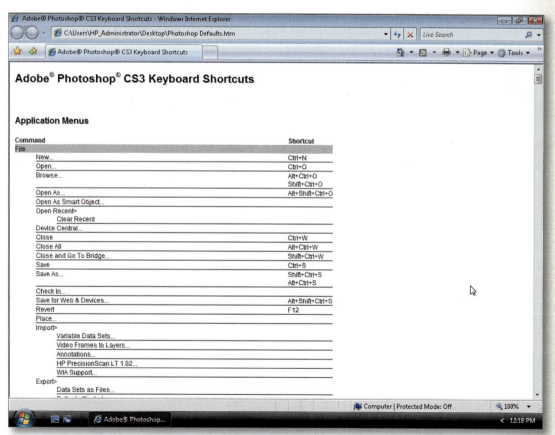

FIGURE 2-70

Cases and Places

The difficulty of these case studies varies:
■ are the least difficult and ■■ are the most difficult. The last exercise is a group exercise.

1 ■ The city of Springfield has an annual hot air balloon festival. They are sending out a brochure to attract balloon enthusiasts from all across the state. The photo submitted by the festival organizers is named, Balloon, and is located in the Chapter02 folder on the CD that accompanies this book. Using the rule of thirds and taking into consideration the layout and perspective, begin by using paper and pencil to sketch several quick roughs that include more than one balloon. Start Photoshop and use the techniques you learned in Chapters 1 and 2 to create several more balloons on the background. You can use the Magnetic Lasso tool to select the balloons or the Magic Wand tool to select the sky and then select the inverse. Save the file with the name, Balloon Edited, on your USB flash drive storage device.

2 ■ Your local bank is starting an initiative to encourage children to open a savings account using their loose change. The bank would like a before and after picture showing how money can grow with interest. A file named Coins is located on the CD that accompanies this book. Start Photoshop and use the Elliptical Marquee tool to select each coin and duplicate it several times to fill the image with coins. Rotate and layer some of the coins to make it look more interesting. Save the photo with the name, Coins Edited on your USB flash drive storage device.

3 ■■ Use your digital camera to take a picture of a small object in your home, such as a can of soup or a piece of fruit. Transfer the picture to your computer system and open it with Photoshop. Duplicate the object several times and perform a different transformation technique on each copy, such as scale, rotate, skew, warp, distort, and perspective. Save the photo and send a copy to your instructor as an attachment to an e-mail.

4 ■■ Look through magazines or newspapers for color photos with distinctive transformations such as perspective, skew, or warp. If possible, cut out three photos. Write a short paragraph for each example describing how you think the image was generated. List the tool, the transformation, and the potential problems associated with duplicating the process. List the idea being conveyed by the photo and describe a second possible conceptual application for the photo. Attach the photos to the descriptions and submit them to your instructor. If directed by your instructor to do so, recreate the image.

5 ■■ **Working Together** Your group has been assigned to create a group photo from individual photos. Using a digital camera or camera phone, take a picture of each team member from the shoulders up. Using Photoshop, open each digital file and select only the team member's head and shoulder area. Invert the selection and press the DELETE key to eliminate the background. Save each file. Choose the picture with the most white space around the team member's picture to be the master photo. In each of the other photos, use the Magnetic Lasso tool to select the individual. Copy the selection and then paste it into the master photo creating a group picture. Scale and move the selections as necessary to make the picture look good. Try to match the proportions for a realistic composition, or exaggerate proportions for more humorous results. Experiment with overlapping shoulder areas. Use the History palette to return to previous states when errors are made. Submit the final result to your teacher.

Using Layers

CHAPTER

3

CASE PERSPECTIVE

You are a freelance graphic designer whose work has caught the eye of Javier Caserne, general manager of Essentials Landscaping Company. Mr. Caserne's clientele includes owners of midsized homes, usually those with new construction, who want to create outdoor landscapes that fit both their style and price range. Essentials Landscaping Company specializes in a tiered approach, adding landscaping components in small sets, as the home owner desires, to improve the grounds in either a practical or aesthetic way.

In order to provide a more realistic view of the finished product to his clients, Mr. Caserne has been using two-dimensional layout sketches and pictures of other homes with similar designs. While that offers a homeowner one vision of what is possible, Mr. Caserne would like an even more realistic and personal approach. He has taken a picture of a client's home and wants you to insert the softscape objects such as lawn, bushes, and trees, and also hardscape, inanimate objects such as a statuary into the photo. Mr. Caserne wants to show his clients what their home will look like five or more years from now as the plants and trees mature.

You decide to investigate Photoshop's layering capabilities to create a composite image from several photographs of landscaping components provided by Mr. Caserne. The Clone Stamp tool will help you apply the image of sod into the corners with precision. You will use the Layers palette combined with Photoshop's color and contrast adjustments to insert flowers, bushes, and trees to give the house a lived-in look. The Move tool will help you position layers in the composite image. Using one of the Photoshop filters, you will create a cloud-filled sky to make the house appear in a summer-like setting. Duplicating a layer, the lion statuary will give the drive a formal elegance and improve the curb appeal. Mr. Caserne's potential client will want to hire the firm right away!

Using Layers

CHAPTER

3

Objectives

You will have mastered the material in this chapter when you can:

- Save a file in PSD format
- Create a layer via cut and use the Layers palette
- Select, name, color, hide, and view layers
- Create a new layer from another image or selection
- Set layer properties
- Resize a layer
- Erase portions of layers and images
- Use the Eraser, Magic Eraser, and Background Eraser tools
- Create layer masks
- Make level adjustments and opacity changes
- Create a layer style and add a render filter
- Use the Clone Stamp tool
- Flatten a composite image

Introduction

Whether it is adding a new person into a photograph, combining artistic effects from different genres, or creating 3-D animation, the concept of layers in Photoshop allows you to work on one element of an image without disturbing the others. A **layer** is an image superimposed or separated from other parts of the document. You may think of layers as sheets of clear film stacked one on top of the other. You can see through **transparent** areas of a layer to the layers below. The nontransparent or **opaque** areas of a layer are solid and eclipse lower layers. You can change the composition of an image by changing the order and attributes of layers. In addition, special features such as adjustment layers, layer masks, fill layers, and layer styles let you create sophisticated effects.

Another tool that graphic designers use when they want to recreate a portion of another photo is the Clone Stamp tool. As you will learn in this chapter, the Clone Stamp tool takes a sample of an image, and then applies, as you draw, an exact copy of that image to your document.

Graphic designers use layers and clones along with other tools in Photoshop to create **composite** images that combine or merge multiple images and drawings to create a new image, also referred to as a montage. Composite images illustrate the power of Photoshop and are used to prepare documents for businesses, advertising, marketing, and media artwork. Composite images such as navigation bars can be created in Photoshop and used on the Web along with layered buttons, graphics, and background images.

Chapter Three — Using Layers

Chapter 3 uses Photoshop to create a composite image from several photographs by using layers. Specifically, it begins with a photo of a recently constructed house, and creates a composite image by inserting layers of flowers, bushes, trees, a statuary, and sod. The process is illustrated in Figure 3-1.

Before   After

Layers and clones

FIGURE 3-1

The enhancements will show how the home will look after some time with appropriate landscaping. Sod will replace the dirt; bushes and trees will be planted. The photo will be edited to display a bright summer day with clouds in the sky. Finally, statuary will be added to give the house maximum curb appeal.

Starting and Customizing Photoshop

If you are stepping through this chapter on a computer and you want your screen to match the figures in this book, you should change your computer's resolution to 1024 × 768 and reset the tools and palettes. For more information about how to change the resolution on your computer, and other advanced Photoshop settings, read Appendix A.

The following steps describe how to start Photoshop and customize the Photoshop window. You may need to ask your instructor how to start Photoshop for your system.

To Start Photoshop

1 **Start Photoshop as described on pages PS 6 and PS 7.**

2 **Choose the Default Workspace as described on page PS 8.**

3 **Select the Rectangular Marquee tool and then reset all tools as described on pages PS 9 and PS 10.**

Photoshop starts and then resets the tools, palettes, and options.

Opening a File

To open a file in Photoshop it must be stored as a digital file on your computer system. The photos and images used in this book are stored on a CD located in the back of the book. Your instructor may designate a different location for the photos.

The next steps show how to open the file House from a CD located in drive E.

To Open a File

1 **Insert the CD that accompanies this book into your CD drive. After a few seconds, if Windows displays a dialog box, click its Close button.**

2 **Click Open on the Photoshop File menu and then navigate to the Chapter03 folder. Double-click the file named House.**

3 **When Photoshop displays the image in the document window, if the magnification is not 25% as shown on the title bar, double-click the magnification box on the document window status bar, type 25, and then press the ENTER key.**

4 **Drag the window to the lower center portion of the workspace.**

5 **If the rulers do not display, press CTRL+R.**

6 **Click the status bar menu button, point to Show, and then click Document Dimensions.**

Photoshop opens the file House and displays it in the document window at 25% magnification (Figure 3-2).

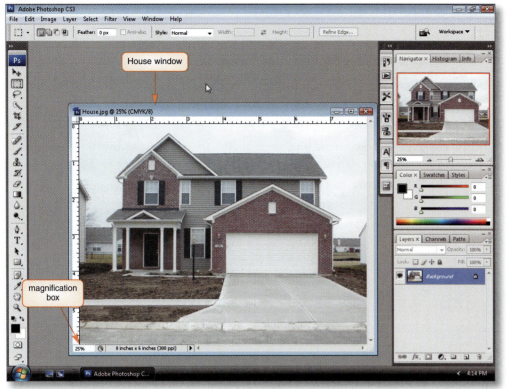

FIGURE 3-2

The Status Bar

If your status bar does not display the document dimensions, you can click the status bar menu button, point to Show, and then click Document Dimensions in the list. You edit the photo in the same way, whether you display the dimensions or display the size of the file.

Table 3-1 displays information about the House photo. It is a photo saved as a JPG file. In the next steps you will convert the image to a PSD file.

The PSD Format

The **Photoshop Document Format** (**PSD**) is the default file format in Photoshop and the only format that supports all Photoshop features. When working with composite objects, to maintain the integrity of each element and to provide maximum flexibility in future editing, it is a good idea to save the file in PSD format. Many Photoshop users save files in multiple formats. For example, a Web version of an image might be saved as a GIF or JPG, the print version as a TIFF or EPS, and the composite file as a PSD. The PSD format maximizes file compatibility and provides a more portable file that can be read by other applications, including previous versions of Photoshop. It also maintains the appearance of blended layers. See Appendix A for instructions on setting Photoshop preferences regarding file formats and saving with different extensions.

Table 3-1 House Image Characteristics	
File Name	House
File Type	JPG
Image Dimensions	8 x 6 inches
Color Mode	CMYK
Resolution	300 pixels/inch
File Size	870 KB

Saving a File in the PSD Format

Because you plan to add multiple objects to the house image, you will save it in the PSD format. To save files in a different format, you use the Save As command on the File menu as the steps on the next page illustrate. In the Save As dialog box, the Format box provides a list of available file formats from which you can choose PSD.

To Save a File in the PSD Format

1 With your USB flash drive connected to one of the computer's USB ports, click File on the menu bar and then click Save As.

2 When the Save As dialog box is displayed, type `House Edited` in the File name text box. Do not press the ENTER key after typing the file name.

3 Click the Format box arrow and then click Photoshop (*.PSD, *.PDD) in the list.

4 Click the Save in box arrow and then click USB (F:), or the location associated with your USB flash drive, in the list (Figure 3-3).

5 Click the Save button in the Save As dialog box.

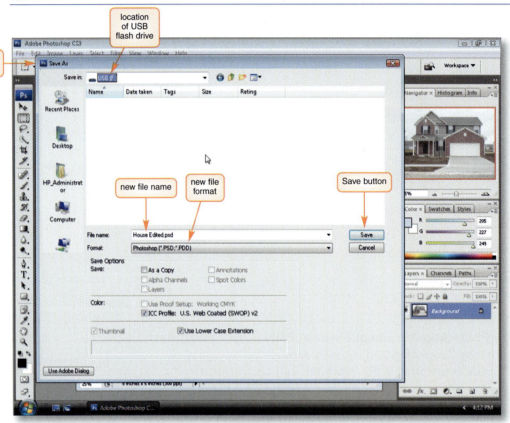

FIGURE 3-3

> ### More About
>
> **Photoshop File Formats**
>
> PSD format is the default file format in Photoshop and the only format that supports all Photoshop features. Other Adobe applications can import PSD files directly and preserve many Photoshop features due to the tight integration between Adobe products. The PDD, or portable document format, is used by other Adobe applications such as PhotoDeluxe and Photoshop Elements.

Photoshop saves the file on the USB flash drive with the file name House Edited in the PSD format, and displays the new name on the document window title bar. As you work through the rest of this chapter, save your file often. That way, if the power goes out, or your system locks, you will have a current copy.

Layers

Creating layers is one of the most powerful tools in Photoshop. A layer is a section within a Photoshop document that you can manipulate independent from the rest of the document. Layers can be stacked one on top of the other, resembling sheets of clear film, to form a composite image.

Layers can be created, copied, deleted, displayed, hidden, merged, locked, grouped, repositioned, and flattened. Layers can be images, patterns, text, shapes, colors, or filters. You can use layers to apply special effects, correct or colorize pictures, repair damaged photos, or import text elements. In previous chapters you worked with images in a single layer called the **background**. In this chapter you will create, name, and manipulate multiple layers.

There are several ways to create a layer. You can:

- Isolate a portion of the image and then cut or make a layer copy
- Create a new layer by copying from a different image
- Duplicate a layer that already exists
- Create a new, blank layer on which you can draw or create text

When you add a layer to an image, a new layer is created above, or on top of, the currently selected layer creating a **stacking order**. By default, layers are named and numbered sequentially. The stacking order of layers in an image can be rearranged to change the appearance of the image. The final appearance of an edited Photoshop document is a view of the layer stack from the top down. These layer manipulations are performed using the Layers palette, which you will learn about later in this chapter.

Creating a Layer via Cut

In the House Edited photo, you will create a new layer that includes only the sky. You will use the Magic Wand tool to select the sky and then use the Layer via Cut command to isolate the sky from the rest of the photo, creating a new layer. To ensure your layers match the figures in this book, you will use the keyboard shortcut by pressing the D key on your keyboard to activate the default color scheme of black and white.

To Create a Layer via Cut

1

• **With the House Edited image displaying in the document window, press the D key.**

• **On the Tools palette, right-click the Quick Selection tool and then click Magic Wand Tool on the context menu. If necessary, on the options bar, type 15 in the Tolerance box and then click the Contiguous check box so it is selected.**

• **In the photo, click the sky.**

The sky displays a selection border (Figure 3-4).

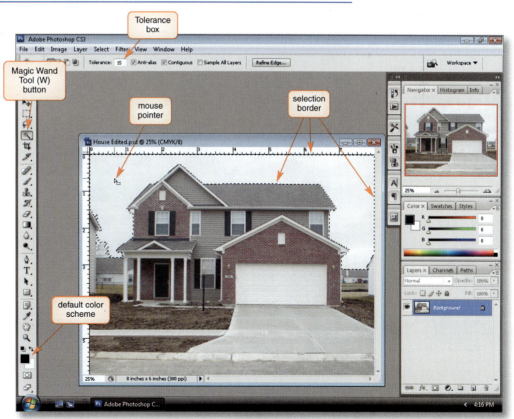

FIGURE 3-4

2 _____

• **Right-click the sky.**

*Photoshop displays the
Selection shortcut menu
(Figure 3-5).*

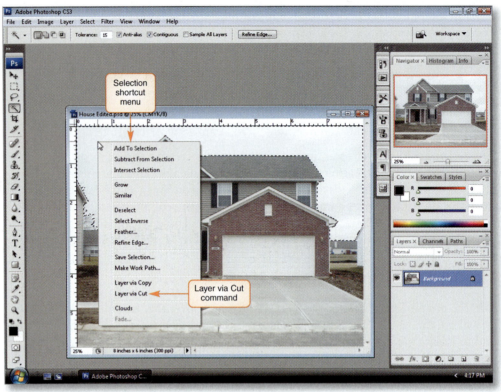

FIGURE 3-5

3 _____

• **Click Layer via Cut on
the shortcut menu.**

*The Layers palette displays a
new layer above the
Background layer (Figure 3-6).*

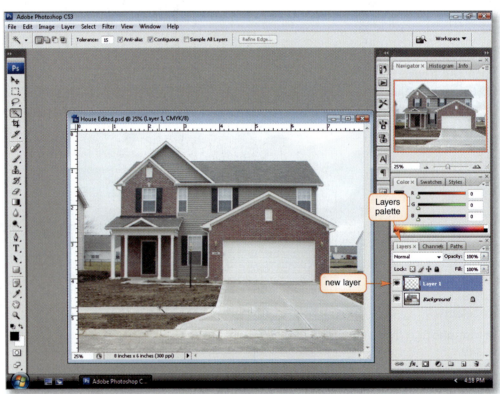

FIGURE 3-6

Other Ways

1. Create selection, press
   SHIFT+CTRL+J
2. On Layer menu, point to
   New, click Layer via Cut

The Layer via Cut command is different from the Layer via Copy command in that it removes the selection from the background. Future edits to the background, such as changing the color or lighting, will not affect the cut layer.

Now that you have a background layer and a second layer of the sky, you can use the Layers palette to customize and manipulate the layers.

The Layers Palette

The **Layers palette**, usually located in the lowest level of palettes on the right of the Photoshop window, lists all layers, groups, and layer effects in an image (Figure 3-7). Each time you insert a layer in an image, the new layer is added to the top of the palette. The default display of a layer in the Layers palette includes a visibility icon, a thumbnail of the layer, and the layer's name. To the right of the layer's name a locking icon may display.

The Layers palette is used in several different ways. You can use the palette to show and hide layers, create new layers, and work with groups of layers. You can access additional commands and attributes by clicking the Layers palette menu button or by right-clicking a layer. The Layers palette defines how layers interact. As you use the buttons and boxes in the Layers palette, each will be explained.

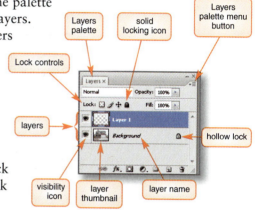

FIGURE 3-7

Photoshop allows you to **lock layers** in several ways. The first button to the right of the word Lock in the Layers palette, Lock transparent pixels, confines editing to the opaque portions of the layer. The second button, Lock image pixels, prevents modification of the layer's pixels using any of the painting tools. The third button, Lock position, prevents the layer from being moved. The fourth button, Lock all, enables all of the other three ways of locking every layer.

When a layer is locked, a lock icon appears to the right of the name in the Layers palette. A fully locked layer displays a solid lock; a partially locked layer displays a hollow lock.

The Background layer is partially locked by default — it displays a hollow lock (Figure 3-7). While Photoshop allows background editing, as you have done in previous chapters, the Background layer cannot be moved, nor can its transparency be changed. In other words, the Background layer fills the document window and there is no layer behind the background. If you want to convert the Background layer into a fully editable layer, double-click the layer in the Layers palette, and then when the New Layer dialog box is displayed, click the OK button.

Changing the Palette Options

The **Palette Options** command, accessible from the Layers palette menu, allows you to change the view and size of the thumbnail related to each layer. A **thumbnail** is a small visual display of the layer in the Layers palette. Clicking Palette Options displays a dialog box in which you can choose small, medium, large, or no thumbnails. In addition, you can specify thumbnail contents by choosing the **Layer Bounds option** that causes the Layers palette to display only the layer, restricting the thumbnail to the object's pixels on the layer.

The steps on the next page show how to display a medium-sized thumbnail of each layer with the Layer Bounds option.

To Change Palette Options

1

• **Click the Layers palette menu button.**

Photoshop displays the palette menu (Figure 3-8).

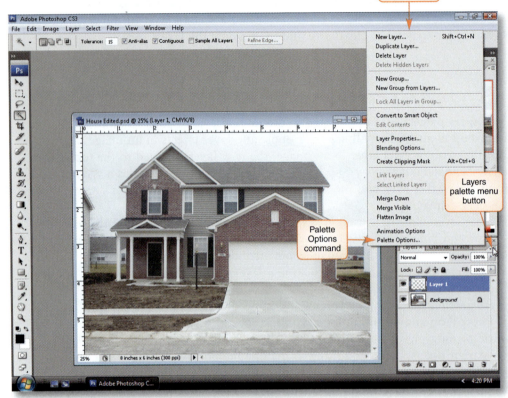

FIGURE 3-8

2

• **Click Palette Options on the menu.**

• **When the Layers Palette Options dialog box is displayed, click the medium thumbnail and Layer Bounds options.**

The Layers Palette Options dialog box displays settings to change the look and feel of the Layers palette (Figure 3-9).

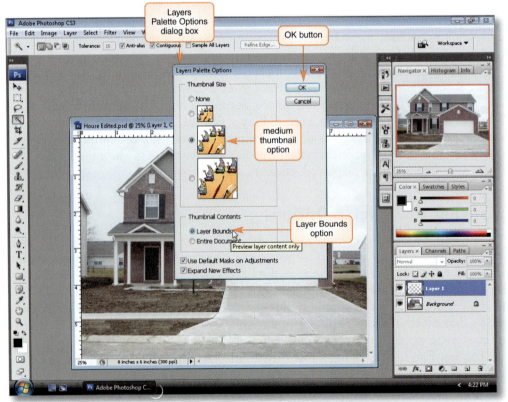

FIGURE 3-9

3

• **Click the OK button.**

The Layers palette now displays small pictures of each layer independent of the background (Figure 3-10).

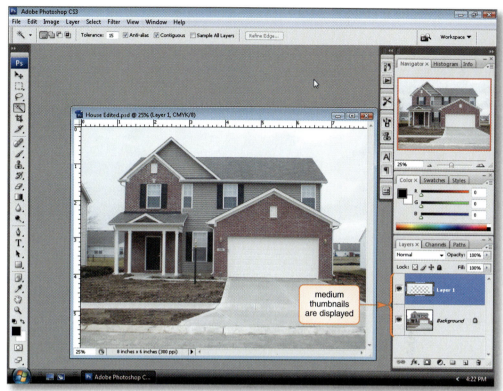

FIGURE 3-10

Displaying thumbnails of each layer allows you to see easily what the layer looks like and helps you to be more efficient when editing a layer. To improve performance and save monitor space, however, some Photoshop users choose not to display thumbnails.

Selecting Layers

When you click a layer in the Layers palette, it becomes the active, editable portion of the image. The selected layer also is referred to as the **active layer** in the Layers palette. To select or activate a layer, you click the layer name or the thumbnail in the Layers palette as the step on the next page show. To select all layers, click All Layers on the Select menu, or press ALT+CTRL+A. While a layer is active, you cannot edit other portions of the image.

More About

CS3 Smart Objects

A new feature in Photoshop CS3 is the ability to convert a layer into a smart object. Similar to a layer mask, smart object layers are nondestructive — they do not change the original pixels. They are useful for warping, scaling, or rotating both raster and vector graphic layers. To convert a layer into a smart object, right-click the layer, and then click Convert to Smart Object on the shortcut menu. Smart object layers display a special icon in the layer's thumbnail.

To Select a Layer

• **In the Layers palette, click the thumbnail of the Background layer.**

The layer is displayed with a blue background indicating that it is the active layer (Figure 3-11).

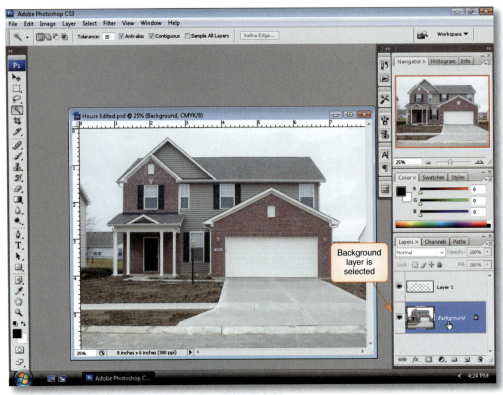

Background layer is selected

FIGURE 3-11

Other Ways

1. To select top layer, press ALT+.
2. To select bottom layer, press ALT+,
3. To select next layer, press ALT+] or ALT+[

Naming Layers

It is a good practice to give each layer a unique name so you can identify it more easily. When you name a layer, the name displays in the Layers palette. The name of the active layer also displays on the title bar of the document window. Photoshop allows you to give each layer its own color identification as well. To name and color a layer, right-click the layer and click Layer Properties to display the Layer Properties dialog box as the following steps illustrate.

More About

Selecting

Creating a selection in the document window should not be confused with selecting the layer. A selection, displayed by a marquee, refers to encompassing pixels in order to edit them. Selecting a layer is done in the Layers palette and allows you to work with only that layer in the document window. In other words, you can create a selection that is all or part of a selected layer.

To Name and Color a Layer

1

• **In the Layers palette, right-click the layer name Layer 1.**

Photoshop displays the layer shortcut menu (Figure 3-12).

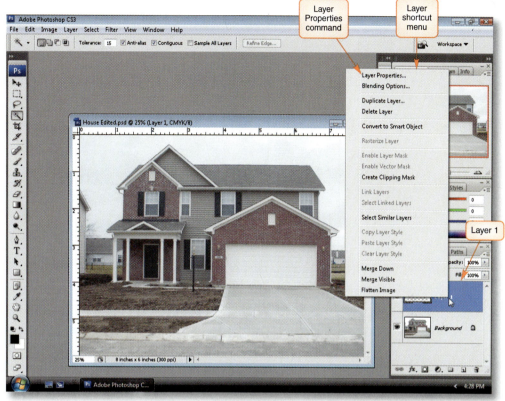

FIGURE 3-12

2

• **Click the Layer Properties command.**

• **When the Layer Properties dialog box is displayed, type** sky **in the Name box.**

• **Click the Color box arrow and then click Blue in the list.**

Photoshop displays the Layer Properties dialog box (Figure 3-13).

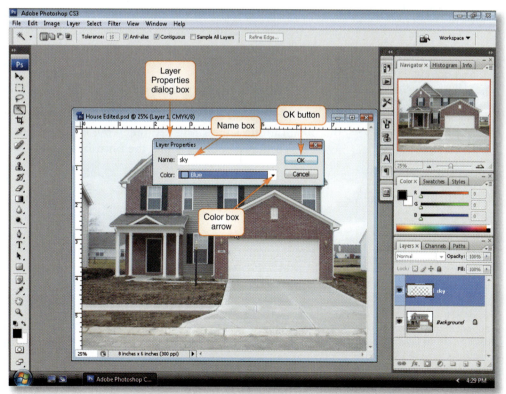

FIGURE 3-13

3

• **Click the OK button.**

The layer is renamed and the color blue displays to the left of the sky layer in the Layers palette (Figure 3-14).

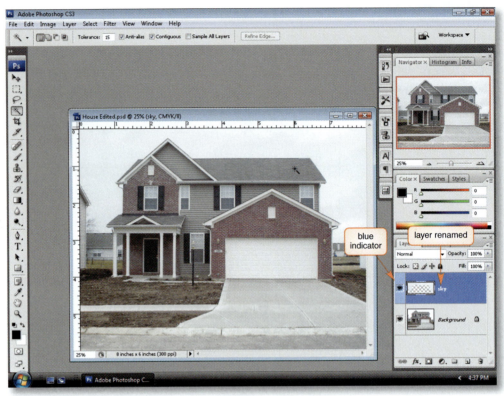

FIGURE 3-14

Photoshop reserves seven colors for color coding layers: red, orange, yellow, green, blue, violet, and gray. If you have more than seven layers, you can group layers that have similar characteristics with one color.

Hiding and Viewing Layers

To hide or view a layer, click the Indicates layer visibility button to the left of the thumbnail in the Layers palette. When the layer is visible, the button displays an eye icon. When the layer is invisible, the button is blank.

To Hide and View a Layer

1

• **Click the Indicates layer visibility button to the left of the sky layer.**

The sky layer is invisible in the document window (Figure 3-15).

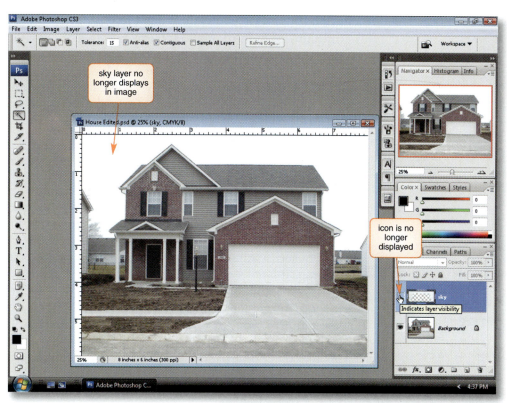

FIGURE 3-15

2

• **Click the Indicates layer visibility button again.**

The sky layer is visible and the Layers palette again displays the eye icon (Figure 3-16).

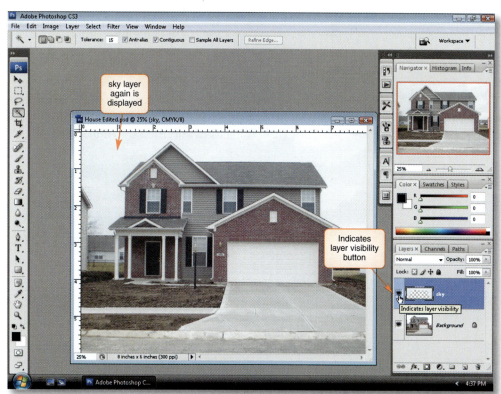

FIGURE 3-16

Other Ways

1. Right-click visibility icon, click Hide this layer or Show this layer
2. On Layer menu, click Hide Layers or Show Layers

Sometimes, if you have multiple layers, you may wish to view only one layer. In that case, rather than turning off all of the other layers one by one, you can press ALT+click on the visibility icon for the layer you wish to view. All other layers will be hidden. Pressing ALT+click again restores the previous visibility settings. You also can show or hide all other layers by selecting Show/Hide all other layers from the shortcut menu.

To hide or view several contiguous layers, drag through the eye column.

To delete a layer permanently, right-click the layer name and then click Delete Layer on the shortcut menu, or activate the layer and press the DELETE key.

Creating a Layer from Another Image

When you create composite images, you may want to create layers from other images. It is important to choose images that closely match or complement color, lighting, size, and perspective if you want your image to look natural. While adjustments can be made, it is easier to start with as close a match as possible. One of the keys to successful image compositions is finding the best source material with similar lighting situations and tonal qualities.

Many sources for components exist for composite images. For example, you can use your own digital photos, scanned images, images from royalty free Web sites, or you can draw your own images. If you use a photo or image from the Web, make sure you have legal rights to use the image. Legal rights include permission from the photographer or artist to use the image, or purchasing these rights, via a contract, through an online store.

The basic process of creating a new layer from another image involves opening a second image, selecting the area you wish to use, and then moving it to the original photo in a drag-and-drop or cut-and-paste fashion. Once the layer exists in the original photo, some editing may need to take place to remove portions of the layer, to resize it, or to make tonal adjustments.

Opening a Second Image

In order to add a landscaped flower bed as a layer to the House Edited image, you will need to open the PSD file Flowerbed from the CD that accompanies this book, or from a location specified by your instructor.

More About

Adobe Stock Images

Photoshop offers the option to download low-resolution, complementary versions of many images. You can work with the complementary images until you make your final decision, at which point you can purchase and download a high-resolution image.

To Open a Second Image

1

• On the File menu, click Open.

• When the Open dialog box is displayed, if necessary, click the Look in box arrow, and then navigate to the Chapter03 folder on the CD that accompanies this book, or a location specified by your instructor.

• If necessary, double-click the Chapter03 folder.

• Click the file named Flowerbed.

The Chapter03 folder is displayed in the Open dialog box (Figure 3-17). Your list of files may differ.

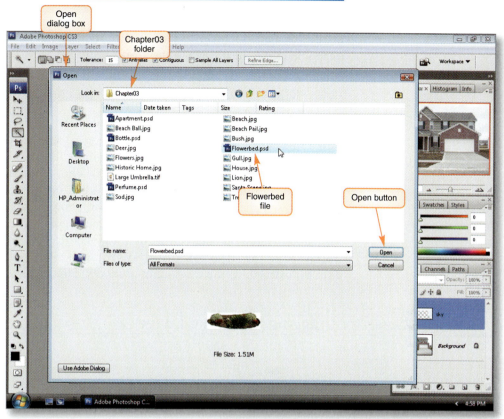

FIGURE 3-17

2

• Click the Open button.

• When the Flowerbed window opens, drag its title bar to a position in the workspace slightly above the House Edited title bar, if necessary.

• If necessary, type 25 in the magnification box at the bottom of the Flowerbed window and then press the ENTER key.

Photoshop displays the second document window (Figure 3-18).

Other Ways

1. Press CTRL+O, select file, click Open
2. Click Go to Bridge button, navigate to location of file, double-click file

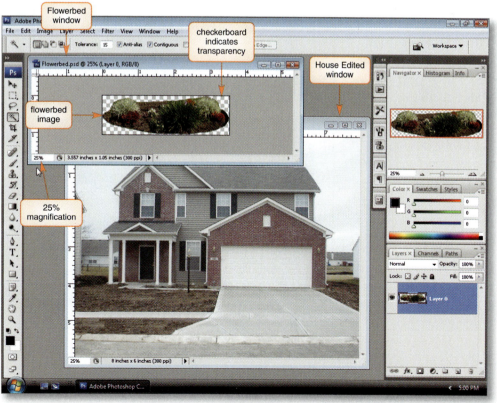

FIGURE 3-18

The gray and white checkerboard effect in the Flowerbed file (Figure 3-18) represents portions of the document window that are transparent, or containing pixels without any color. In other words, that part of the document window is blank. Because document windows are rectangular in nature, a nonrectangular image usually will display some transparent parts.

Creating a Layer by Dragging an Entire Image

When you drag from one document window to the other, Photoshop creates a layer. If you want to include the entire image from the source window, click the Move Tool (V) button and then drag from any location in the source window to the destination window. When dragging layers, Photoshop users adjust their document windows to display in various ways depending upon personal preference. You may want to resize the document window by dragging a border or move the document window by dragging the title bar so you can see both images more clearly.

The flowerbed image will be used in its entirety as a landscaping feature in the front yard to the left of the driveway. You will move the image from the source window, Flowerbed, to the destination window, House Edited.

To Create a Layer by Dragging an Entire Image

1

• **If necessary, click the Flowerbed window title bar to make it the active document window.**

• **Click the Move Tool (V) button on the Tools palette.**

• **Point to the center of the image.**

The mouse pointer displays the move icon (Figure 3-19).

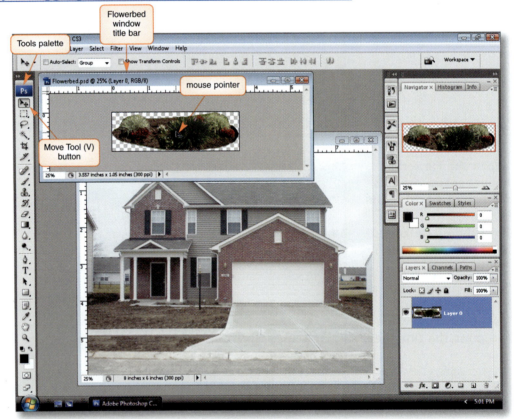

FIGURE 3-19

2

• **Drag the flowerbed image into the House Edited window and drop it to the left of the driveway.**

The superimposed flowerbed is displayed in the House Edited window, and a layer is created at the top of the Layers palette (Figure 3-20).

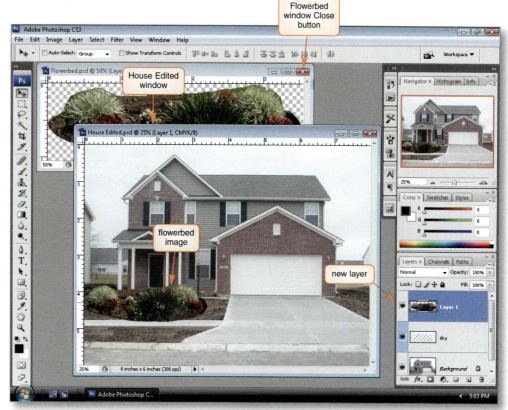

FIGURE 3-20

The original or source image remains unchanged. Dragging between document windows is an automatic duplication rather than a true move. The following step shows how to close the Flowerbed window.

Other Ways

1. To select all, press CTRL+A, drag image
2. To select Move tool, press V key, drag image

To Close the Flowerbed Window

1 **Click the Close button in the Flowerbed window. If Photoshop asks if you want to save changes to the document, click the No button.**

The window closes and the House Edited window becomes active.

The new layer is displayed in the Layers palette above the layer of the sky. The following steps illustrate how to set the layer properties.

To Set the Flowerbed Layer Properties

1 **Right-click Layer 1 in the Layers palette. Click Layer Properties on the shortcut menu.**

2 **Type** `flowerbed` **in the Name box. Click the Color box arrow and then click Green.**

3 **Click the OK button.**

The flowerbed layer displays a green indicator in the Layers palette as shown in Figure 3-21 on the next page.

Resizing a Layer

The flowerbed layer is too large for the amount of yard in front of the house. The following steps illustrate how to resize a layer. The process is the same as resizing any selection.

To Resize a Layer

1

• **If necessary, in the Layers palette, click the flowerbed layer to activate it.**

• **Click the Move Tool (V) button on the Tools palette.**

• **If necessary, click the Show Transform Controls check box on the options bar to select it.**

Photoshop displays the layer with a bounding box (Figure 3-21).

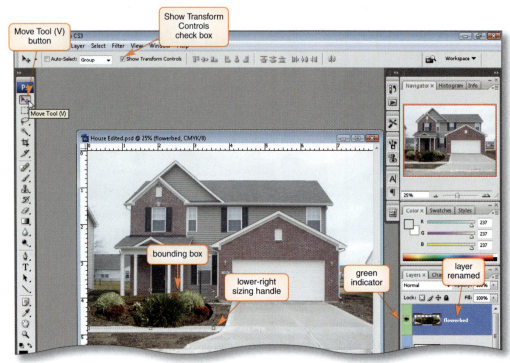

FIGURE 3-21

2

• **SHIFT+drag the lower-right sizing handle toward the center of the layer until the layer is approximately the size of the front porch of the house.**

The resized layer is displayed (Figure 3-22). Recall that SHIFT+drag maintains the width to height ratio when resizing selections.

3

• **Press the ENTER key to apply the transformation.**

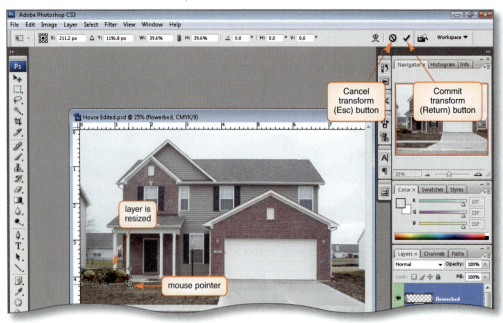

FIGURE 3-22

Applying or committing a transformation tells Photoshop that you are finished resizing. You cannot choose another tool until you apply the transformation. To cancel the transformation, click the Cancel transform (Esc) button on the options bar (Figure 3-22) or press the ESC key.

The next step shows how the layer is moved.

To Move the Flowerbed Layer

1 With the layer selected, drag the layer so its horizontal center is approximately even with the left column on the porch and its vertical center is between the house and the street. Do not drag the center reference point.

The layer is moved (Figure 3-23).

In the next section, you will create a layer that includes only a selected area from another image. First, the following steps illustrate how to open a file named Flowers.

To Open the Flowers Image

1 On the File menu, click Open.

2 When the Open dialog box is displayed, click the Look in box arrow, and then navigate to the Chapter03 folder on the CD that accompanies this book, or a location specified by your instructor.

3 Click the file named Flowers, and then click the Open button.

4 Change the magnification to 25%. Resize the window and scroll as necessary to display the red and pink flowers as shown in Figure 3-24.

Photoshop displays the Flowers window (Figure 3-24).

FIGURE 3-23

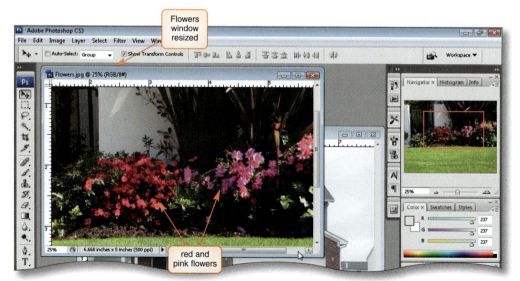

FIGURE 3-24

Creating a Layer by Dragging a Selection

The flowers that will display between the porch and sidewalk are a part of a larger image. Therefore, you will have to select a portion of the image and then drag the selection to create a layer. You will move the selection from the source window, Flowers, to the destination window, House Edited. The following steps illustrate how to create a layer by dragging.

To Create a Layer by Dragging a Selection

1

• **With the Flowers window active, if necessary, right-click the Lasso Tool (L) button and then click Magnetic Lasso on the context menu.**

• **Drag around the red and dark pink flowers including some greenery. Avoid including in the selection the building behind the flowers and the ground below the flowers. Use the Add to selection and Subtract from selection buttons on the options bar, as necessary, to create your selection. If you make a mistake while selecting, press CTRL+D to deselect, then begin again.**

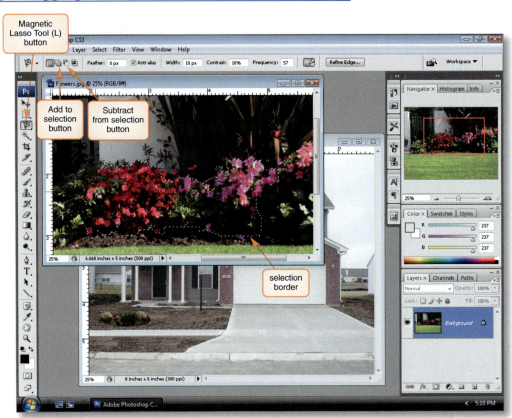

FIGURE 3-25

Photoshop displays the selection border around the flowers (Figure 3-25). Your exact selection does not have to match the one in the figure.

2

• **Click the Move Tool (V) button on the Tools palette.**

• **ALT+drag the selection and drop it in the House Edited window.**

• **On the options bar, if necessary, click the Show Transform Controls check box to select it.**

The flowers are displayed in the House Edited window with the bounding box (Figure 3-26). Recall that ALT+drag of a selection creates a copy of the selection rather than a cut.

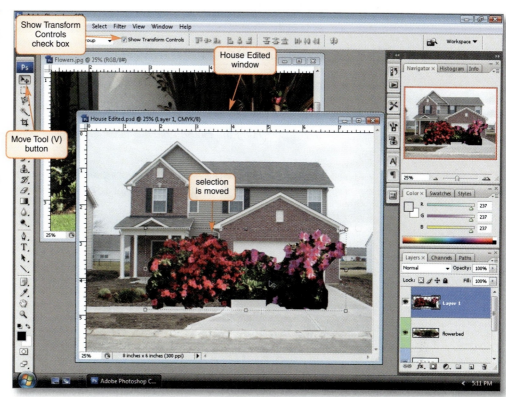

FIGURE 3-26

3

• **SHIFT+drag a corner sizing handle to reduce the size of the flowers to approximately 1.0 by 0.5 inches.**

Drag the selection to the area between the porch and sidewalk as shown in Figure 3-27.

4

• **Press the ENTER key to apply the transformation.**

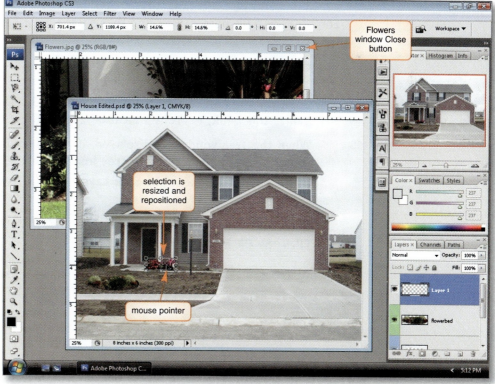

FIGURE 3-27

Other Ways

1. In source window, create selection, on Edit menu, click Copy, in destination window, click Paste

The next step shows how to close the Flowers window.

To Close the Flowers Window

1 **Click the Close button in the Flowers window. If Photoshop displays a dialog box asking if you want to save the changes, click the No button.**

The window closes and the House Edited window becomes active.

The new layer displays in the Layers palette above the layer of the flowerbed. The following steps illustrate how to set the layer properties.

To Set the Flowers Layer Properties

1 **Right-click Layer 1 in the Layers palette. Click Layer Properties on the shortcut menu.**

2 **Type** flowers **in the Name box. Click the Color box arrow and then click Red.**

3 **Click the OK button.**

The flowers layer displays a red indicator in the Layers palette as shown in Figure 3-28.

The flowers fit the space but may need some tonal adjustment, which you will learn about later in this chapter.

In preparation for editing a layer that includes a tree, the following steps show how to open a file named Tree, and then set the layer properties.

To Create the Tree Layer

1 **Open the file named Tree from the Chapter03 folder on the CD that accompanies this book, or from a location specified by your instructor.**

2 **When the Tree window is displayed, if necessary press the v key to access the Move tool, and then drag the tree image into the House Edited window.**

3 **In the Layers palette, right-click Layer 1. Click Layer Properties on the shortcut menu.**

4 **Type** tree **in the Name box. Click the Color box arrow and then click Gray.**

5 **Click the OK button.**

The tree layer is displayed in the document window and is renamed and colored in the Layers palette (Figure 3-28).

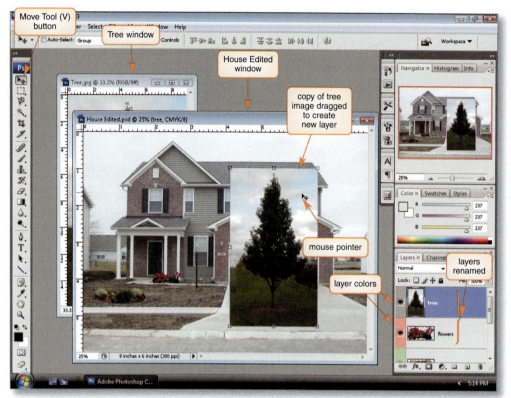

FIGURE 3-28

The Eraser Tools

When creating a composite image, you can limit the selected area of the source image as you did in the flowers layer, but sometimes a layer still has extra color or objects that are not appropriate for the composite image. The image may be oddly shaped making selecting a portion tedious; or, there are other images in the background that come along with the selection no matter what you do. In those cases, dragging the image into a layer and then erasing part of that layer gives you more freedom and control in how the layer is displayed.

Using the Eraser Tools

The **Eraser tool** changes pixels in the image as you drag through them. On most layers, the Eraser tool simply erases the pixels or changes them to transparent. On the background layer, the pixels are changed to white. On a locked layer, the Eraser tool changes the pixels to the background color.

When you right-click the Eraser Tool (E) button on the Tools palette, you can choose other eraser tools. The **Magic Eraser tool** is similar to the Eraser tool except it erases all similarly colored pixels with one click. You have the choice of contiguous or noncontiguous pixels.

The **Background Eraser tool** erases the background while maintaining the edges of an object in the foreground, based on a set color that you choose for the background.

On the next page, Table 3-2 describes the eraser tools.

Table 3-2 Eraser Tools

TOOL	PURPOSE	SHORTCUT	BUTTON
Eraser tool	erases pixels beneath the cursor or brush tip	E SHIFT+E toggles through all three eraser tools	
Background Eraser tool	erases sample color from center of brush	E SHIFT+E toggles through all three eraser tools	
Magic Eraser tool	erases all similarly colored pixels	E SHIFT+E toggles through all three eraser tools	

Erasing with the Magic Eraser

The following steps illustrate how to use the Magic Eraser tool to remove the sky around, and in back of, the tree. The Magic Eraser options bar (Figure 3-30) allows you to enter a **tolerance** value to define the range of colors that can be erased. A lower tolerance erases pixels within a range of color values very similar to the pixel you click. A higher tolerance erases pixels within a broader range. You will choose to erase noncontiguous pixels, which means all pixels with similar colors in the selected layer will be erased.

To Erase Using the Magic Eraser

1

• **With the tree layer still selected, right-click the Eraser Tool (E) button on the Tools palette.**

Photoshop displays the context menu (Figure 3-29).

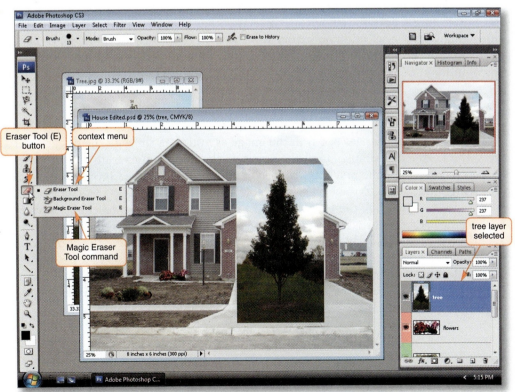

FIGURE 3-29

2

• **Click Magic Eraser Tool.**

• **On the Magic Eraser options bar, type** 50 **in the Tolerance box. If necessary, click the Anti-Alias check box to select it. If necessary, click the Contiguous check box to deselect it.**

• **Move the mouse to a portion of the tree layer containing sky.**

The mouse pointer changes to a Magic Eraser icon (Figure 3-30). Choosing non-contiguous will select all pixels of similar color.

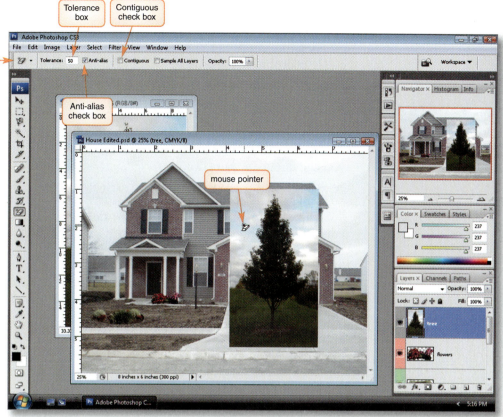

FIGURE 3-30

3

• **Click the sky.**

Photoshop deletes all of the sky color (Figure 3-31).

4

• **If some sky still remains in your layer, click it.**

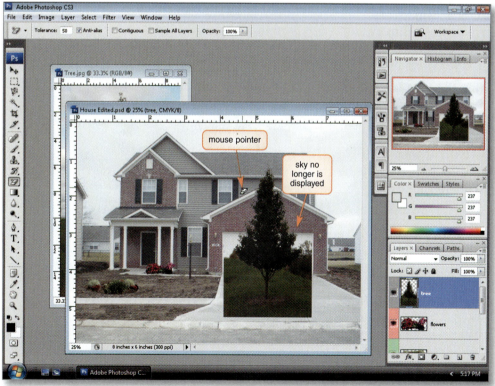

FIGURE 3-31

Other Ways

1. From another eraser tool, press SHIFT+E until Magic Eraser tool is selected, click in document

Recall that the Anti-alias check box creates a smooth edge that can apply to both selecting and erasing. The tolerance setting of 50 affects a fairly broad range in the color spectrum.

Erasing with the Eraser Tool

To erase more of the background in the tree layer, the following steps use the Eraser tool. The Eraser tool options bar (Figure 3-32) displays a Mode box in which you can choose a shape for erasure, an Opacity box to specify the depth of the erasure, and a Flow box to specify how quickly the erasure is performed. In addition, you can specify whether or not the erasure becomes a state in the History palette.

The right-bracket key on your keyboard ( ]) is used to increase the size of the eraser. The left bracket key ([ ) decreases the size of the eraser. Some users find it easier to erase in a layer when only that layer is displayed. If you want to display only the layer, click the visibility icon next to the background and all layers other than the tree layer. When you are finished erasing, click the visibility box again to redisplay the background and other layers. The following steps illustrate how to use the Eraser tool.

To Erase Using the Eraser tool

1

• **Increase the magnification of the document window to 50%. Scroll to display the lower portion of the tree layer.**

• **With the tree layer still selected, right-click the Eraser Tool (E) button on the Tools palette, and then click Eraser Tool on the context menu.**

• **Move the mouse to a portion of the tree layer containing grass.**

• **Press the] key several times to resize the eraser until the mouser pointer changes from a dot to a small circle.**

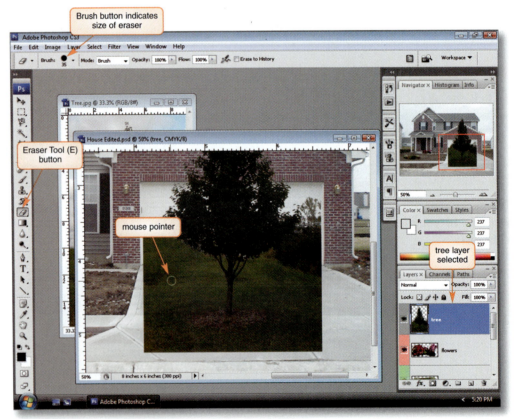

FIGURE 3-32

Photoshop displays the mouse pointer as a circle (Figure 3-32). Notice the eraser brush size setting changes on the options bar as you click the bracket key.

2

• **Drag the mouse across a portion of the grass. Do not drag across the tree or its trunk.**

The Eraser tool erases the pixels under the mouse (Figure 3-33).

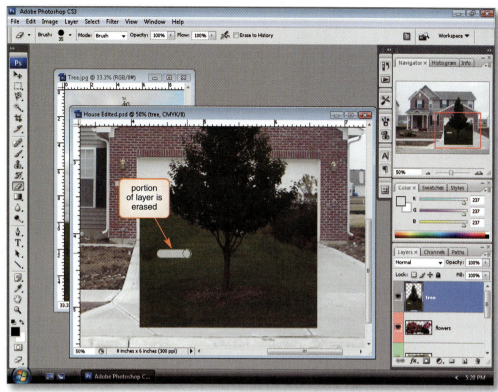

FIGURE 3-33

3

• **Continue dragging, using the [and] keys to change the size of your eraser. Zoom in as necessary, to erase the majority of the grass and background bushes. Do not try to erase the grass showing behind the tree limbs.**

Most of the grass is deleted (Figure 3-34).

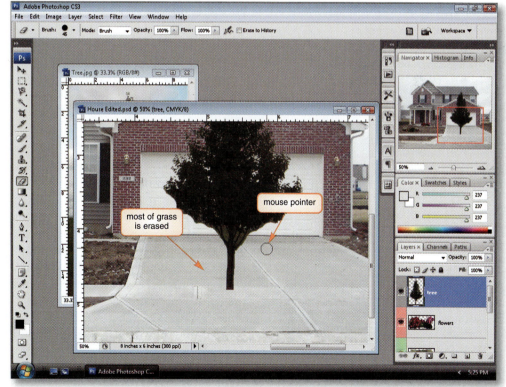

FIGURE 3-34

4 ———

• **To delete close to the tree trunk, click the Mode box arrow on the options bar and then choose Block.**

• **Increase the magnification and scroll as necessary to view the trunk of the tree.**

• **Using the Block shape, drag close to the trunk on each side of the tree.**

The Eraser tool erases the pixels under the mouse (Figure 3-35). Some grass color will remain close to the leaves of the trees.

5 ———

• **If necessary, change the magnification back to 50% by typing** 50 **in the magnification box on the status bar.**

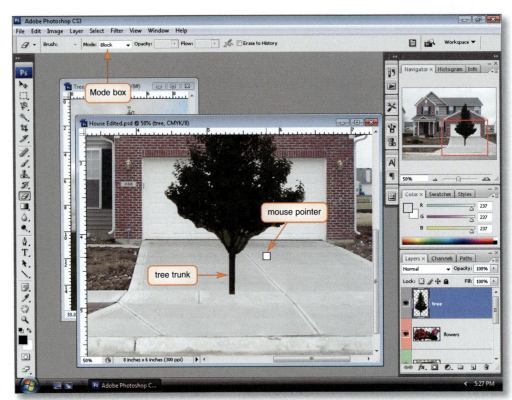

FIGURE 3-35

The Block and Pencil mode on the options bar are not resizable like the Brush mode.

Erasing with the Background Eraser

The Background Eraser samples the color in the center of the mouse pointer which is called the **hot spot** and then erases that color as you drag, leaving the rest of the layer as foreground. You release the mouse to sample a different color. On the Background Eraser options bar (Figure 3-36) you can use the tolerance setting to control the range of the transparency, sample the color selections, and adjust the sharpness of the boundaries by setting limits. The three sampling buttons on the Background Eraser options bar sample in different ways. Sampling: Continuous samples colors and erases continuously as you drag; Sampling Once: erases only the areas containing the color you first click; and Sampling: Background Swatch erases only areas containing the current background color.

The following steps show how to use the Background Eraser tool to remove the grass from behind the branches of the tree. If you make a mistake while erasing, click the previous state in the History palette and begin erasing again.

To Erase Using the Background Eraser

1

• **With the tree layer still selected and the magnification at 50%, right-click the Eraser Tool (E) button on the Tools palette.**

• **Click Background Eraser Tool on the context menu.**

• **On the options bar, click the Sampling: Once button. Click the Limits box arrow and then choose Discontiguous. Type 25 in the Tolerance box and press the ENTER key. Click the Protect Foreground Color check box to select it.**

• **Move the mouse to the document window and then press the] key several times to increase the size of the eraser. Position the mouse pointer directly over a portion of the grass that still is displayed.**

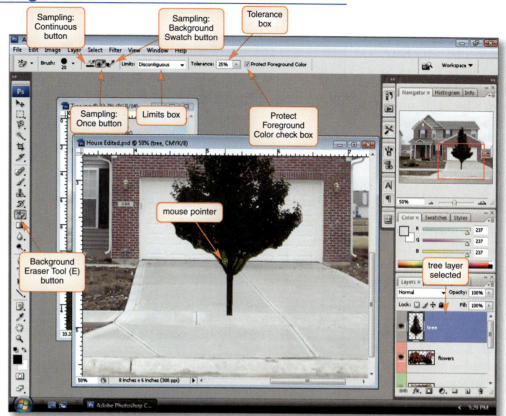

FIGURE 3-36

Photoshop displays the mouse pointer as a circle with a cross in the middle (Figure 3-36).

2

• **With the cross directly over green grass, click and hold the mouse button. Slowly drag across the lower limbs of the tree.**

Photoshop erases all of the grass in the background (Figure 3-37).

3

• **If any parts of the layer still need to be erased to display only the tree, right-click the Eraser Tool (E) button on the Tools palette and then click Eraser Tool. Adjust the brush size as necessary with the bracket keys and carefully erase small portions at a time.**

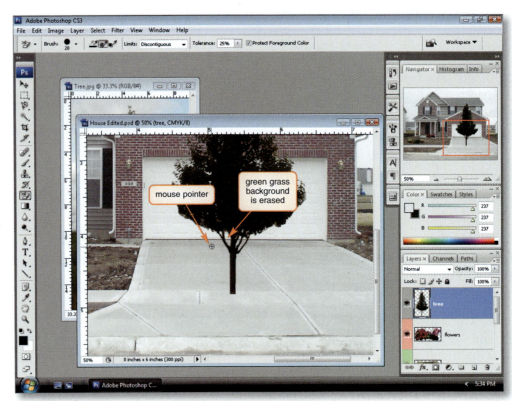

FIGURE 3-37

To alternate among the three eraser tools, press SHIFT+E. To access the eraser tools after using a different tool, press the E key.

When using the eraser tools, it is best to erase small portions at once. That way each erasure is a separate state in the History palette. If you make mistakes you can click earlier states in the palette. Small erasures also can be undone. To **undo** an erasure, click Edit on the menu bar and then click Undo Eraser, or press CTRL+Z to undo.

When working with layers, it is important to make sure which layer you are editing by looking at the active layer in the Layers palette. If a layer is partially eclipsed, or overlapped, by another layer do the following. Select the layer in the Layers palette. Click Layer on the menu bar, point to Arrange, and then click one of the options to bring the layer to the front or send it to the back.

The final step in editing the tree layer is to move it to a position in the flowerbed.

To Reposition the Tree Layer

1 Decrease the magnification to 25%.

2 With the tree layer selected, press the V key to activate the Move tool.

3 Drag the layer to a location left of the front door of the house, so the base of the tree is in the flowerbed (Figure 3-38). Part of the tree will be eclipsed by the left margin.

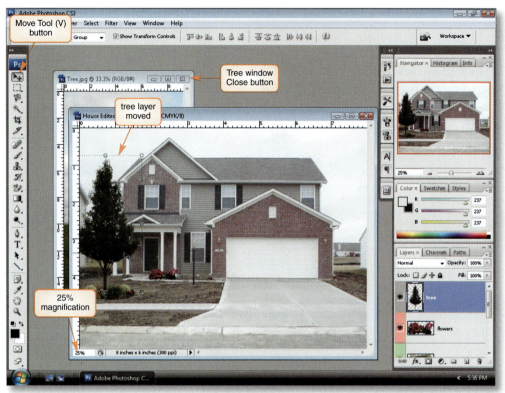

FIGURE 3-38

Because you are finished with the original tree image, it is time to close the Tree window as shown in the following step.

To Close the Tree Window

1 **Click the Close button on the Tree window title bar. If Photoshop displays a dialog box asking if you want to save the changes, click the No button.**

The window closes and the House Edited window becomes active.

The next piece of landscaping is to add a lion statue on each side of the driveway. The two layers are created as the following steps illustrate.

To Insert the Lion Layers

1 **Open the file named Lion from the Chapter03 folder on the CD that accompanies this book, or from a location specified by your instructor.**

2 **When Photoshop displays the Lion window, drag its title bar above the House Edited window title bar.**

3 **Press the w key to activate the Magic Wand tool. Click in the white space. Right-click the selection and then click Select Inverse on the shortcut menu.**

4 **Press the v key to activate the Move tool. If necessary, click the Show Transform Controls check box to select it. Drag the selection to the House Edited image and position it on one side of the garage door, close to the house. Resize as necessary.**

More About

Arranging Layers

If you want to rearrange your layers in order to change their visibility or to better organize them, simply drag the layer up or down in the Layers palette. Release the mouse button when the highlighted line appears where you want to place the layer or group. The topmost layer in the Layers palette displays in front of any other layers in the document window. The Layer menu on the Photoshop menu bar also contains an Arrange submenu to help you organize your layers.

5 ALT+drag another copy of the lion to the other side of the garage door.

6 In the Layers palette, right-click Layer 1 and then click Layer Properties on the shortcut menu. Type lion in the Name box. Click the Color box arrow and then click Yellow in the list. Click the OK button.

7 In the Layers palette, right-click Layer 2 and then click Layer Properties on the shortcut menu. Type second lion in the Name box. Click the Color box arrow and then click Yellow in the list. Click the OK button.

Photoshop creates two more layers (Figure 3-39).

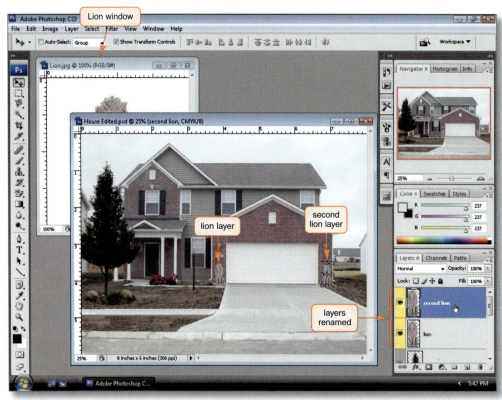

FIGURE 3-39

The next step closes the Lion window.

To Close the Lion Window

1 Click the Close button on the Lion window title bar. If Photoshop displays a dialog box asking if you want to save the changes, click the No button.

The window closes and the House Edited window becomes active.

Instead of dragging an image twice to create two layers, you can **duplicate a layer,** by right-clicking a layer in the Layers palette, and then click Duplicate Layer on the shortcut menu. Photoshop then allows you to name the new layer and specify to which open document window the layer should be added. A duplicate layer can be used to create an entirely new document in the same manner.

In preparation for editing a layer that includes a bush, the followings steps show how to open the file named Bush and set the layer properties.

To Create the Bush Layer

1 Open the file named Bush from the Chapter03 folder on the CD that accompanies this book, or from a location specified by your instructor.

2 When the Bush window is displayed, drag the title bar slightly above the House Edited title bar. Reduce the magnification to 25% and reduce the size of the window by dragging the lower-right corner of the window toward the center.

3 Press the v key to access the Move tool, and then drag the bush image into the House Edited image.

4 Right-click Layer 1 in the Layers palette. Click Layer Properties on the shortcut menu.

5 Type bush in the Name box. Click the Color box arrow and then click Violet.

6 Click the OK button.

The bush layer is displayed in the House Edited window and is renamed in the Layers palette as shown in Figure 3-40.

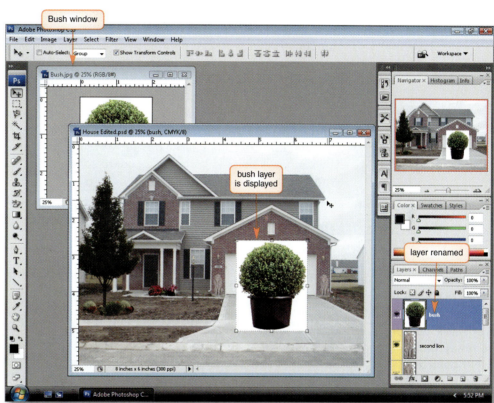

FIGURE 3-40

Layer Masks

Another way to edit layers is by creating a mask. A **mask** is used to show or hide portions of a layer or protect areas from edits. A mask does not change the layer as the Eraser tool did; it merely overlays a template to conceal a portion of the layer.

Photoshop provides two types of masks. **Layer masks** are resolution-dependent bitmap images that are created with the painting or selection tools. **Vector masks** are resolution independent and are created with a pen or shape tool. In this chapter you will create a layer mask.

You can edit a layer mask to add or subtract from the masked region. A layer mask is a **grayscale** image, which means each pixel in the image is represented by a single sample value, or shade of overall luminance, on a scale from black to white. Therefore in the mask, areas you create in black are hidden because the mask is in front of the layer. Areas you create in white are visible. Shades of gray display in various levels of transparency.

Masks have advantages over other kinds of layer editing. If you change your mind or make mistakes, you have not altered the original layer image. With the Eraser tool you would have to delete the layer, open the second image again, recreate the layer, and then begin to edit again. With masks, you simply create a new mask.

A special kind of mask is a **clipping mask** that masks the layers above it. The transparent pixels of the bottom layer mask or clip the content of layers above it, much like a color overlay.

Creating a Layer Mask

To create a layer mask, Photoshop provides an Add layer mask button in the lower part of the Layers palette. When clicked, the button adds a second thumbnail to the layer's description in the palette. By default the mask is **linked** or connected to the selected layer. A link icon displays between the layer thumbnail and the mask thumbnail.

After you add the mask, you will paint with black to identify masked portions of the layer. Pressing the B key on the keyboard will activate the brush to paint in the layer. To paint, simply drag in the layer. The layer added to the House Edited image is a photo of a bush planted in a pot. You will need to mask all of the layer except for the area containing the bush.

The following steps show how, if you make a mistake while creating the mask, you can press the X key on the keyboard to toggle to the default foreground color, white, and paint to unmask the error.

To Create a Layer Mask

1

• **With the bush layer selected, click the Add layer mask button in the lower part of the Layers palette.**

• **If necessary, press the D key to activate the default color scheme. If black is not the foreground color, press the X key to reverse the colors.**

Photoshop adds a layer mask to the selected layer in the palette (Figure 3-41). The link icon links the mask to the layer. The mask is selected.

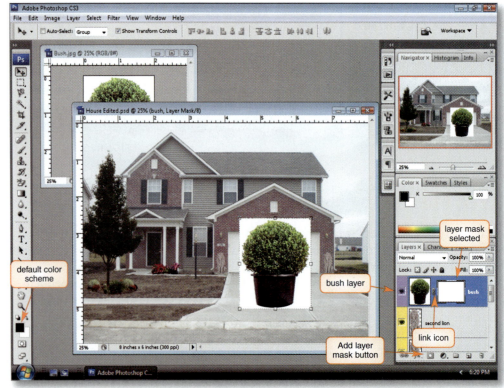

FIGURE 3-41

2

• **With the mask selected, press the B key to activate the brush.**

• **Move the mouse pointer to the document window and press] to increase the size of the brush's circle, as necessary.**

• **Drag the mouse across a lower portion of the layer.**

The black color masks the layer to reveal the background underneath (Figure 3-42).

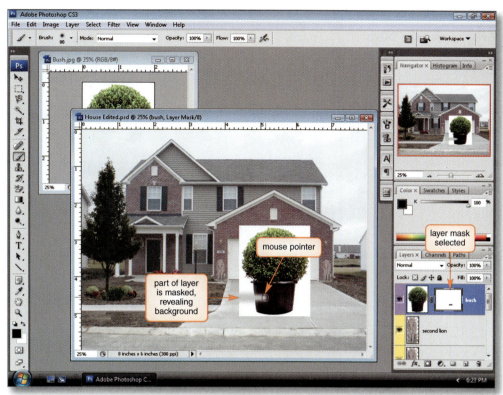

FIGURE 3-42

3

• **Continue dragging through the layer to remove everything except the bush itself. Adjust the size of the brush as necessary using the [and] keys.**

Only the bush is visible (Figure 3-43). The rest of the layer is masked.

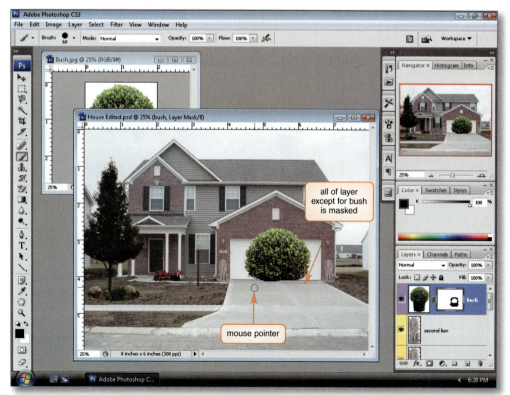

FIGURE 3-43

4

• **Drag across the bush.**

Part of the bush is masked (Figure 3-44).

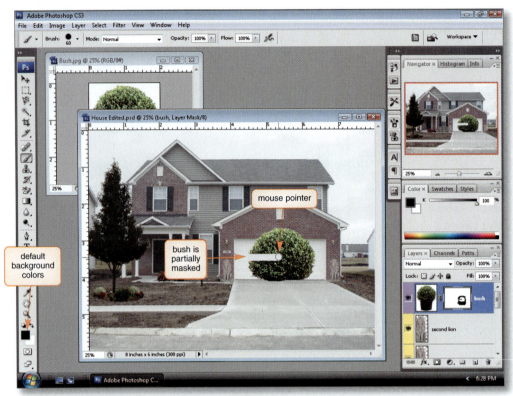

FIGURE 3-44

5

• **Press the x key and then drag across the same portion of the bush.**

The x key toggles the foreground and background colors, effectively painting with white to unmask the error (Figure 3-45).

6

• **Press the x key again to return to the default foreground and background colors.**

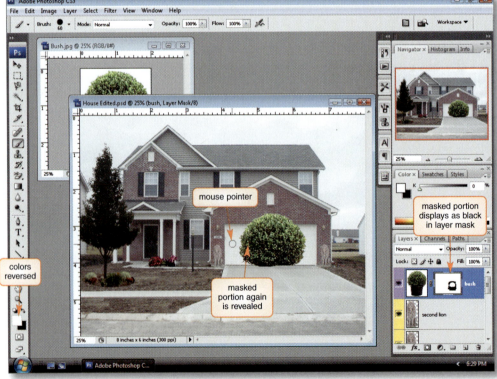

FIGURE 3-45

Other Ways

1. On Layer menu, point to Layer Mask, click Reveal All

Once you have created a mask, you may want to perform other manipulations on the mask. For example, if you want to unlink a mask to move it independently of its layer, click the link icon in the Layers palette. To unlink a mask temporarily, SHIFT+click the link icon. If you want to mask the entire layer completely, you can ALT+click the Add layer mask button. In that case, painting with white in the mask would reveal portions of the mask. To make the mask permanent and reduce overall file size, apply the mask using a command on the mask's shortcut menu.

The following steps show how the bush layer is moved to a location between the sidewalk and the house.

To Resize and Move the Bush Layer

1 With the layer selected, press the V key to activate the Move tool. Click the Show Transform Controls check box to select it, if necessary.

2 SHIFT+drag a corner sizing handle to decrease the size of the layer to approximately 25% as displayed in the Transformation options bar scale boxes.

3 Press the ENTER key to confirm the transformation.

4 Drag the layer to a location between the house and sidewalk as shown in Figure 3-46 on the next page. Do not drag the center reference point.

Later in this chapter you will make tonal adjustments to the layer so it better blends into the composite image.

Creating a Layer Mask from a Selection

A **selection layer mask** is a layer mask created by making a selection in the layer. Instead of painting in the layer mask, the selection border dictates the transparent portion of the layer.

The steps on the next page illustrate how to add a second bush to the House Edited image by creating a layer, selecting an area, and then adding a layer mask.

To Create a Selection Mask

1

• **Select the Bush window.**

• **If necessary, press the v key to activate the Move tool.**

• **Drag the image into the House Edited window.**

The new layer is displayed (Figure 3-46).

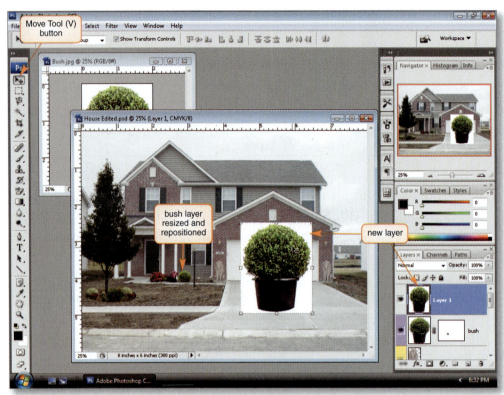

FIGURE 3-46

2

• **On the Tools palette, right-click the Rectangular Marquee Tool (M) button, and then select Elliptical Marquee Tool from the context menu.**

• **Drag an area of the layer to include as much of the bush as possible, but not the pot.**

The bush is selected (Figure 3-47).

FIGURE 3-47

3

- **In the Layers palette, click the Add layer mask button.**

Only the selected area is visible (Figure 3-48).

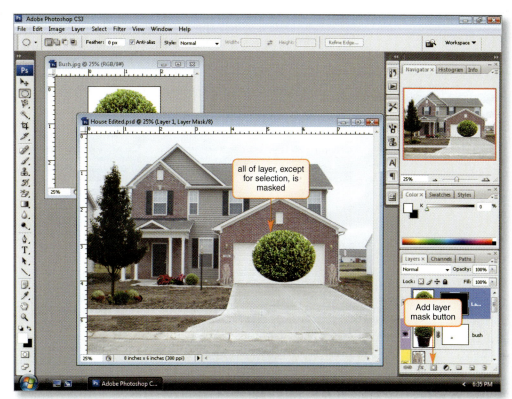

FIGURE 3-48

If you want to change the masked portion of the layer, you can change the visible area by moving the mask around the image. To move the mask, first click the link icon in the Layers palette to unlink the mask from the layer. Select the Move tool on the Tools palette. Then, in the document window, click the layer and drag to reposition it. When the mask is correctly positioned, click between the layer and layer mask in the Layers palette to relink the mask and the layer.

To complete the bush layer, it must be resized, repositioned, and named as shown in the following steps.

To Resize, Reposition, and Name the Layer

1 With the layer selected, press the v key to activate the Move tool. If necessary, click the Show Transform Controls check box to select it.

2 SHIFT+drag a corner sizing handle to decrease the size of the layer to approximately 25% as displayed in the Transformation options bar scale boxes.

3 Press the ENTER key to apply the transformation.

4 Drag the layer to a location between the house and sidewalk, on the other size of the lamppost. Do not drag the center reference point.

5 **Right-click the selected layer in the Layers palette and then click Layer Properties. When the Layer Properties dialog box is displayed, type** second bush **in the Name box. Click the Color box arrow and then click Violet in the list. Click the OK button.**

The second bush layer is renamed and repositioned (Figure 3-49).

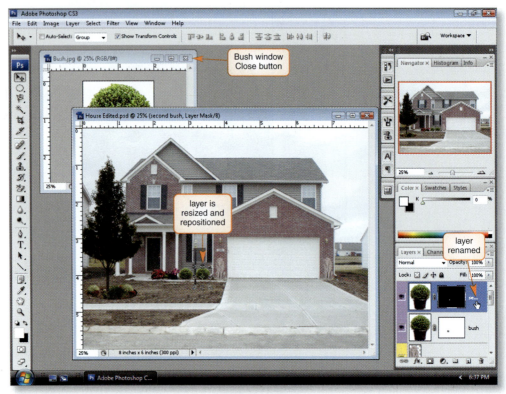

FIGURE 3-49

When you are finished using the Bush window, close it to save resources and memory on your system. The following step closes the window.

To Close the Bush Window

1 **Click the Close button in the Bush window. If Photoshop displays a dialog box asking if you want to save the changes, click the No button.**

The window closes and the House Edited window becomes active.

Fine-Tuning Layers

Sometimes layers need special adjustments in order to fit into their new surroundings in the document window. This fine-tuning usually involves **tonal adjustments** that affect the tonal range of color, lighting, opacity, level, or fill; **style adjustments** such as special effects or blends; or **filter adjustments** that let you apply predetermined pictures, tiles, or patterns.

You can make tonal, style, and filter changes to the pixels of the layer itself, or you can create an adjustment layer or fill layer that is applied over the top without changing the original layer. With the right adjustment, a layer seems to meld into the image and maintains a consistency of appearance for the overall composite image.

Making an Opacity Change to a Layer

In the Layers palette, the **Opacity box** allows you to change the opacity or transparency of a layer. Setting an opacity percentage specifies the level at which you can see through the layer to reveal the image or layer beneath it. You can control exactly how solid the objects on a specific layer appear. For example, if you wanted to display an American flag in an image, superimposed over the top of a memorial or monument, you might change the flag layer's opacity to 50%. The monument would be easily visible through the flag.

The next steps show how to lighten the color in the flowers layer by lowering the opacity.

To Make an Opacity Change to a Layer

1

• **In the Layers palette, scroll down and then click the flowers layer.**

• **Click the Opacity box arrow.**

Photoshop displays a slider to adjust the opacity (Figure 3-50).

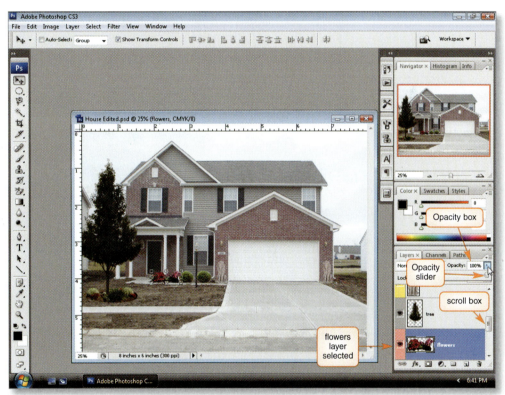

FIGURE 3-50

2

• **Drag the Opacity slider to the left until the Opacity box displays 85%.**

The color of the flowers lightens (Figure 3-51).

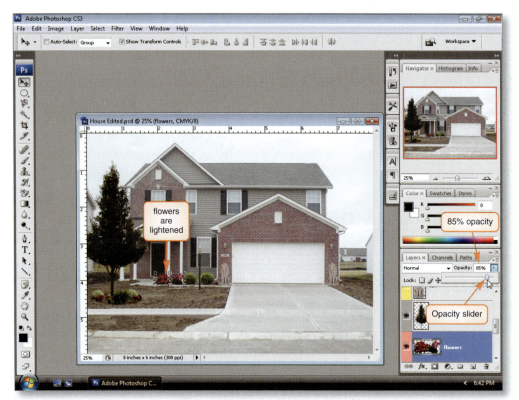

FIGURE 3-51

Beneath the Opacity box is the **Fill box** (Figure 3-52). Changing the fill of a layer is similar to changing its opacity, but editing the Fill percentage changes only the pixels in the layer rather than any layer styles or blending modes. When you click either the Opacity box arrow or the Fill box arrow, a slider displays to adjust the percentage. You also can type a percentage in either box.

Making Level Adjustments

A **level adjustment** is one way to make tonal changes to the shadows and highlights in a layer or to the entire image. In the Levels dialog box, Photoshop displays black, gray, and white sliders to adjust any or all of the three tonal ranges. Experimenting with the gray slider changes the intensity values of the middle range of gray tones without dramatically altering the highlights and shadows.

In the bush layer of the image, you will adjust the gray tones slightly to make the layer match the picture. The following steps illustrate how to make level adjustments in a layer.

To Make a Level Adjustment

1

• **In the Layers palette, scroll up and then click the bush layer thumbnail, not the layer mask.**

• **Increase the magnification to 50% and scroll to display the bush in the center of the document window.**

• **Click Image on the menu bar and then point to Adjustments.**

The Adjustments submenu displays many possible adjustments (Figure 3-52).

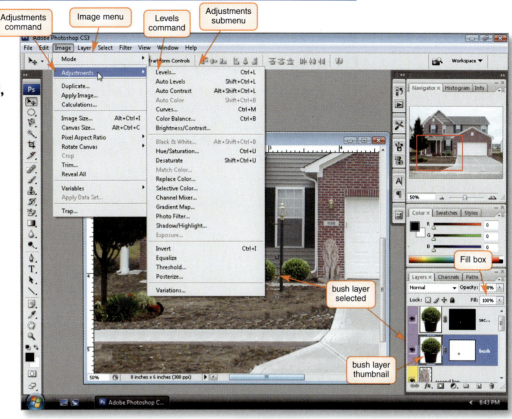

FIGURE 3-52

2

• **Click Levels.**

• **When the Levels dialog box is displayed, in the Input area, drag the gray slider to the right until the middle Input levels box displays .75.**

The gray slider adjusts the midtone colors (Figure 3-53).

3

• **Click the OK button.**

• **Repeat the process for the second bush layer.**

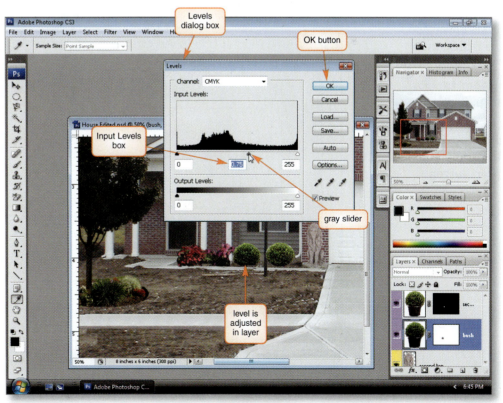

FIGURE 3-53

Other Ways

1. Press CTRL+L, adjust levels

More About

Level Sliders

In the Levels dialog box, the Input Level sliders on each end map the black point (on the left) and white point (on the right) to the settings of the Output sliders. The middle Input slider adjusts the gamma in the image. It moves the midtone and changes the intensity values of the middle range of gray tones without dramatically altering the highlights and shadows. If you move one of the Input Level sliders, the black point, midtone, or white point changes in the Output sliders and all the remaining levels are redistributed. This redistribution increases the tonal range of the image, in effect increasing the overall contrast of the image.

The opacity and level changes in the previous steps were made to the actual pixels in the layer. In the next section, you will learn how to create an extra layer to make the changes while preserving the original pixels.

Creating an Adjustment Layer

An **adjustment layer** is a new layer added to the image to affect a tonal change to a large portion of the image. You can create adjustment layers for the entire composite image or just the background.

The following steps show how to add contrast to the background by creating an adjustment layer.

To Create an Adjustment Layer

1

• In the Layers palette, scroll down and then click the Background layer.

• Zoom to 25% magnification.

• In the Layers palette, click the Create new fill or adjustment layer button.

The button menu is displayed (Figure 3-54).

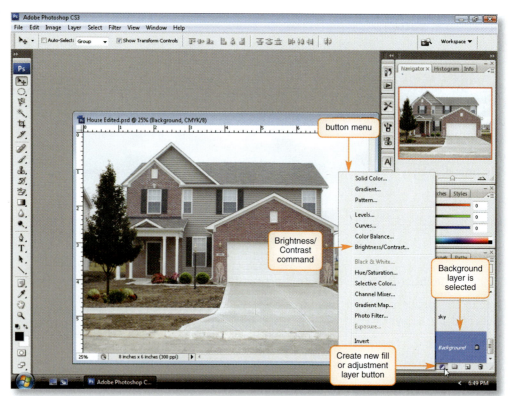

FIGURE 3-54

2

• **Click the Brightness/ Contrast command.**

• **When the Brightness/Contrast dialog box is displayed, drag the Brightness slider to –3 and the Contrast slider to +10.**

The increase in brightness and contrast will create the illusion of a sunnier day in the image (Figure 3-55).

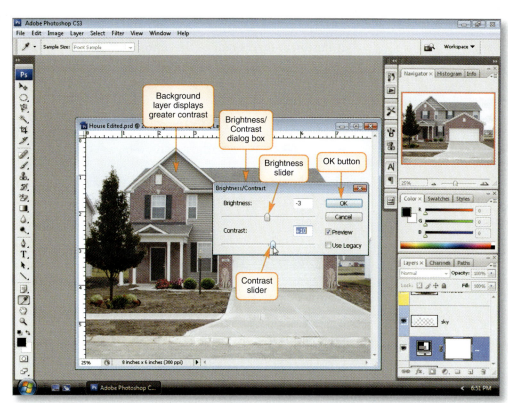

FIGURE 3-55

3

• **Click the OK button.**

The Layers palette displays the new layer (Figure 3-56).

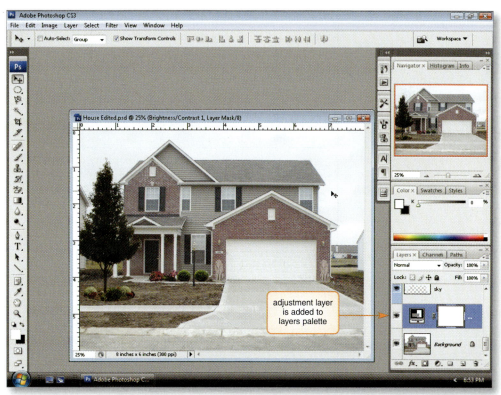

FIGURE 3-56

Other Ways

1. On Layer menu, point to New Adjustment Layer, click Brightness/Contrast, name layer

Adjustment layers have several advantages. They are nondestructive, which means you can try different settings and re-edit the adjustment layer at any time. Adjustment layers reduce the amount of damage you do to an image by making direct edits. Adjustment layers also can be copied to other images, which saves time and maintains consistency.

Adding a Layer Style

Similar to a layer adjustment, **a layer style** is applied to a layer rather than changing the layer's actual pixels. Layer styles, or layer effects, include shadows, glows, bevels, overlays, and strokes, among others. A layer can display multiple styles or effects. Table 3-3 describes some of the Layer Style options. The options apply to many different effects.

Table 3-3 Layer Style Options

OPTION	DESCRIPTION
Angle	sets a degree value for the lighting angle at which the effect is applied
Anti-alias	blends the edge pixels of a contour or gloss contour
Blend Mode	determines how a layer style blends with its underlying layers
Color	assigns the color of a shadow, glow, or highlight
Contour	allows you to create rings of transparency such as gradients, fades, beveling and embossing, and sculpting
Depth	sets the depth of a bevel or pattern
Distance	specifies the offset distance for a shadow or satin effect
Fill Type	sets the content of a stroke
Global Light	turns on global lighting for the effect
Gloss Contour	creates a glossy, metallic appearance on a bevel or emboss
Gradient	indicates the gradient of a layer effect
Highlight or Shadow Mode	specifies the blending mode of a bevel or emboss highlight or shadow
Jitter	varies the color and opacity of a gradient
Layer Knocks Out Drop Shadow	controls the drop shadow's visibility in a semitransparent layer
Noise	assigns the number of random elements in the opacity of a glow or shadow
Opacity	sets the opacity or transparency
Pattern	specifies the pattern
Position	sets the position of a stroke
Range	controls which portion or range of the glow is targeted for the contour
Size	specifies the amount of blur or the size of the shadow
Soften	blurs the results of shading to reduce unwanted artifacts
Source	specifies the source for an inner glow
Style	specifies the style of a bevel or emboss

When a layer has a style, an *fx* icon appears to the right of the layer's name in the Layers palette. You can expand the style in the Layers palette to view all of the applied effects and edit them to change the style.

The following steps show how the Add a layer style button is used to apply a shadow to the lion statue.

To Add a Layer Style

1

• **In the Layers palette, scroll up and then click the lion layer. Adjust the magnification to 100% and then scroll to center the lion in the document window.**

• **Click the Add a layer style button.**

The button menu is displayed (Figure 3-57).

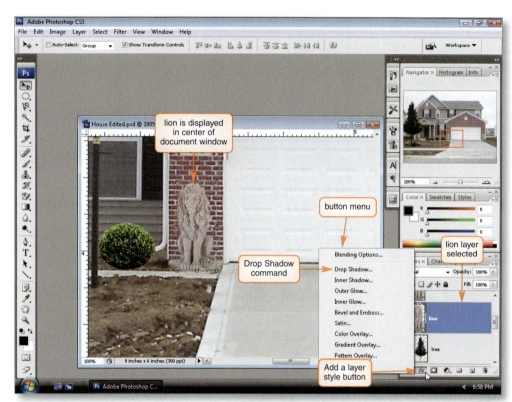

FIGURE 3-57

2

• **Click Drop Shadow.**

• **When Photoshop displays the Layer Style dialog box, drag the dialog box title bar up and to the right so the lion is visible.**

• **In the Layer Style dialog box, drag the Opacity slider to 50. Drag the radius line to rotate the Angle radius to 135 degrees, which will adjust the direction of the shadow. If necessary, type 5 in the Distance box and type 5 in the Size box.**

The Drop Shadow dialog box displays many different settings to change how, where, and from what distance the shadow is created (Figure 3-58). A shadow now displays to the right of the lion statue.

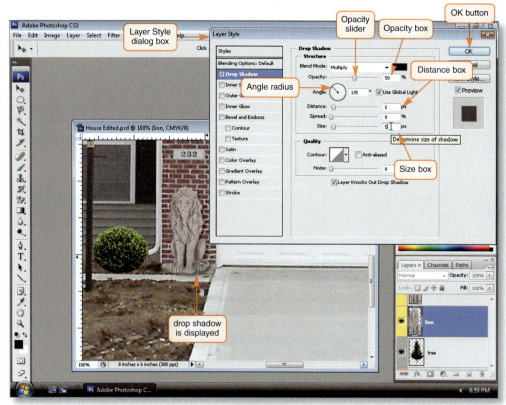

FIGURE 3-58

3

• **Click the OK button.**

• **In the Layers palette, click the Reveals layer effects in the palette button, if necessary.**

Photoshop displays the added effects in the Layers palette (Figure 3-59).

4

• **Click the button again to hide the layer effects.**

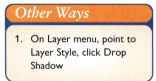

Other Ways

1. On Layer menu, point to Layer Style, click Drop Shadow

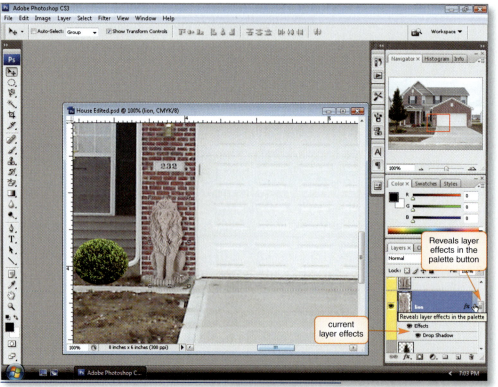

FIGURE 3-59

As you can tell from Figure 3-58, there are a large number of layer styles and settings in Photoshop. As you use them, many of these settings will be explained in future chapters.

The next steps illustrate how to copy the layer style to the second lion.

To Copy a Layer Style

1 **In the Layers palette, right-click the lion layer. Do not right-click the thumbnail. When the shortcut menu is displayed, click Copy Layer Style.**

2 **Right-click the second lion layer. When the shortcut menu is displayed, click Paste Layer Style. Change the magnification to 50%.**

Both lions now display a small shadow, as if the sun is shining from the top, left of the picture (Figure 3-60).

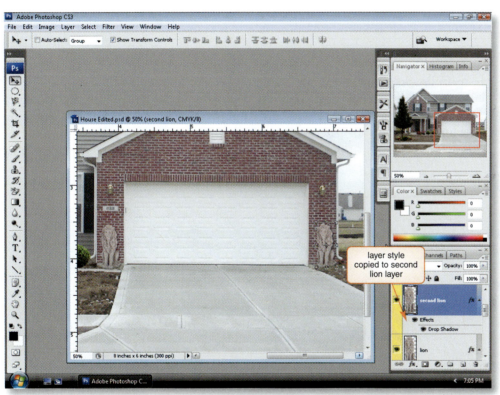

layer style copied to second lion layer

FIGURE 3-60

Adding a Render Filter

Photoshop uses many different filters, blends, styles, and color changes to produce special effects. One special effect that will be useful in the House Edited image is that of clouds. Clouds is a **render filter** that purposefully distorts the colors in a layer or mask to simulate clouds in the sky. Among the more than 100 filters that come installed with Photoshop, the render filters help you create cloud patterns, fiber patterns, refraction patterns, and simulated light reflections. Other examples of filters include artistic filters, blurs, textures, and sketches, among others.

On the next page, Table 3-4 displays the render filters included in an initial installation of Photoshop.

RENDER FILTER	DESCRIPTION
Clouds	Filter produces a cloud pattern using the current foreground and the background colors. To generate a bolder cloud pattern, hold down the ALT key while creating the filter.
Difference Clouds	Filter produces a softer, hazier cloud pattern using the current foreground and the background colors. Applying the filter several times creates marble-like rib and vein patterns.
Fibers	Filter produces a woven fiber pattern using the foreground and background colors. Variance and Strength settings control the color, length, and weave of the fibers.
Lens Flare	Filter produces a glare that simulates refraction caused by shining a bright light into a camera lens.
Lighting Effects	Filter produces a lighting effect based on choices made in style, type, property, and channel. It cannot be used with a mask.

Table 3-4 Render Filters

In the following steps, the sky is selected. Because the render filter applies the current foreground and background colors, light blue and white are used to render a cloud filter, creating a stronger cloud pattern in the photograph. You will learn more about colors and the Color palette in a later chapter.

To Create a Render Filter

1

• **In the Navigator palette, click the Zoom Out button until the magnification is 25%.**

• **In the Layers palette, scroll down and then click the sky layer.**

• **Press W to activate the Magic Wand tool and then, in the document window, click the sky.**

• **In the Color palette, click a very light blue color on the color bar.**

The mask is selected in the sky layer (Figure 3-61).

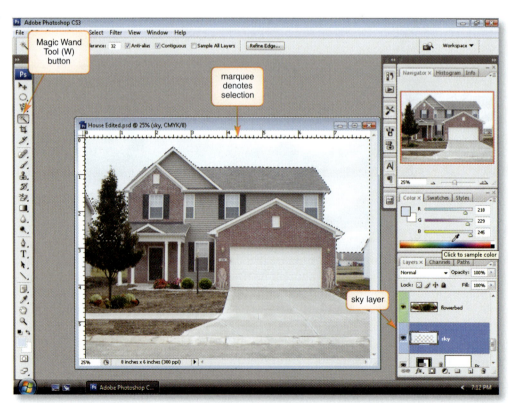

FIGURE 3-61

2

• **Click Filter on the menu bar and then point to Render.**

Photoshop displays the Render submenu (Figure 3-62).

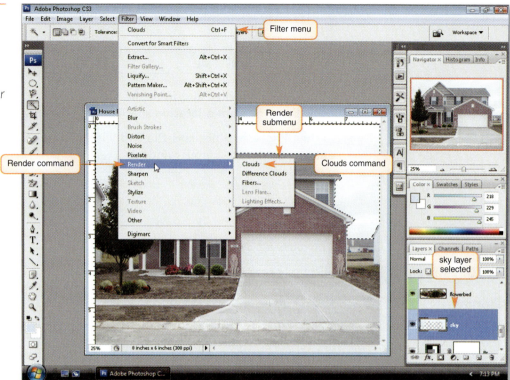

FIGURE 3-62

3

• **Click Clouds on the Render submenu.**

• **Press CTL+D to remove the selection marquee.**

Because the cloud pattern randomizes colors, your pattern will differ (Figure 3-63).

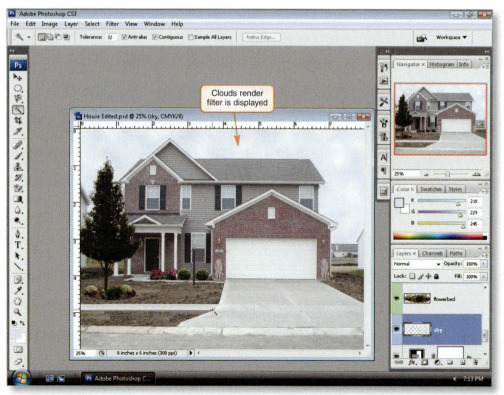

FIGURE 3-63

To finish the composite image of the house and landscaping you will add sod to the yard. The following steps open the Sod file.

To Open the Sod File

1 Open the file named Sod from the Chapter03 folder on the CD that accompanies this book, or from a location specified by your instructor.

2 When Photoshop displays the Sod window, drag its title bar to a location above the House Edited window.

Photoshop displays the Sod window as shown in Figure 3-64.

The Clone Stamp Tool

The **Clone Stamp tool** is used to reproduce portions of an image changing the pixels, rather than by creating a layer. After clicking the Clone Stamp Tool (S) button on the Tools palette, you press and hold ALT while clicking in the portion of the picture that you wish to copy. Photoshop takes a **sample** of the image, remembering where the mouse pointer clicked. You then move the mouse pointer to the position where you wish to create the copy. As you drag with the brush, like you did with the layer mask, the image is applied. Each stroke of the tool paints on more of the sample. The Clone Stamp tool is useful for duplicating an object or correcting defects in an image. The **Clone Source palette** (shown in Figure 3-64) is displayed by clicking the Clone Source button in the dock of collpased palettes on the right side of the workspace. It allows you to work with up to five cloning sources at the same time, so you do not have to resample over and over. Additionally, the palette has options to rotate or scale the sample, or specify the size and orientation. The Clone Source palette makes it easy to create variegated patterns using multiple sources, and unique clones positioned at different angles and perspectives from the original.

The Clone Stamp options bar (Figure 3-64) displays some of the same settings as you used with layer masks, along with an Aligned check box and Sample box. When Aligned is selected, the sample point is not reset if you start dragging in a new location; in other words, the sampling moves to a relative point in the original image. When Aligned is not selected, the sample point begins again as you start a new clone. The default value is to sample only the current layer or background. When All Layers is selected in the Sample box, the clone displays all layers. One restriction when using the Clone Stamp tool from one image to another is that both images have to be in the same color mode such as RGB.

Creating a Clone

In the House Edited image, there is no grass. Using the Clone Stamp tool, you will sample the sod image and then clone it all around the yard in the House Edited image, as shown in the following steps. As you clone the sod, adjust the magnification of the image to view clearly the corners and small areas. If you make a mistake while cloning, click the History button in the dock of collapsed palettes on the right side of the workspace. When the History palette is displayed, click the previous state and begin dragging again.

To Create a Clone

1

• **With the Sod window active, click the Clone Source button in the collapsed palettes on the right side of the workspace.**

• **In the palette, click the Invert box to remove its check mark, if necessary.**

• **On the Tools palette, right-click the Clone Stamp Tool (S) button.**

Photoshop displays the context menu (Figure 3-64).

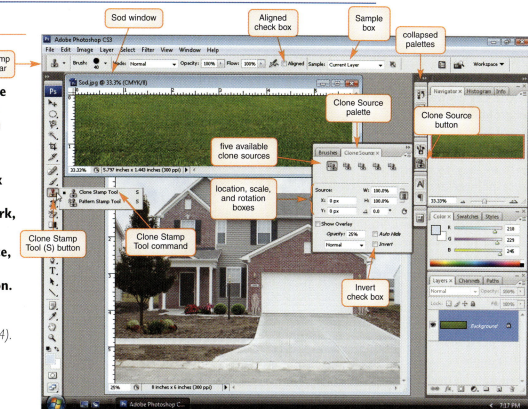

FIGURE 3-64

2

• **Click Clone Stamp Tool on the context menu.**

• **On the options bar, click the Aligned check box to deselect it.**

• **Move the mouse pointer to the Sod window and ALT+click in the upper-left corner of the sod.**

As you ALT+click, the Clone Stamp tool displays a crosshair mouse pointer (Figure 3-65). The Clone Source palette displays the source of the clone.

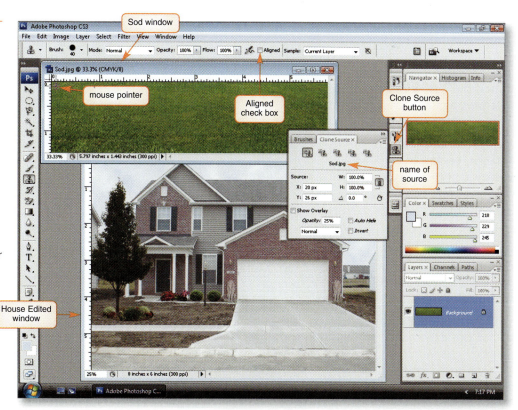

FIGURE 3-65

3

• Click the Clone Source button again to collapse the palette.

• Click the border of the House Edited window to make it active.

• In the Layers palette, select the Background layer.

• Move the mouse pointer into the document window and then press the] or [key to display the mouse pointer as a small circle.

• Working from left to right, click and drag in the House Edited image, to fill in the area from the left margin to the driveway, above the flowerbed. Change the magnification as necessary to fill in small areas. Use short strokes, so if you make a mistake, you can click a previous state in the History palette.

• Because you are dragging the background image, you can drag through any of the layers, such as the tree. Do not drag through the house, sidewalk, or driveway.

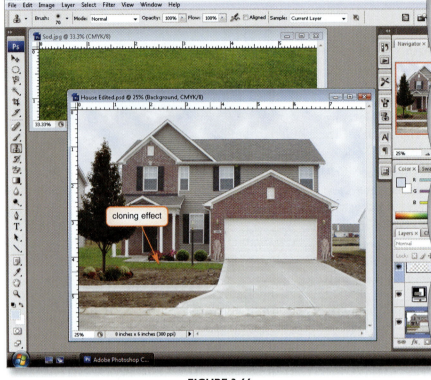

FIGURE 3-66

Photoshop displays grass (Figure 3-66).

4

• Click the Sod window title bar, again.

• To create a more variegated and realistic pattern, resample the sod by ALT+clicking in the lower-left corner of the sod image.

• Click the House Edited window title bar, and then begin dragging in the lower-left corner of the image.

• Fill in all of the areas left of the driveway.

The grass on the left side of the driveway is complete (Figure 3-67).

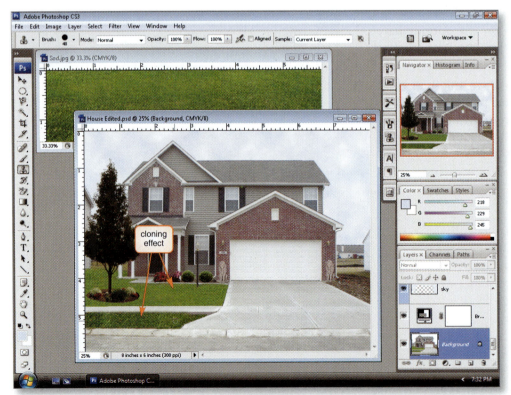

FIGURE 3-67

5

- **Using the techniques in the previous steps, clone as necessary to fill in the grass on the right side of the driveway.**

The grass is complete (Figure 3-68).

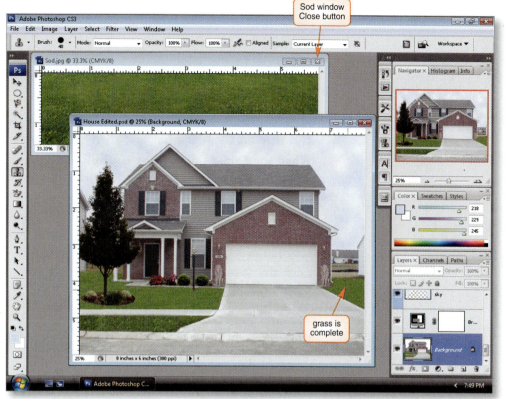

FIGURE 3-68

On the Clone Stamp Tool (S) context menu (Figure 3-64 on page PS 175), a second kind of stamp, the **Pattern Stamp Tool (S)**, allows you to paint with a pattern chosen from Photoshop's pattern library. A **pattern** is an image that is repeated, or tiled, when you use it to fill a layer or selection. On the Pattern Stamp options bar, a Pattern Picker box arrow displays patterns in a list. You can import additional patterns into the Pattern Picker box.

The next step is to close the Sod window.

To Close the Sod Window

1 **Click the Close button in the Sod window. If Photoshop asks if you want to save changes to the document, click the No button.**

The window closes and the House Edited window becomes active.

Flattening a Composite Image

Flattening composite images reduces the file size by merging all visible layers into the background, discarding hidden layers and applying masks. A flattened file is easier to print, export, and display on the Web. It is a good practice, however, to save the layered version in PSD format in case you want to make further changes to the file. It is very important to remember that once a file is flattened and saved, no changes can be made to individual layers.

First you will save the file in PSD format with the name, House Composite. Then you will flatten the composite image. Finally, you will save the file in TIF format with the name, House Complete.

To Save the Composite Image

1 **With your USB flash drive connected to one of the computer's USB ports, click File on the menu bar and then click Save As.**

2 **When the Save As dialog box is displayed, type** House Composite **in the File name text box. Do not press the ENTER key after typing the file name.**

3 **If necessary, click the Format box arrow and then choose Photoshop (*.PSD, *.PDD) in the list.**

4 **If necessary, click the Save in box arrow and then click USB (F:), or the location associated with your USB flash drive, in the list.**

5 **Click the Save button in the Save As dialog box. If Photoshop displays an options dialog box, click the OK button.**

Photoshop saves the file on the USB flash drive with the file name House Composite, in the PSD format, and displays the new name on the document window title bar.

To Flatten a Composite Image

1

• **Click Layer on the menu bar.**

Photoshop displays the Layer menu (Figure 3-69).

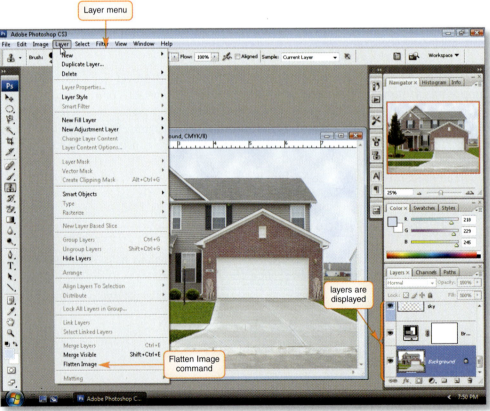

FIGURE 3-69

2

• **Click Flatten Image on the Layer menu.**

After a few moments, the image is flattened and a single Background layer displays in the Layers palette (Figure 3-70).

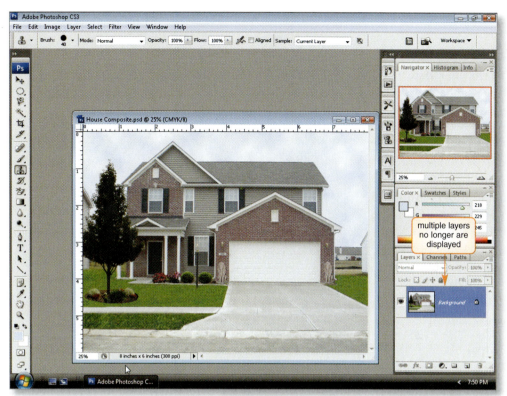

FIGURE 3-70

If you flatten an image and then change your mind, if the file is still open, you can click the previous state in the History palette to restore all of the layers.

If you want to save each layer as a separate file, click File on the menu bar, point to Scripts, and then click Export Layers to Files. This script is useful if you think you may want to use your layers from this document in other composite images.

Saving a File in the TIF Format

TIF or TIFF is a flexible raster image format. A raster image is a digital image represented by a matrix of pixels. TIFF stands for Tagged Image File Format and is a common file format for images acquired from scanners and screen capture programs. Because TIFF files are supported by virtually all paint, image-editing, and page-layout applications, it is a versatile format for cross platform applications.

The steps on the next page save the flattened image as a TIF file.

To Save a File in the TIF Format

1

• **With your USB flash drive connected to one of the computer's USB ports, click File on the menu bar and then click Save As.**

• **When the Save As dialog box is displayed, type** House Complete **in the File name text box. Do not press the ENTER key after typing the file name.**

• **Click the Format box arrow and then click TIFF (*.TIF, *TIFF) in the list.**

• **Click the Save in box arrow and then click USB (F:), or the location associated with your USB flash drive, in the list.**

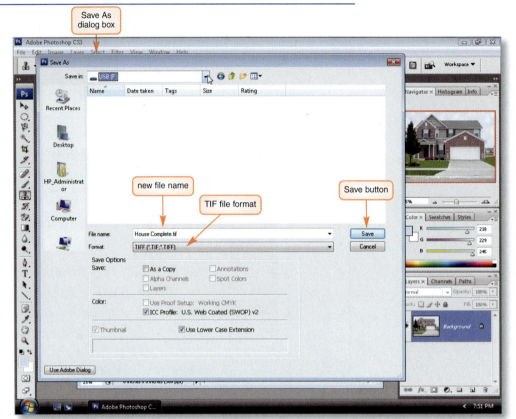

FIGURE 3-71

The Save As dialog box displays the file name, format, and location settings (Figure 3-71).

2

• **Click the Save button in the Save As dialog box.**

• **When Photoshop displays the TIFF Options dialog box, click the OK button.**

Other Ways

1. Press CTRL+SHIFT+S

The following steps illustrate how to print a copy of the House Complete image.

To Print the House Complete Image

1 Ready the printer according to the printer instructions.

2 Click File on the menu bar and then click Print One Copy on the File menu.

The image prints on the default printer.

Closing a Photo

The chapter is complete. The final steps close the document window and quit Photoshop.

To Close the Document Window and Quit Photoshop

1 With the House Complete window selected, click the Close button in the document window.

2 If Photoshop displays a dialog box, click the No button to ignore the changes since the last time you saved the photo.

3 Click the Close button on the right side of the Photoshop title bar.

The Photoshop window closes.

Chapter Summary

In editing the landscape of the house image, you gained a broad knowledge of Photoshop's layering capabilities. First, you were introduced to the PSD format and the concept of layers. You created a layer via cut, a layer from another image, and a layer from a selection, using the Layers palette to set options, select, rename, color, view, and hide layers. Then you used the eraser tools to erase portions of the layer that were not needed in the final composite image.

You learned how to hide portions of layers with layer masks and selection masks. You fine tuned layers with layer adjustments, styles, and render filters. Finally, you used the Clone Stamp tool to recreate grass in the composite image. The file was flattened and saved in the TIF format.

More About

The TIF Options Dialog Box

The TIF Options dialog box displays commands to compress the image. Some compression techniques are not supported by older versions of applications that handle TIF files. Pixel Order writes the TIF file with the channels data interleaved or organized by plane. Byte Order selects the platform on which the file can be read. Save Image Pyramid preserves multi-resolution information. Save Transparency preserves transparency as an additional alpha channel when the file is opened in another application. Transparency is always preserved when the file is reopened in Photoshop. Layer Compression specifies a method for compressing data for pixels in layers.

What You Should Know

Having completed this chapter, you should be able to perform the tasks below. The tasks are listed in the same order they were presented in this chapter. For a list of the buttons, menus, toolbars, and other commands introduced in this chapter, see the Quick Reference Summary at the back of this book and refer to the Page Number column.

1. Start Photoshop (PS 124)
2. Open a File (PS 124)
3. Save a File in the PSD Format (PS 126)
4. Create a Layer via Cut (PS 127)
5. Change Palette Options (PS 130)
6. Select a Layer (PS 132)
7. Name and Color a Layer (PS 133)
8. Hide and View a Layer (PS 135)
9. Open a Second Image (PS 137)
10. Create a Layer by Dragging an Entire Image (PS 138)
11. Close the Flowerbed Window (PS 139)
12. Set the Flowerbed Layer Properties (PS 139)
13. Resize a Layer (PS 140)
14. Move the Flowerbed Layer (PS 141)
15. Open the Flowers Image (PS 141)
16. Create a Layer by Dragging a Selection (PS 142)
17. Close the Flowers Window (PS 144)
18. Set the Flowers Layer Properties (PS 144)
19. Create the Tree Layer (PS 144)
20. Erase Using the Magic Eraser (PS 146)
21. Erase Using the Eraser Tool (PS 148)
22. Erase Using the Background Eraser (PS 151)
23. Reposition the Tree Layer (PS 152)
24. Close the Tree Window (PS 153)
25. Insert the Lion Layers (PS 153)
26. Close the Lion Window (PS 154)
27. Create the Bush Layer (PS 155)
28. Create a Layer Mask (PS 156)
29. Resize and Move the Bush Layer (PS 159)
30. Create a Selection Mask (PS 160)
31. Resize, Reposition, and Name the Layer (PS 161)
32. Close the Bush Window (PS 162)
33. Make an Opacity Change to a Layer (PS 163)
34. Make a Level Adjustment (PS 165)
35. Create an Adjustment Layer (PS 166)
36. Add a Layer Style (PS 169)
37. Copy a Layer Style (PS 171)
38. Create a Render Filter (PS 172)
39. Open the Sod File (PS 174)
40. Create a Clone (PS 175)
41. Close the Sod Window (PS 177)
42. Save the Composite Image (PS 178)
43. Flatten a Composite Image (PS 178)
44. Save a File in the TIF Format (PS 180)
45. Print the House Complete Image (PS 180)
46. Close the Document Window and Quit Photoshop (PS 181)

Learn It Online

Instructions: To complete the Learn It Online exercises, start your browser, click the Address bar, and then enter the Web address scsite.com/pscs3/learn. When the Photoshop CS3 Learn It Online page is displayed, follow the instructions in the exercises below. Each exercise has instructions for printing your results, either for your own records or for submission to your instructor.

1 Chapter Reinforcement TF, MC, and SA

Below Photoshop Chapter 3, click the Chapter Reinforcement link. Print the quiz by clicking Print on the File menu for each page. Answer each question.

2 Flash Cards

Below Photoshop Chapter 3, click the Flash Cards link and read the instructions. Type 20 (or a number specified by your instructor) in the Number of playing cards text box, type your name in the Enter your Name text box, and then click the Flip Card button. When the flash card is displayed, read the question and then click the ANSWER box arrow to select an answer. Flip through Flash Cards. If your score is 15 (75%) correct or greater, click Print on the File menu to print your results. If your score is less than 15 (75%) correct, then redo this exercise by clicking the Replay button.

3 Practice Test

Below Photoshop Chapter 3, click the Practice Test link. Answer each question, enter your first and last name at the bottom of the page, and then click the Grade Test button. When the graded practice test is displayed on your screen, click Print on the File menu to print a hard copy. Continue to take practice tests until you score 80% or better.

4 Who Wants to Be a Computer Genius?

Below Photoshop Chapter 3, click the Computer Genius link. Read the instructions, enter your first and last name at the bottom of the page, and then click the PLAY button. When your score is displayed, click the PRINT RESULTS link to print a hard copy.

5 Wheel of Terms

Below Photoshop Chapter 3, click the Wheel of Terms link. Read the instructions, and then enter your first and last name and your school name. Click the PLAY button. When your score is displayed, right-click the score and then click Print on the shortcut menu to print a hard copy.

6 Crossword Puzzle Challenge

Below Photoshop Chapter 3, click the Crossword Puzzle Challenge link. Read the instructions, and then enter your first and last name. Click the SUBMIT button. Work the crossword puzzle. When you are finished, click the Submit button. When the crossword puzzle is redisplayed, click the Print Puzzle button to print a hard copy.

7 Tips and Tricks

Below Photoshop Chapter 3, click the Tips and Tricks link. Click a topic that pertains to Chapter 3. Right-click the information and then click Print on the shortcut menu. Construct a brief example of what the information relates to in Photoshop to confirm you understand how to use the tip or trick.

8 Expanding Your Horizons

Below Photoshop Chapter 3, click the Expanding Your Horizons link. Click a topic that pertains to Chapter 3. Print the information. Construct a brief example of what the information relates to in Photoshop to confirm you understand the contents of the article.

9 Search Sleuth

Below Photoshop Chapter 3, click the Search Sleuth link. To search for a term that pertains to this chapter, select a term below the Chapter 3 title and then use the Google search engine at google.com (or any major search engine) to display and print two Web pages that present information on the term.

10 Photoshop Online Training

Below Photoshop Chapter 3, click the Photoshop Online Training link. When your browser displays the Web page, click one of the Photoshop tutorials that covers one or more of the objectives listed at the beginning of the chapter on page PS 122. Print the first page of the tutorial before stepping through it.

Apply Your Knowledge

1 Creating Layers

Instructions: Start Photoshop, and set the workspace and tools to default settings. Open the Beach file from the Chapter03 folder, located either on the CD that accompanies this book or in a location specified by your instructor. The purpose of this exercise is to create a composite photo by creating layers, and to create both a PSD and TIF version of the final photo. The edited photo is displayed in Figure 3-72.

FIGURE 3-72

1. Use the Save As command to save the image on your USB flash drive as a PSD file, with the file name Beach Composite.
2. Remove the visitors from the beach:
   a. Press the S key to select the Clone Stamp tool. On the options bar, click Aligned so it does not display a check. ALT+click the sand to the right of the people on the beach. Drag over the people to erase them from the beach.
3. Insert the gull and create a duplicate:
   a. Press CTRL+O and open the gull image from the Chapter03 folder.
   b. When Photoshop displays the image, use the Magic Wand tool with a tolerance setting of 50 to select the sky around the bird. On the Select menu, click Inverse.
   c. Right-click the selection and then click Grow to increase the selection slightly.
   d. Press the V key to select the Move tool. Drag the gull into the beach scene.
   e. Click the Show Transform Controls check box to select it. SHIFT+drag the gull to resize it. Drag the gull to a position as shown in Figure 3-72.

Apply Your Knowledge

    f. Rename the layer, gull, and use a Violet identification color.

    g. Right-click the gull layer and then click Duplicate Layer. Name the duplicate layer, second gull. (*Hint*: The second gull will display directly over the top of the first gull.)

    h. If necessary, press the V key to activate the Move tool and then drag the second gull to a position above the first. If necessary, press CTRL+T to display the bounding box. SHIFT+drag a corner sizing handle to make the second gull smaller, thereby giving the composite image a sense of perspective.

    i. Close the Gull window.

4. Next, insert the large umbrella and add a layer mask:

    a. Press CTRL+O and open the Large Umbrella image from the Chapter03 folder.

    b. When Photoshop displays the image, if necessary, press the V key to select the Move tool. Drag from the Large Umbrella image to the beach scene. Position the layer between the trees.

    c. In the Layers palette, click the Add a layer mask button. Press the E key to access the eraser tools and then, if necessary, press SHIFT+E to access the Eraser tool.

    d. Press the D key to select the default colors and then press the B key to activate the brush. Drag to erase any portions of the umbrella that eclipse the trees. (*Hint*: If you make a mistake and erase too much, press the X key to alternate to white and drag over the error.)

    e. Rename the layer, umbrella, and use a Blue identification color.

    f. Close the Large Umbrella window.

5. Insert the beach ball and add a Drop Shadow:

    a. Press CTRL+O and open the Beach Ball file from the Chapter03 folder.

    b. When Photoshop displays the image, press the V key to select the Move tool. Drag from the Beach Ball image to the beach scene.

    c. Press the E key to select the eraser tools and then, if necessary, press SHIFT+E to toggle to the Magic Eraser tool. On the options bar, type 15 in the Tolerance box. Click the Contiguous check box so it displays a check. Click the white portions around the edges of the beach ball.

    d. Drag the beach ball to a position in the lower part of the scene.

    e. In the Layers palette, click the Add a layer style button and then click Drop Shadow. When the Layer Styles dialog box is displayed, type 70 in the Opacity box; drag the Angle radius to 97. Type 8 in the Distance box. Click the OK button.

    f. Rename the layer, ball, and use a Red identification color.

    g. Close the Beach Ball window.

6. Finally, insert the beach pail:

    a. Press CTRL+O and open the Beach Pail file from the Chapter03 folder.

    b. When Photoshop displays the image, drag a rectangular marquee around the beach pail staying as close to the edges of the pail as possible. Press the V key to select the Move tool. Drag the selection into the beach scene.

    c. Right-click the Eraser Tool (E) button and then click the Eraser Tool. Erase any areas around the pail that should not display in the layer. Do not erase the shadow beneath the bucket.

    d. Rename the layer, pail, and use a Yellow identification color.

    e. Close the Beach Pail window.

7. Save the file again, by pressing CTRL+S. Flatten the image.

8. Press SHIFT+CTRL+S to open the Save As dialog box. Type Beach Complete in the Name box. Click the Format box arrow and then click TIF in the list. Click the Save button. If Photoshop displays a dialog box, click the OK button.

9. Turn in a hard copy of the photo to your instructor.

10. Quit Photoshop.

Adobe
Photoshop CS3

In the Lab

1 Making Level Adjustments Using Masks

Problem: A local tourist company has hired you to create its latest brochure about historic homes. You encounter a photo that is too dark to use in the brochure. You decide to try adjusting the levels to lighten the trees, grass, and bushes in the photo and prepare it for print in the brochure. The edited photo displays in Figure 3-73.

Instructions:

1. Start Photoshop. Set the default workspace and reset all tools.
2. Open the file Historic Home from the Chapter03 folder on the CD that accompanies this book, or from a location specified by your instructor.
3. Click the Save As command on the File menu. Type Historic Home Edited as the file name. Click the Format box arrow and click PSD in the list. Browse to your USB flash drive storage device. Click the Save button. If Photoshop displays a Format Options dialog box, click the OK button.

FIGURE 3-73

4. Use the Navigator palette to zoom the photo to 100% magnification, if necessary.
5. On the Tools palette, right-click the current lasso tool. Click Lasso Tool on the context menu. Drag with the Lasso tool to draw around the house. Stay as close to the house itself as possible. Do not include trees, bushes, or the sky.
6. Press the W key to activate the Magic Wand tool. On the options bar, click the Add to selection button and then, if necessary, click the Contiguous check box so it displays a check.
7. In the document window, click the Sky.
8. Click Select on the menu bar and then click Inverse to select the inverse of the house and sky which would be the trees, bushes, and grounds.
9. Click Layer on the menu bar, point to New, and then click Layer via Cut.
10. In the Layers palette, rename the layer, grounds.
11. With the layer selected, press CTRL+L to open the Levels dialog box. In the Input Levels area, drag the white slider to the left until the grounds are lighter and the features easily discerned, and then click the OK button in the dialog box.
12. On the Tools palette, double-click the Set foreground color button. When the Color Picker (Foreground Color) dialog box is displayed, click a light blue color, and then click the OK button.
13. Press the W key to activate the Magic Wand tool. On the options bar, click the New selection button and then, if necessary, click the Contiguous check box so it displays a check. In the Layers palette, click the Background layer. In the document window, click the sky.
14. Click Filter on the menu bar, point to Render, and then click Clouds.
15. Press CTRL+S to save the photo again.
16. Press SHIFT+CTRL+S to access the Save As dialog box. Choose the TIF format and name the file Historic Home Complete.
17. Print a copy and turn it in to your instructor.

2 Creating a Composite from Multiple Images

Problem: You are thinking about moving to a new apartment. After visiting the complex, the landlord gave you a floor plan of a corner unit with two bedrooms. You decide to use Photoshop to experiment with different placements of the furniture to create the best layout and maintain the most free space. In a file called Apartment, the floor plan is stored as the background, and sample furniture images as layers. The floor plan is displayed in Figure 3-74.

FIGURE 3-74

Instructions:

1. Start Photoshop. Set the default workspace and reset all tools.
2. Open the file Apartment from the Chapter03 folder on the CD that accompanies this book, or from a location specified by your instructor. If Photoshop displays a dialog box, click the OK button.
3. Click the Save As command on the File menu. Type `Apartment Edited` as the file name. If necessary, click the Format box arrow and then click PSD in the list. Browse to your USB flash drive storage device, if necessary. Click the Save button. If Photoshop displays a Format Options dialog box, click the OK button.
4. One at a time, click each layer in the palette. Look at the layer and rename it with a descriptive name such as chair or desk.
5. Choose a layer to place in the apartment. Click the layer's visibility icon. When Photoshop displays the layer in the document window, click the Move Tool (V) button on the Tools palette and drag the layer to an appropriate place. If you need to resize the layer so it better fits the location, select the Show Transform Controls check box and then SHIFT+drag a corner sizing handle. If you need to flip the layer, click Edit on the menu bar, point to Transform, and then click Flip Horizontal.
6. Repeat Step 5 choosing each of the remaining layers.
7. Once you have placed all of the layers, duplicate at least three layers to create more furniture. Resize and flip as necessary.
8. When you are finished, save the changes and then use the Flatten Image command to flatten all of the layers into the background.
9. Save the flattened image as Apartment Complete.
10. For extra credit, take digital pictures of your own furniture. Open the pictures in Photoshop and use the Layer via Copy command to create new layers in the apartment image.

In the Lab

3 Using the Clone Tool and Creating a Layer with Outer Glow

Problem: The marketing agency that you work for has asked you to edit the latest advertisement for Qintara perfume. You decide to use Photoshop's layering capabilities to insert the image of the perfume bottle. You also decide to clone the Q of their logo multiple times to create a stylistic band of color across the advertisement. A sample of the advertisement is displayed in Figure 3-75.

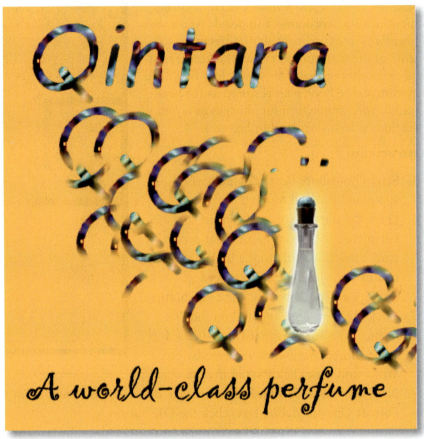

FIGURE 3-75

Instructions:

1. Start Photoshop. Set the default workspace and reset all tools.

2. Open the file Perfume from the Chapter03 folder on the CD that accompanies this book, or from a location specified by your instructor. If Photoshop displays a dialog box, click the OK button.

3. Click the Save As command on the File menu. Type `Perfume Edited` as the file name. If necessary, click the Format box arrow and then click PSD in the list. Browse to your USB flash drive storage device. Click the Save button. If Photoshop displays a Format Options dialog box, click the OK button.

4. Select the layer named slogan. Move the layer to the lower portion of the image.

5. Open the file Bottle from the Chapter03 folder on the CD that accompanies this book, or from a location specified by your instructor. Select all of the image and then, using the Move tool drag a copy to the Perfume Edited window.

6. In the Perfume Edited window, name the new layer, bottle.

7. Use the Add layer mask button to create a layer mask in the bottle layer. Use the Brush tool with black to make the area around the bottle transparent.

8. Use the Add a layer style button in the Layers palette to create an Outer Glow layer style. When the Layer Style dialog box is displayed, type 25 in the Size box.

9. Click the background layer. Click the Clone Stamp tool on the Tools palette. ALT-click the top of the letter Q in the logo. Move the mouse down and to the right. Drag to create a clone of the Q.

10. Repeat step 9, creating multiple, overlapped clones of the letter Q as shown in Figure 3-75. Use short strokes. If you make a mistake, click the previous state in the History palette and drag again.

11. When you are satisfied with your clones, flatten the image.

12. Save the file again and submit a copy to your instructor.

Cases and Places

The difficulty of these case studies varies:
■ are the least difficult and ■■ are the most difficult. The last exercise is a group exercise.

1 ■ You have been hired as an intern with a greeting card company. You were given several photos to use in preparing holiday cards. The photo named Santa Scene is located in the Chapter03 folder. You want to use the figure of Santa Claus only, on the front of a card. Save the photo in the PSD format on your USB flash drive storage device as Santa Layered. Create a rectangular marquee selection around the figure. Use the Layer via Cut command and name the new layer, Santa. Hide the background. Create a layer mask, painting with black to display only the figure. Print with the background hidden.

2 ■ Earlier in this chapter, a suggestion was made to create a flag with 50% opacity superimposed over a memorial. Locate a photo of a memorial in your city and a picture of your flag. Obtain permission to use a digital photo or scan the images. Open the photos. Select only the flag and then drag it as a new layer into the memorial photo. Resize the layer to fit across the memorial. Change the opacity to 50%. Make other corrections as necessary. Save the composite photo and print a copy.

3 ■■ You are planning a family reunion at a vacation spot and want to create a photo to advertise the event to your family. Use a scanner to scan photos of the vacation spot and photos of your family members. Using the scanner's software, save the photos in the highest possible resolution, using the most color settings. Bring the vacation photo into Photoshop and save it on your storage device. One at a time open each of the family member photos and drag the images into layers on top of the vacation spot photo. Use Layer masks to hide the background in the layers and adjust the levels so the family members fit into the picture. Flatten the photo and save it in the TIF format. Send the edited photo via e-mail to members of your family or to your instructor as directed.

4 ■■ You recently took a photo of a deer at the local forest preserve. To make the picture more interesting you decide to create a layer and clone the deer. Open the photo named Deer, located in the Chapter03 folder. Click the Layer command on the menu bar, point to New and then click Layer. Click the background, choose the Clone tool, and take a sample of the middle of the deer. Click the new layer and clone the deer. On the Edit menu, click Free Transform and resize the deer so it appears to be further away. Save the file as Deer Edited on your storage device.

Cases and Places

5 ██ **Working Together** Graphic layers in advertising and marketing are commonplace. Designers who know how to work effectively with layers are in demand. In preparation for an upcoming job fair, your instructor has asked you to research layers used in advertising. Ask each member of your team to bring in their favorite cereal box. As a group, examine the boxes. Choose 3 boxes that you believe have layered images and/or text. Create a list of each layer in order, from the top layer to the background. List notable characteristics of each layer including items from the Layer styles button menu in the Layers palette (Figure 3-57 on page PS 169) and the Adjustments submenu (Figure 3-52 on page PS 165).

An Introduction to the Fundamentals of Graphic Design

Defining Graphic Design

Graphic design is a term generally used to describe the act of arranging words and images to convey a particular, intended message effectively to a specific audience. The graphic designer takes an idea and makes it into something tangible. Graphic design sometimes is referred to as design, graphic arts, visual communication, graphic communication, or visual problem solving. The term, graphic design, also is used to describe an area of study, which can lead to a seemingly infinite number of related professions, including the following:

- printing
- advertising
- interactive design
- publications, including newspapers, magazines, and books
- Web design
- computer information technology
- marketing collateral, which specifically means printed marketing material including brochures, newsletters, annual reports, etc.
- illustration
- animation
- software design
- packaging
- computer-aided design / computer-aided manufacturing (CAD/CAM)
- mechanical engineering technology

Photoshop and other computer software enables you to manipulate and reproduce graphic images for countless varied uses. The best designers have an innate ability at recognizing a well-designed graphic layout. But even if graphic design sensibility does not come naturally to you, you can develop basic skills for consistently producing competent, effective, and well thought-out graphic design layouts. Practice, learning from mistakes, and careful analysis of work done by others are ways of increasing your graphic design ability. Knowing the fundamentals of graphic design, and developing a working knowledge of computers and software, is essential.

Graphic Designer's Considerations

Graphic designers deal with *the client, the design of an idea,* and the *process.* To produce competent, comprehensive results, graphic designers must consider three simple facts about graphic design described in Figure SF 1-1.

1. *You are usually creating a product for someone else.* It is important to identify and research your **client, audience,** and **topic.** The client is the person or company who hires you. The audience, also referred to as the target consumer, the user, or the end user, are the people who will be seeing and using your design. The topic is the subject matter of your graphic design. For example, if your topic is to design a catalog for a candle and candy company, you need to research the client, in this case the company itself, so you can satisfy the marketing needs of the company's owners. You also need to understand your audience, who in this example are people who will be receiving this catalog.

One of the best tools for preliminary research is listening. Listen to what your client tells you and take notes of their ideas. For example your client may own a sports uniform mail order catalog company. The client explains that the company was established in 1949 and has a reputation for being traditional and reliable. Yet they are concerned with keeping abreast of current trends in sports uniform fashion. They want you to design a new catalog which would appeal to a younger audience. Listening to your client you glean the importance of blending the new with the old by giving the catalog a contemporary look while simultaneously emphasizing the company's longstanding reputation.

Follow that up with market research. For example, if your topic is a shopping catalog, your research would include analyzing and comparing the visual effectiveness of several existing catalogs.

2. *The design is defined by its purpose; it must function as intended.* Once you know what you are creating and for whom, the next step is to come up with the best possible ideas. You must answer the following questions:

- What am I trying to do?
- What is the problem I am trying to solve?
- What is the intended outcome?

For example, you may be asked to design a public service poster for your community advertising "Free Testing". The problem you must solve is how to include the required information about where and when to go for this service while at the same time making a poster which is highly visible and graphically engaging. The goal is to grab the attention of your audience and present them with all the necessary information in readable form. The design should function as intended by making the message you need to convey clear to the audience. Most graphic design concepts and layouts evolve from having a clear vision of the desired outcome of the project.

3. *Technical and creative methods are combined to achieve results.* Graphic designers are the conduit between an idea or concept and the actual finished product. Creative consideration means producing a design based on research, intuition, and skillful application of basic design principles. Technical ability refers to an understanding of computers, printing, and Web processes, and knowing how to use design-related software such as Photoshop. Graphic designers, and anyone in related fields, need to possess an understanding of both technical and creative aspects to create and produce a design.

GRAPHIC DESIGNER'S CONCERNS

1. CLIENT/AUDIENCE/CONSUMER
You are usually making it for someone else.

2. DESIGN OF AN IDEA
Defined by its purpose, it must function as intended.

3. PROCESS
Technical & creative methods are combined to achieve results.

FIGURE SF 1-1

Because design is a complex field with constantly changing technology, no single person can know everything. Success often is achieved by cooperation between people who share their expertise in a given area. Many designers will focus on the conceptualization of a project, then work with a technician who has advanced skills with software to fine-tune the final project. Many Web programmers rely on the expertise of designers to make their Web site competitively marketable.

Professionals involved in graphic design share a basic fundamental body of required knowledge, language, materials, concepts, and tools. No matter what the assignment is, all graphic designers use similar visual techniques and methods to ensure their designs are effective and persuasive.

Planning and Developing a Project

Planning and developing a project includes primarily two critical steps: organizing and documenting materials, and developing an idea.

Organizing and Documenting Materials

Graphic designers develop good organizational skills for documenting a project's development. It is the designer's responsibility to keep track of computer files, backup disks, and hard copy (paper printouts) related to a project.

Label actual folders, computer desktop folders, and disks with the name of the project; keep track of the dates, the software you used, the font (or type style), and types of images. It also is your responsibility to keep track of original versions of the work, art and text documents, and schedules.

Developing an Idea

Once you know what you are designing and for whom, your job is to take the idea and work out some real, visual examples. Usually you have two or three different concepts that you would like to explore with your client. Computer software programs like Photoshop give designers the opportunity to experiment, save, and view or print different versions of ideas.

The graphic designer's vocabulary, also called design **vernacular**, contains many words used to describe the developmental stage of an idea. Although these terms often are used interchangeably, they have specific meaning.

Graphic designers develop individual methods for conceiving and documenting ideas, and coming up with strong concepts. Most designers use their research to brainstorm on paper by drawing a mind map. Mind maps are used to document multiple random

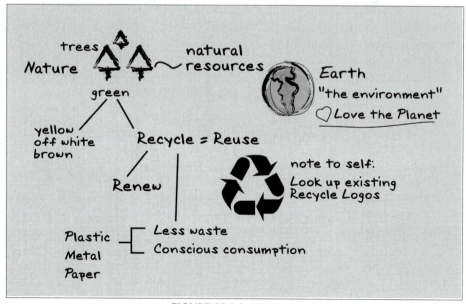

FIGURE SF 1-2 Mind map

thoughts and related ideas associated with a topic. Figure SF 1-2 is an example of a mind map a designer might sketch to begin a design project such as a poster or brochure about recycling and renewable resources.

Sketches, roughs, and **thumbnails** are quick pencil or pen drawings used to get the idea from your head onto paper. Designers often begin their sketches during the initial meeting with the client.

Dummies and **mock-ups** are roughs made for two-sided or multipage pieces like brochures, books, or magazines. For example, a piece of 8½" × 11" paper could be folded into 3 panels to make a tri-fold brochure dummy. The dummy enables you to see both sides of the brochure.

Comps, or comprehensive layouts, are developed from the best ideas taken from your roughs. They are renderings which look as close as possible to how you imagine the finished project. Comps, dummies, and mock-ups are made by hand or using a computer.

Storyboards are used for sequential designs, like movies, video, and animation — anything that involves a scene-by-scene plot plan. Storyboards

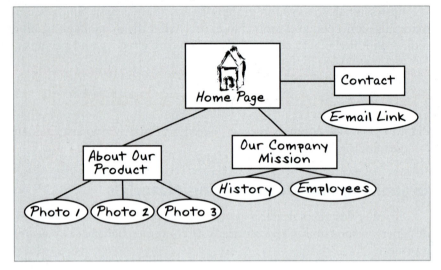

FIGURE SF 1-3 Rough sketch for a Web site

also explain in frames, using drawings or photos, the planned actions of a scene. The rough sketch for a Web site in Figure SF 1-3 may serve as a preliminary draft for a storyboard because it illustrates the planned sequence of pages.

A **prototype** is another word for a mock-up. A graphic designer makes a version, or prototype, of a layout or product. This version of the design is tested on the client or audience to determine how well it functions. The development of a graphic design piece is **iterative**. The word iterative means to repeat. From a graphic design point of view, it means the client or audience suggests changes in the prototype. The designer will make the changes suggested, and present a new and improved prototype to the client. If the client proposes more changes, the designer incorporates the additional changes and again presents the client with the next prototype iteration. As many iterations are done as necessary until the client and designer agree that the project development is complete.

About Images

A picture really IS worth a thousand words. Graphic designers must understand about the different types of images, their meaning and impact, and how they can be manipulated. Designers and artists use a specific vernacular to describe images within a visual and aesthetic context.

(a)

(b)   FIGURE SF 1-4

Images are classified as being representational, symbolic, or abstract. A **representational image** is the real thing. The image, whether it is a photograph or rendered as an illustration, is realistic (Figure SF 1-4a).

Symbolic images use something graphical to represent a different, nongraphical concept. A letter is a symbol that represents a sound. A red circle with a slash is a common symbol indicating something not permitted (Figure SF 1-4b).

Abstract images are nonrepresentational. No specific implied meaning exists in the visual arrangement of color, shape, or form. Abstract images often convey feeling and emotion that are open to personal interpretation (Figure SF 1-4c).

FIGURE SF 1-4(c)

Table SF 1-1   Elements

ELEMENTS	DESCRIPTION
Dot, line, and shape	the most basic elements of which all images are made
Graphic image	the visible object also known as the graphic, the image, or design — including type, symbols, abstract shapes, and pictures
Image area	describes the area of a plane or surface on which images are placed, such as a computer screen or a piece of paper
Nonimage area	describes the area around graphic images, also known as white space
Color	shade or hue of emotion or feeling

Table SF 1-2   Techniques

TECHNIQUES	DESCRIPTION
Composition	the arrangement of elements
Juxtaposition	images placed next to one another
Unity	compositional harmony of diverse elements
Balance	how images relate to the horizontal and vertical centerline of a surface or plane
Simplicity	understated and direct message from a minimum of elements
Contrast	elements placed in opposition to show emphasis
Exaggeration	distorted or overstated from true and real form
Scale	size and proportion of elements in relationship to one another
Perspective	using scale to give the illusion of depth or dimension (3D) on a flat surface
Motion	kinetic, nonstatic quality of elements on a surface
Repetition	same image repeated for visual or conceptual impact
Sequence	changing images shown in logical, narrative order
Transparency	less saturated images or see-through colors
Opacity	solid, dense, nontransparent color or image
Texture	the look and feel of a surface or image

Elements & Techniques

All designers, artists, and photographers use the same universal, visual, and conceptual **elements** and **techniques**. Elements are manipulated using techniques to create layouts with graphic intent. Table SF 1-1 lists elements and Table SF 1-2 lists techniques commonly used by graphic designers.

Every image, such as a photograph, or graphic design layout contains recognizable elements and techniques. Figure SF 1-5a is a close-up photograph of a cactus. A graphic designer could describe the qualities of this photograph in terms of the basic elements it exhibits. Dot, line, and shape create the form. Light and shadow provide contrast. The natural dots inherent in a cactus create a visual rhythm through repetition. These dots engage the viewer's eye, indicating vertical motion from top to bottom of the page. The overall surface has a textured quality.

Contrast is a commonly applied technique. Contrast can mean a comparison of tones of colors, or images of different sizes. In Figure SF 1-5b the composition made from juxtaposing two photographs emphasizes contrast in light and scale. By placing the close-up of the baby next to the smaller image of the woman, meaning is implied by the contrast of young and old. The composition of these images creates a sense of unity and balance.

Unity, which is the compositional harmony of elements, often depends on the balance of the image or layout. **Balance** can be **symmetrical**, in which the same image is placed in the same position on each side of a center line. With **asymmetrical** balance the image is not identical, but still has a sense of visual unity. Repeating the shell photograph in Figure SF 1-5c demonstrates symmetrical balance. The single shell in Figure SF 1-5d demonstrates asymmetrical balance.

(a)

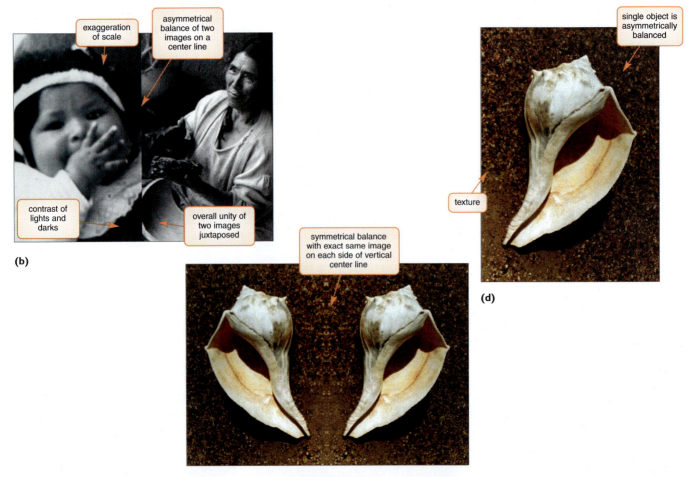

(b)

(c)

(d)

FIGURE SF 1-5

Continue to analyze Figure SF 1-5d to identify the other elements and techniques. The shell itself could be considered the image, and the sand could be considered the nonimage area because it is the background. Both the sand and shell have texture. The smooth shell and rough sand create contrast. Simplicity and unity are conveyed through the single image and noncontrasting, soothing colors.

Color

Color is the most powerful design element. It catches attention and leaves a lasting impression. Color can evoke a physiological response from your audience; it can sooth or stimulate. Color used symbolically tells you when to stop, when to go, and when to go slow. Color also is referred to as **hue**.

For an artist mixing paint or pigment to use on paper or canvas, the primary colors are red, yellow, and blue. Combinations of primary colors make secondary colors. A general rule is that warm colors (red, yellow, and orange) advance, and cool colors (blue, green, and violet) recede. Complementary colors face each other on the color model as shown in Figure SF 1-6. For example, yellow and violet are complementary colors. Complementary colors provide good contrast, and when juxtaposed make each other stand out more brightly. **Shades** of a color are created by adding black to the hue; **tints** are created by adding white.

Colors on a TV screen or a computer monitor are visual illusions made from reflected light. All colors you see on a monitor are created from combinations of red, green, and blue, which are referred to as RGB as you see in Figure SF 1-7.

To print on paper, designers and printers use **process colors**, which are always cyan, magenta, yellow, and black, or **CMYK**. As shown in Figure SF 1-8, CMYK are called process colors because they are fundamental to the printing process. Carefully controlled percentages of these colors mixed together create the illusion of all the colors you see in print.

Design Systems

In addition to creativity, inspiration, and intuition, design requires common sense and adherence to a few rules and established systems.

Layout

Layout involves applying design principles within a given space, page, or screen for maximum visual impact. Design layout encompasses the whole process of thoughtfully and skillfully arranging elements and content on a plane or surface. Content is both **visual** — words, images, colors, etc. that you see, and **perceptual** — meanings or ideas that you feel. Layouts include either images or type, also referred to as objects, or a combination of both.

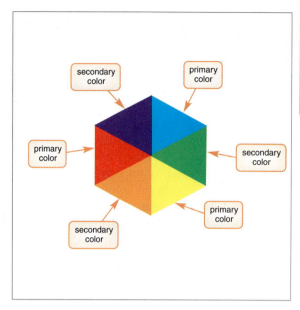

FIGURE SF 1-6

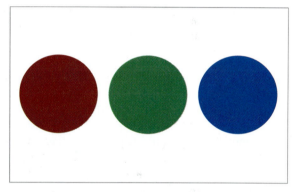

FIGURE SF 1-7

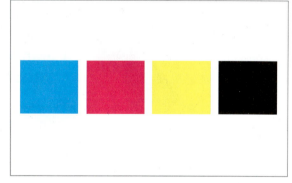

FIGURE SF 1-8

In a layout the images in front are in the foreground. Elements that are of secondary importance are in the background. The term **figure-ground** refers to the relationship between an object or image, and its surroundings.

Images that you want your viewer to focus on often are placed slightly above, and to the right of, the actual center line of a layout. This is called the **visual center**. Usually you should avoid placing images too close to the bottom of a page, because it directs the viewer off the page.

Cropping means to cut or resize an image for maximum visual impact. Whether a layout is dynamic or static often depends on how the images are cropped. A **static layout** is very stable and predictable as illustrated in Figure SF 1-9a. This centered layout is static and illustrates unity and simplicity in composition. Notice the objects, which include text and an image, are centered within the layout.

A **dynamic layout** is active and promotes audience participation as illustrated in Figure SF 1-9b. A more dynamic layout makes use of different type, color in the foreground and background, layers of complexity, and repetition of a basic shape to indicate motion. Notice the objects are centered slightly above the horizontal center.

Grids

Visual elements often are organized according to an underlying grid. Grids are invisible guides used to determine the best placement of images and text on a surface, providing overall visual unity. Grids can be simple, when used for a small advertisement for example, or complex, when used for a multiple paged publication such as a catalog. The most basic grid might

(a)

(b)

FIGURE SF 1-9

random placement of photographs

New Ceramics Studio

OPENING

poorly cropped photo directs viewer's eye off page instead of to images in photo

opening date
store hours
address + city
phone number here

no clear system for aligning text makes information difficult to read

FIGURE SF 1-10a

place margins at the top, bottom, and sides of a piece of paper, using the space within the margins for your layout. A complex grid might indicate a standard for placement of several photographs and columns of text.

The amount of text, the length of a headline, **information hierarchy**, meaning what is most and least important, and the size and number of images you are using are all factors in determining a grid structure.

Figure SF 1-10a is of a layout made without using a grid. The juxtaposition of elements is random. The overall layout lacks unity and balance.

Figure SF 1-10b displays the same images as Figure SF 1-10a, but a simple grid is used to help with placement. The overall composition is unified and balanced.

Understanding limitations provided by a grid gives you a framework to apply your creative thinking. Grids provide a structure of guides to help with placement, but do not limit your possibilities. You usually can break your own rules to make a layout "look right" by placing an image outside the grid structure. Some layouts, like packaging for 3D objects, might require strict adherence to the grid to prevent losing key images or information on a fold or flap.

Grids are excellent design tools for the following reasons:

- For the layout of a single page project, the grid helps determine the point of visual focus.
- For the layout of a multipage project (Figures SF 1-11), grids provide unity, consistency, rhythm, structure, and balance from page to page.
- Ideas are unlimited. Time is not. For decision making and production, grids save time.

grid lines are placed equal distance from top and sides of page

text lines up with photos making it easy for viewer to read top to bottom and across page, smoothly integrating words and images

space between photos is equal

bottom margin is slightly bigger than top and side margins

OPENING

New Ceramics Studio

opening date
store hours
address + city
phone number here

FIGURE SF 1-10(b)
Simple grid provides unity and visual structure
by organizing the placement of images and text.

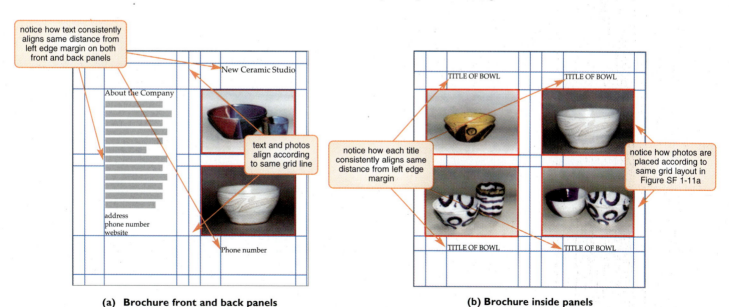

notice how text consistently aligns same distance from left edge margin on both front and back panels

New Ceramic Studio

About the Company

address
phone number
website

Phone number

text and photos align according to same grid line

notice how each title consistently aligns same distance from left edge margin

TITLE OF BOWL   TITLE OF BOWL

TITLE OF BOWL   TITLE OF BOWL

notice how photos are placed according to same grid layout in Figure SF 1-11a

(a) Brochure front and back panels
For this two-sided brochure, a more complex
grid provides a structure so the whole piece has
continuity and unity from panel to panel and
front to back.

(b) Brochure inside panels

FIGURE SF 1-11

Summary

To plan a graphic design project you need to identify the assignment or topic, the client, the audience, and the basic processes used to complete the job. Photoshop and other computer software allows you to manipulate images for different types of graphic design layouts.

Color, a powerful and useful design element, conveys emotion and feeling. Color also has technical considerations depending on what you are designing. Designing for a computer screen makes use of the RGB model, while designing for print uses the CMYK color model.

Understanding the graphic designer's vernacular helps you to describe the way images are used. Using elements such as image and type, and techniques such as composition, unity, and balance, helps you to develop good ideas into successful graphic design layouts. Design layouts are made by arranging images and text on a surface. Grids provide a structure for placing images within a layout. Layouts made using grids often exhibit more visual unity and balance in their overall composition.

Appendix A

Changing Screen Resolution and Editing Preferences

This appendix explains how to change the screen resolution in Windows Vista to the resolution used in this book. It also describes how to customize the Photoshop window by setting preferences, resetting user changes, and changing the screen modes.

Screen Resolution

Screen resolution indicates the number of pixels (dots) that the computer uses to display the graphics, text, and background you see on the screen. The screen resolution usually is stated as the product of two numbers, such as 1024×768. That resolution results in a display of 1,024 distinct pixels on each of 768 lines, or about 786,432 pixels. The figures in this book were created using a screen resolution of 1024×768.

Changing Screen Resolution

The following steps show how to change your screen's resolution from 1280 by 720 pixels to 1024 by 768 pixels. Your computer already may be set to 1024×768 or some other resolution.

To Change Screen Resolution

1

• If necessary, minimize all programs so that the Windows Vista desktop is displayed.

• Right-click the Windows Vista desktop to display the Windows Vista desktop shortcut menu.

The shortcut menu is displayed (Figure A-1).

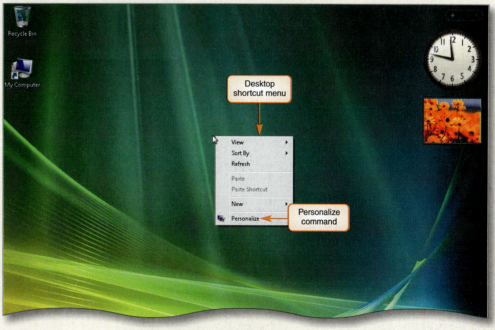

FIGURE A-1

2

• **Click Personalize on the shortcut menu.**

The Personalization window opens (Figure A-2).

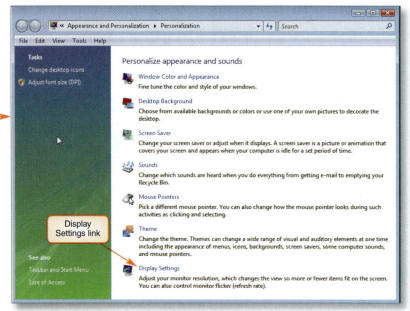

FIGURE A-2

3

• **Click Display Settings in the Personalization window.**

The Display Settings dialog box is displayed (Figure A-3). The current screen resolution is displayed in the Resolution area.

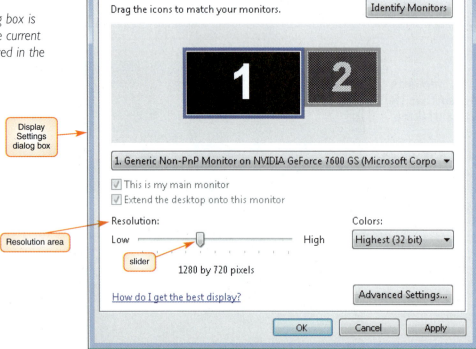

FIGURE A-3

4

• **Drag the slider in the Resolution area so that the screen resolution changes to 1024 × 768, if necessary.**

As the slider is moved one mark to the right, the screen resolution displayed below the slider changes to 1024 by 768 pixels (Figure A-4).

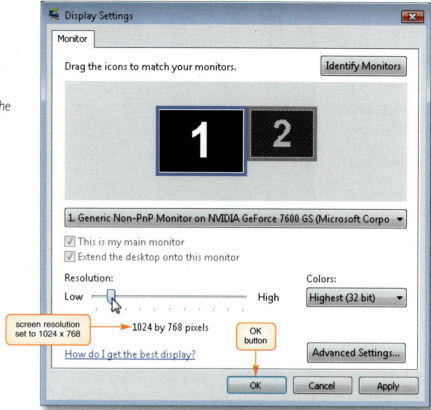

FIGURE A-4

5

• **Click the OK button to change the screen resolution.**

Windows displays a Display Settings dialog box confirming the change (Figure A-5).

FIGURE A-5

6

- **Click the Yes button.**

- **Click the Close button in the Personalization window.**

The Personalization window closes. The screen is displayed at a resolution of 1024 by 768 pixels (Figure A-6). Your screen may flicker while the resolution change takes place.

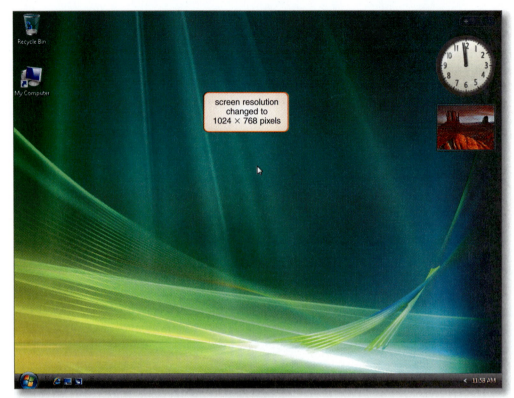

screen resolution
changed to
1024 × 768 pixels

FIGURE A-6

When you increase the screen resolution, Windows displays more information on the screen, but the information decreases in size. The reverse also is true; as you decrease the screen resolution, Windows displays less information on the screen, but the information increases in size.

You can experiment with various screen resolutions. Depending on your monitor and the video adapter installed in your computer, the screen resolutions available on your computer will vary.

Editing Photoshop Preferences

In Chapter 1, you learned how to start Photoshop and reset the default workspace, select the default tool, and reset all tools to their default settings. There are other preferences and settings you can edit to customize the Photoshop workspace and maximize your efficiency.

Editing General Preferences

General preferences include how Photoshop displays and stores your work. For example, you can change how many states are saved in the History palette, change the number of files shown on the Open Recent menu, or reset the display and cursors. As shown in the following steps, Photoshop allows you to traverse through several Preferences dialog boxes to reset values and change preferences. You can access this set of dialog boxes by pressing CTRL+K or by clicking Preferences on the Edit menu.

To Edit General Preferences

1

• Start Photoshop.

• Press CTRL+K.

• When the Preferences dialog box is displayed, make sure your Options check boxes are selected as shown in Figure A-7.

• Click the Reset All Warning Dialogs button, so your dialog boxes will match the ones in this book.

• When Photoshop displays a dialog box, click the OK button.

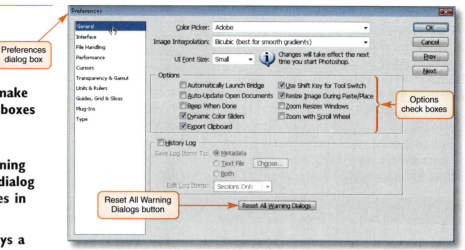

FIGURE A-7

The General preferences are displayed with many option settings (Figure A-7). Photoshop will show all warning dialog boxes as you work in the application.

2

• Click File Handling in the list of Preferences.

• If necessary, click the File Extension box arrow and then click Use Lower Case in the list, so Photoshop will use lowercase letters when you save files.

• Make sure your check boxes are selected as shown in Figure A-8.

• Click the Maximize PSD and PSB File Compatibility box arrow and then click Ask, in order for Photoshop to ask you about saving files in PSD format.

• Type 10 in the Recent file list contains box, in order for Photoshop to display the last 10 files you have worked on, creating easier access through the menu system.

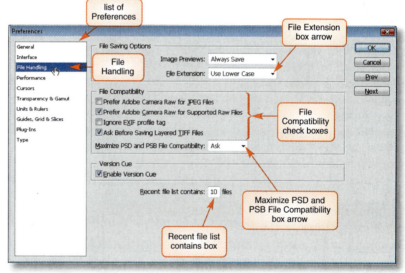

FIGURE A-8

The File Handling preferences are displayed (Figure A-8).

3

• **Click Performance in the list of Preferences.**

• **When the Preferences dialog box is displayed, if necessary, type 20 in the History States box, so Photoshop will allow you to back up through the last 20 steps of any editing session.**

The Performance preferences are displayed (Figure A-9). Photoshop will save 20 states in the History palette.

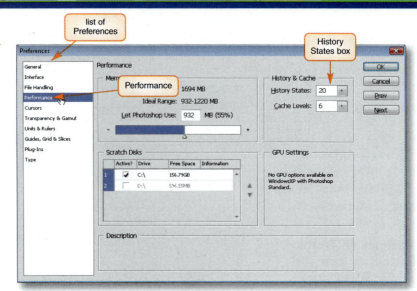

FIGURE A-9

4

• **Click Cursors in the list of Preferences.**

• **If necessary, select Normal Brush Tip in the Painting Cursors area and Standard in the Other Cursors area, to reset those options back to their default values.**

The Cursors preferences are displayed (Figure A-10).

FIGURE A-10

5

• **One at a time, click each of the other preference settings in the list. If you want your screens to match the ones in the book, accept the default settings. Or, you may make changes to the colors and sizes as desired.**

• **When you are finished, click the OK button.**

The preferences are changed.

Other Ways

1. On Edit menu, point to Preferences, click General, select individual preferences

The Preferences dialog boxes contain a variety of settings that can be changed to suit individual needs and styles. The Reset All Warning Dialogs button in Figure A-7 on page APP 5 is especially useful to display the dialog boxes if someone has turned them off by clicking the Don't show again check box.

In Figure A-10, **Normal Brush Tip** causes the mouse pointer outline to correspond to approximately 50 percent of the area that the tool will affect. This option shows the pixels that would be most visibly affected. It is easier to work with Normal Brush Tip than **Full Size Brush Tip**, especially when using larger brushes. A **Standard painting cursor** displays mouse pointers as tool icons; a **Precise painting cursor** displays the mouse pointer as a crosshair.

If there is one particular setting you wish to change, you can open that specific Preferences dialog box from the menu. For example, if you want to change the color of a ruler guide, you can point to Preferences on the Edit menu and then click Guides, Grid & Slices on the Preferences submenu to go directly to those settings and make your edits. To restore all preferences to their default settings, you can press and hold ALT+CONTROL+SHIFT as you start Photoshop, which causes the system to prompt that you are about to delete the current settings.

Menu Command Preferences

Photoshop allows users to customize both the application menus and the palette menus in several ways. You can hide commands that you seldom use. You can set colors on the menu structure to highlight or organize your favorite commands. Or, you can let Photoshop organize your menus with color based on functionality. If changes have been made to the menu structure, you can reset the menus back to their default states.

Hiding and Showing Menu Commands

If there are menu commands that you seldom use, you can hide them in order to access other commands more quickly. A **hidden command** is a menu command that does not display currently on a menu. If menu commands have been hidden, a Show All Menu Items command will display at the bottom of the menu list. When you click the Show All Menu Items command or press and hold the CTRL key as you click the menu name, Photoshop displays all menu commands including hidden ones.

The steps on the next page illustrate how to hide a menu command and then show it. The last step turns the hidden menu command back on so it always is displayed.

To Hide and Show Menu Commands

1

• **Click Edit on the menu bar, and then click Menus.**

The Keyboard Shortcuts and Menus dialog box is displayed (Figure A-11).

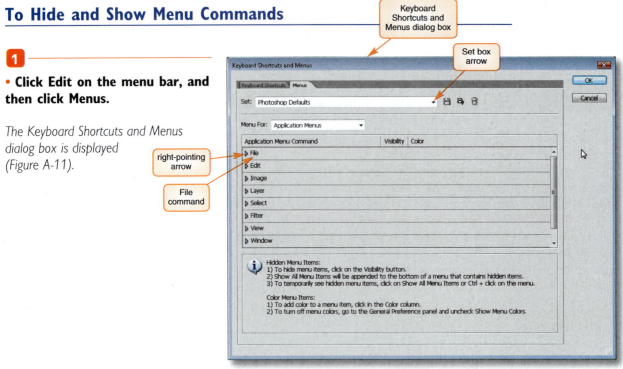

FIGURE A-11

2

• **If necessary, click the Set box arrow and then click Photoshop Defaults.**

• **Click the right-pointing arrow next to the word File.**

The File commands are displayed (Figure A-12). The right-pointing arrow changes to a down-pointing arrow.

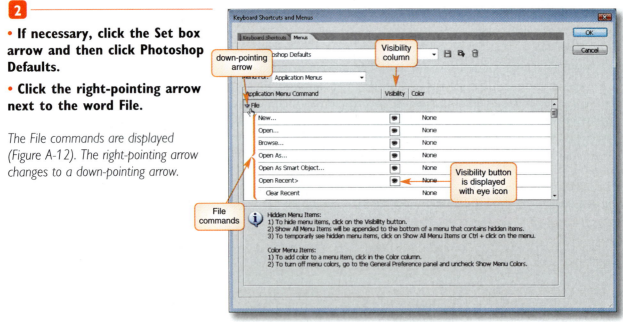

FIGURE A-12

3

• **In the Visibility column, click the Visibility button next to the Open Recent command.**

The eye on the Visibility button no longer is displayed (Figure A-13). Photoshop notes that the default settings have been modified.

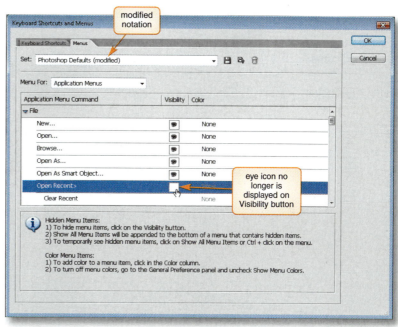

FIGURE A-13

4

• **Click the OK button in the Keyboard Shortcuts and Menus dialog box.**

• **Click File on the menu bar.**

The Keyboard Shortcuts and Menus dialog box closes and Photoshop displays the File menu (Figure A-14). The Show All Menu Items command is added to the bottom of the menu. The Open Recent command is not displayed.

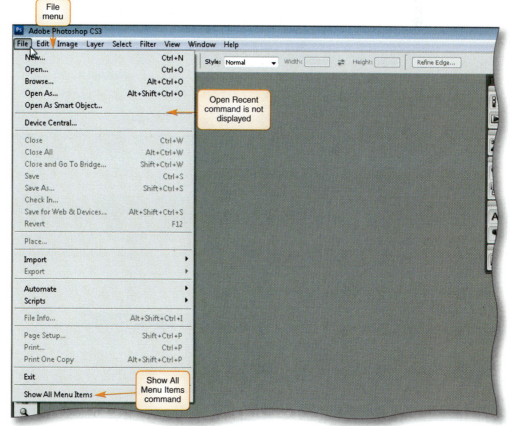

FIGURE A-14

5

• **On the File menu, click Show All Menu Items.**

The File menu displays the Open Recent command (Figure A-15).

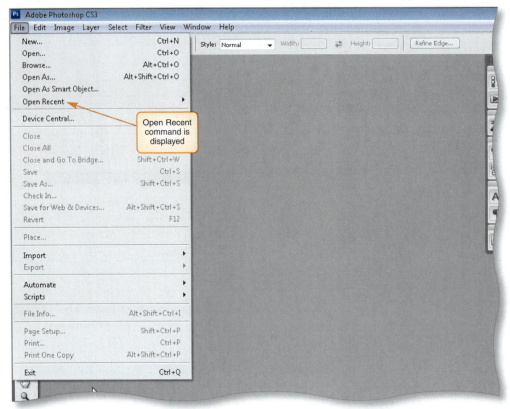

FIGURE A-15

6

• **Click Edit on the menu bar and then click Menus.**

• **When the Keyboard Shortcuts and Menus dialog box is displayed, if necessary, click the right-pointing arrow next to the word File. Click the Visibility button next to the Open Recent command.**

The eye icon again is displayed (Figure A-16). The next time the File menu is accessed, Photoshop will display the Open Recent command.

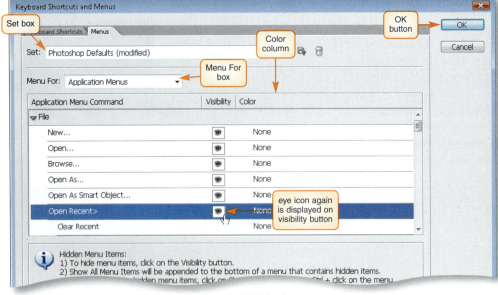

FIGURE A-16

Other Ways

1. On menu bar, click Window, point to Workspace, click Keyboard Shortcuts and Menus
2. Press ALT+SHIFT+CTRL+M

You can add color to your menu commands to help you find them easily or to organize them into groups based on personal preferences, as shown in the following steps.

To Add Color to Menu Commands

1

• **With the Keyboard Shortcuts and Menus dialog box still displayed, click the word None in the row associated with the Open command.**

Photoshop displays a list of possible colors (Figure A-17).

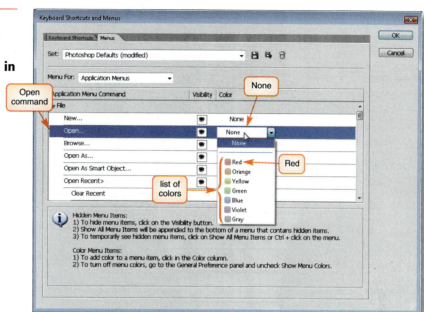

FIGURE A-17

2

• **Click Red in the list.**

• **Click the word None in the row associated with the Open As command, and then click Red in the list.**

The changes are displayed (Figure A-18).

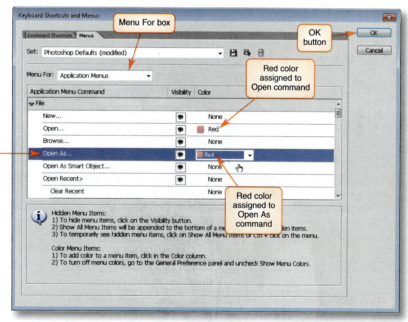

FIGURE A-18

3

• **Click the OK button to close the Keyboard Shortcuts and Menus dialog box.**

• **Click File on the Photoshop menu bar.**

The menu is displayed with the Open and Open As commands highlighted in red (Figure A-19).

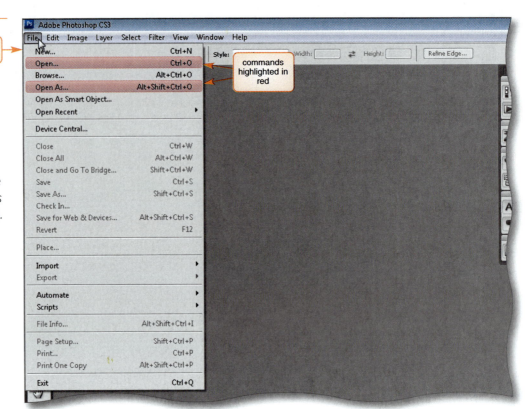

FIGURE A-19

The Set box (Figure A-20) lists several different categories of menu commands related to common tasks. Choosing a set causes Photoshop to display related commands with color. For example, if you choose Web Design, the commands on all menus that directly relate to Web design will display in purple. This category list also is displayed when you click Window on the menu bar and then point to Workspace.

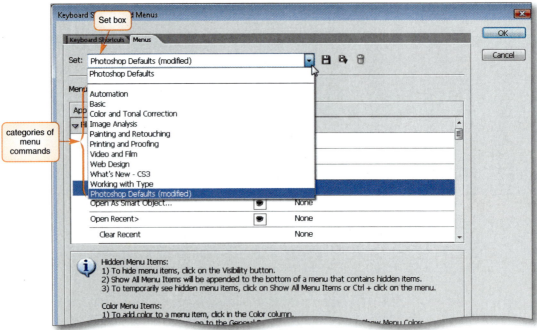

FIGURE A-20

The Menu For box (Figure A-18 on page APP 11) allows you to set options for Applications Menus or Palette Menus.

Resetting User Changes

If you are working in a lab situation and you notice that Photoshop does not display the workspace, menus, and brushes the way you are used to, someone may have changed the settings. The next sections describe how to reset those changes.

Resetting the Palettes, Keyboard Shortcuts, and Menus

The following steps show how to reset the location of the palettes, reset the keyboard shortcuts to their default settings, and remove any changes to the menus.

To Reset the Palettes, Keyboard Shortcuts, and Menus

1

• **Click Window on the menu bar, and then point to Workspace.**

The Workspace submenu is displayed (Figure A-21).

2

• **Click Reset Palette Locations.**

• **Click Window on the menu bar, point to Workspace, and then click Reset Keyboard Shortcuts.**

• **Click Window on the menu bar, point to Workspace, and then click Reset Menus.**

• **If Photoshop displays a dialog box asking you to save the current settings, click the No button.**

Each of the options is reset.

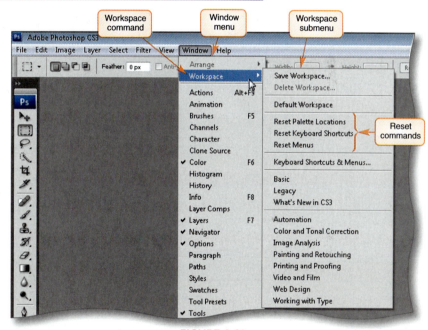

FIGURE A-21

Resetting the Brushes

One of the most used tools in Photoshop is the Brush tool. Users make many choices in the Brushes palette and options bar that carry over from one session to another. In order to begin with a clean set of brushes in the default settings, the steps on the next page illustrate how to clear the brush controls and reset the brush tips.

Other Ways

1. To reset all three, on menu bar, click Window, point to Workspace, click Default Workspace

To Reset the Brushes

• On the Tools palette, click the Brush Tool (B) button.

• In the group of docked palettes, click the Brushes palette button and then drag the palette group away from the docking area.

• Click the Brushes palette menu button.

Photoshop displays the Brushes palette menu (Figure A-22).

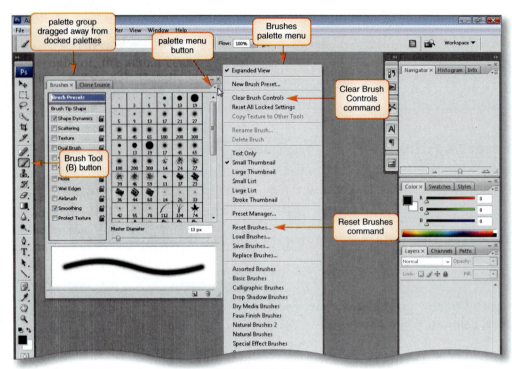

FIGURE A-22

2

• Click Clear Brush Controls.

• Click the Brushes palette menu button again, and then click Reset Brushes.

• When Photoshop asks if you want to use the default brushes, click the OK button.

• Drag the palette group back to its original location, between the 2nd and 3rd palette groupings in the dock of additional palettes as shown in Figure A-23.

Other Ways

1. On Brush options bar, click Toggle Brushes Palette, click palette menu button, click Reset Brushes

Users may have changed the color settings related to your brushes as well. As you learned in Chapter 3, pressing the D key restores the Color palette to its default setting of black and white.

Changing the Screen Mode

Photoshop offers four screen modes from which users may choose. The modes are listed on the context menu associated with the Change Screen Modes (F) button on the Tools palette. The **standard screen mode** is the default setting where the menu bar, options bar, palettes, and document window are displayed. The **maximized screen mode** displays a maximized document window that fills all available space between docked palettes and resizes when dock widths change. The **full screen mode with menu bar** removes the title bars from the Photoshop window and document window while maximizing the screen. The **full screen mode** removes the title bars and the menu bar, and changes the background of the workspace to black. Using the Hand tool, full screen mode also allows you to move a maximized document window around on the black background. In full screen mode, the menu system is available via a Tools palette menu button.

To Change Screen Modes

1

- **Open any image file in Photoshop.**
- **On the Tools palette, right-click the Change Screen Mode (F) button.**
- **Click Maximized Screen Mode on the context menu.**

Photoshop displays the workspace in maximized screen mode (Figure A-23).

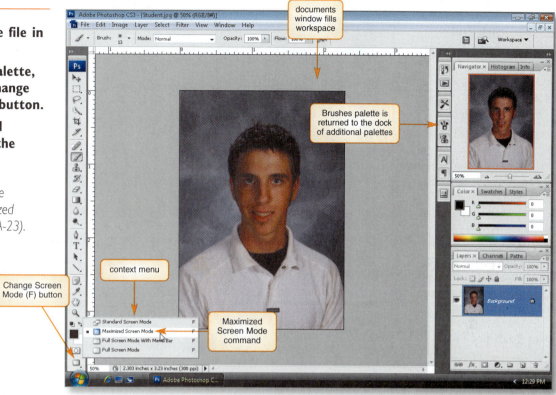

FIGURE A-23

2

- **Right-click the Change Screen Mode (F) button and then click Full Screen Mode With Menu Bar in the list.**

Photoshop displays the workspace in full screen mode with a menu bar (Figure A-24).

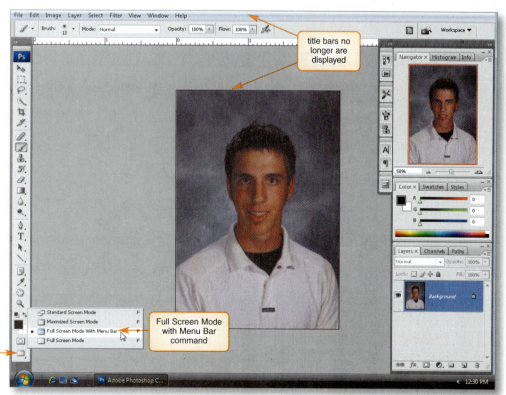

FIGURE A-24

3

• **Right-click the Change Screen Mode (F) button and then click Full Screen Mode in the list.**

Photoshop displays the workspace in full screen mode (Figure A-25). The Tools palette displays a menu button to allow access to the Photoshop menus. Notice that the workspace background changes to black.

4

• **Right-click the Change Screen Mode (F) button and then click Standard Screen Mode in the list.**

Photoshop returns the display to standard screen mode.

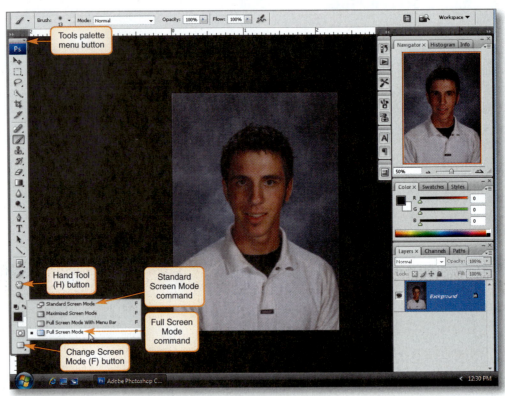

FIGURE A-25

Other Ways

1. Press F key to cycle through screen modes

The final step is to quit Photoshop.

To Quit Photoshop

1 **Click the Close button on the Photoshop title bar. If Photoshop displays a dialog box, click the No button.**

The Photoshop window closes.

Changing Preferences

1 Changing the Color and Style of Guides, Grid & Slices

Instructions: You would like to use some different colors and styles for grids and guides because the current colors are very similar to the colors in your image, making them hard to see. You decide to change the color and style preferences on your system as described in the following steps.

1. Start Adobe Photoshop CS3 on your system.
2. On the Edit menu, point to Preferences, and then click Guides, Grid, and Slices. Your command name may differ slightly.
3. When the Preferences dialog box is displayed, change the color and Style settings as shown in Figure A-26.

FIGURE A-26

4. Click the OK button.
5. Open any image file you have saved on your system and drag a guide from the horizontal ruler. Note the Light Red colored line.
6. On the View menu, point to Show, and then click Grid. Note the grid with dashed Light Red lines.
7. To clear the guides, on the View menu, click Clear Guides.
8. To clear the gird, on the View menu, point to Show and then click Grid.
9. To reset the colors and styles, either change them back in the Preferences dialog box, or quit Photoshop and then restart Photoshop while pressing ALT+CTRL+SHIFT. If Photoshop asks if you wish to delete the previous settings, click the Yes button.

Changing Preferences

2 Changing Menu Command Preferences

Instructions: You plan on creating Web graphics over the next few Photoshop sessions, so you would like to highlight Web commands on the menu system as described in the following steps.

1. Start Adobe Photoshop CS3 on your system.
2. On the Window menu, point to Workspace, and then click Web Design.
3. When Photoshop displays a dialog box, click the Yes button.
4. One at a time, click each menu command on the menu bar. Make a list of each highlighted command. Next to each listed command, make a notation on how that command affects Web design and Web graphics. Turn the list in to your instructor.
5. On the Window menu, point to Workspace and then click Reset Menus.
6. Quit Photoshop.

3 Searching the Web

Instructions: You want to learn more about optimizing Photoshop settings and your computer system's memory by setting preferences for file size, history states, and cached views. Perform a Web search by using the Google search engine at google.com (or any major search engine) to display and print three Web pages that pertain to optimizing Photoshop CS3. On each printout, highlight something new that you learned by reading the Web page.

Appendix B

Using Adobe Help

Adobe Help

This appendix shows you how to use Adobe Help. At any time, whether you are accessing Photoshop currently or not, there are ways to interact with Adobe Help and display information on any Photoshop topic. It is a complete reference manual at your fingertips. The figures in this appendix use Adobe Help Viewer 1.1. If you have a different version, your screens may differ slightly.

Adobe Help documentation for Photoshop CS3 is available in several formats as shown in Figure B-1. **In-product Help** provides access to all documentation and instructional content available at the time the software ships. In-product Help is accessed via the Help menu or by pressing the F1 key. **LiveDocs Help** includes all the content from In-product Help, plus updates and links to additional instructional content available on the Web. LiveDocs is accessed via links found in the In-product Help pages or on the Web at the Adobe Help Resource Center (www.adobe.com/go/documentation). Both In-product and LiveDocs documentation use a browser-based system with buttons to navigate back and forth, as well as a table of contents, index, bookmarks, and hyperlinks.

In-product Help is included in a PDF format that is optimized for printing. To view the documentation, open the Documents folder on the installation or content DVD for your software, and then double-click In-product Help. Use the Print button in the Adobe Reader toolbar to print the documentation. Additionally you can purchase documentation in printed form.

The Adobe Web site also contains many other kinds of assistance including tutorials about each of their products (www.adobe.com/designcenter/tutorials).

Adobe
Photoshop CS3

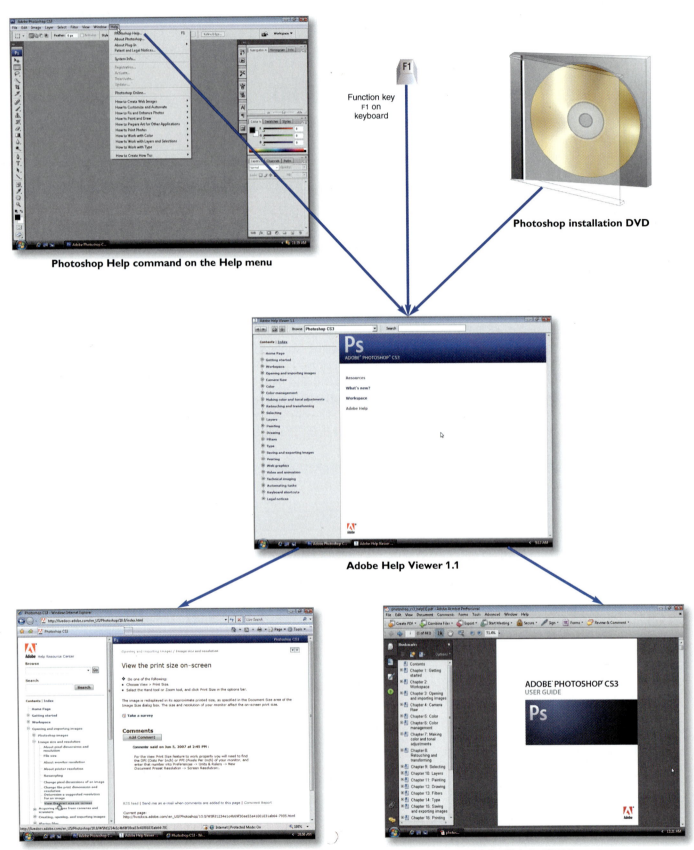

Photoshop Help command on the Help menu

Function key
F1 on
keyboard

Photoshop installation DVD

Adobe Help Viewer 1.1

LiveDocs

Adobe Help in PDF format

FIGURE B-1

The documentation for Adobe Help displays in a new window. If you access Live Docs, or if you have multiple Adobe products installed, you may have to click the Browse box arrow and then select Photoshop CS3 from the list. If you use the Help menu or the function key, Adobe Help displays help for Photoshop CS3 automatically.

Adobe Help displays two main panes. The left pane displays a navigation system. The right pane displays help information on the selected topic.

Above the panes are buttons and boxes to assist you in making help selections as described in the following sections of this appendix.

Searching for Help Using Words and Phrases

The quickest way to navigate Adobe Help is through the **Search box**, or the Type in a word or phrase box in some versions of Adobe Help, on the right side of the tool-bar at the top of the screen. Here you can type words, such as layer mask, hue, or file formats; or you can type phrases, such as preview a Web graphic, or create master palette. Adobe Help responds by displaying search results with a list of topics you can click.

Here are some tips regarding the words or phrases you enter to initiate a search: (1) check the spelling of the word or phrase; (2) keep your search specific, with fewer than seven words, to return the most accurate results; (3) if you search using a specific phrase, such as shape tool, put quotation marks around the phrase — the search returns only those topics containing all words in the phrase; and, (4) if a search term does not yield the desired results, try using a synonym, such as Web instead of Internet.

For the following example, assume that you want to learn more about changing the ruler so it displays the zero origin or starting measurement in a different location. The likely keywords are zero origin. The following steps show how to open Adobe Help and use the Search box to obtain useful information by entering the keywords zero origin.

To Obtain Help Using the Search Box

1

• **With Photoshop running on your system, press the F1 key on the keyboard.**

• **When the Adobe Help Viewer 1.1 window is displayed, double-click the title bar to maximize the window, if necessary.**

Adobe Help is launched and opens in a new window (Figure B-2).

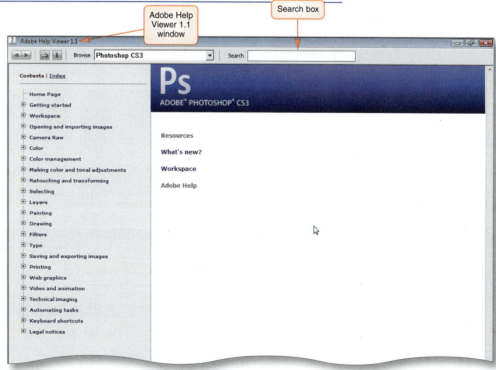

FIGURE B-2

2

• **Click the Search box on the right side of the toolbar, type** zero origin **as the entry, and then press the ENTER key.**

Adobe Help displays five topics in the search results (Figure B-3). Depending on your version of Adobe Help, your display may differ.

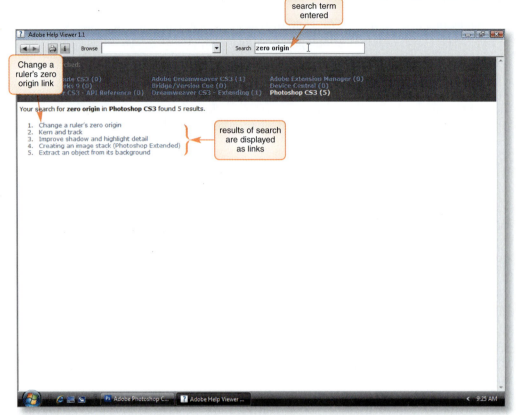

search term entered

Change a ruler's zero origin link

results of search are displayed as links

FIGURE B-3

3

• **Click the link, Change a ruler's zero origin.**

Adobe Help displays information about the topic in the right pane and the table of contents in the left pane (Figure B-4).

Forward to next page button

Print the current page button

About Adobe Help Viewer button

Browse box arrow

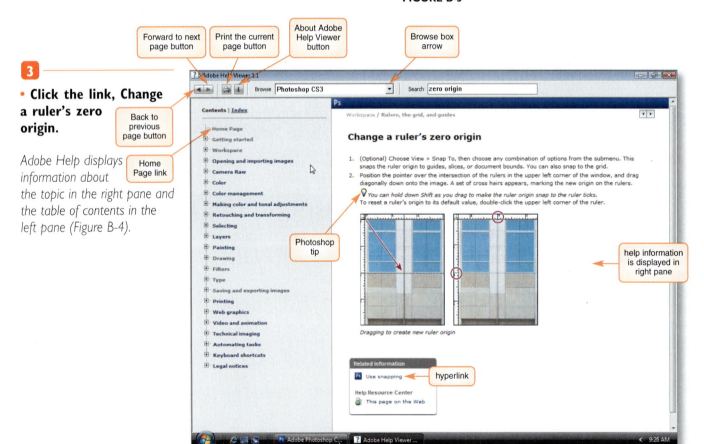

Back to previous page button

Home Page link

Photoshop tip

help information is displayed in right pane

hyperlink

FIGURE B-4

In the right pane, Adobe Help displays hyperlinks, which you can click to seek additional information. A light bulb icon indicates a Photoshop tip.

If none of the topics presents the information you want, you can refine the search by entering another word or phrase in the Search box.

Use the buttons in the Adobe Help window toolbar (Figure B-4) to move back and forth between pages, print the contents of the window, or display information about the viewer. If other Adobe products are installed on your system, clicking the Browse box arrow will display a list. Click another product in the list to access its help system.

As you click topics on the left, Adobe Help displays new pages of information. Adobe Help remembers the topics you visited and allows you to redisplay the pages visited during a session by clicking the Back to previous page and Forward to next page buttons.

Using the Contents and Index Panes

On the Home Page of Adobe Help, the left pane displays topics in a list called Contents. A link at the top changes the left pane to an Index list.

Using the Contents Pane

The **Contents pane** is similar to a table of contents in a book. To use the Contents pane, click the Contents link from the Home Page in Adobe Help. Then click any plus sign in the Contents pane to display subtopics as shown in the following steps.

To Use the Contents Pane

1

• **If the Index page is displayed in the left pane, click the Contents link.**

• **Click Home Page in the Contents list.**

Adobe Help displays the table of contents (Figure B-5).

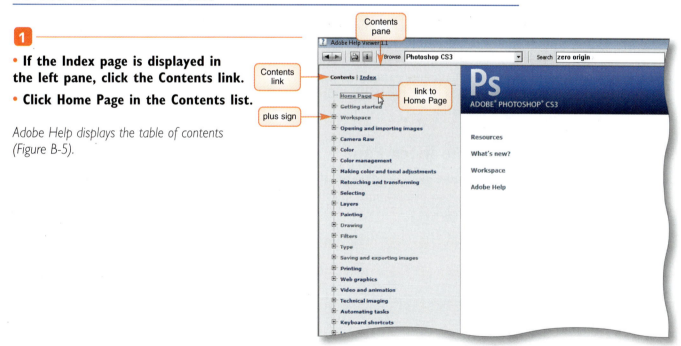

FIGURE B-5

2

• **Click the plus sign next to Workspace and then click the plus sign next to Workspace basics.**

• **Click Workspace overview.**

Information is displayed about the workspace (Figure B-6). After clicking a plus sign, it changes to a minus sign, and its subtopics are displayed.

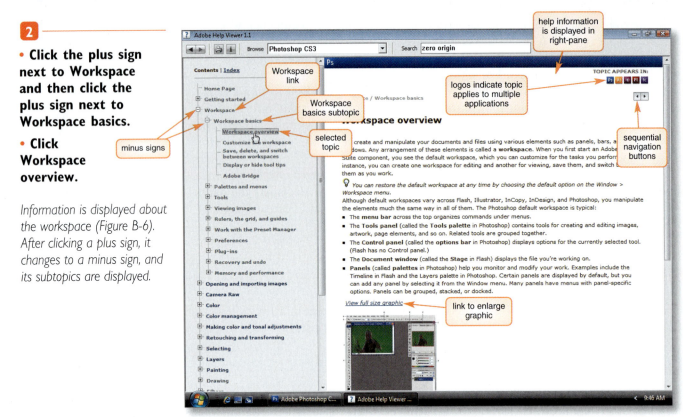

FIGURE B-6

When viewing any of the help topics, previous and next buttons are displayed in the upper-right corner of the right pane (Figure B-6). Clicking one of those buttons moves to the next sequential topic. If a topic applies to more than one CS3 application, logos are displayed in the upper-right corner as well.

In the Contents pane, plus signs indicate that subtopics exist. Clicking the plus sign expands the topic to list those subtopics. The minus sign can be clicked to collapse the listing.

Using the Index Pane

The **Index pane** displays an alphanumerical listing of topics. Click the letter of the alphabet to display subtopics beginning with the selected letter as the following steps illustrate.

To Use the Index Pane

1

• **Click the Index link.**

Adobe Help displays the alphabetical listing (Figure B-7).

FIGURE B-7

2

• **Click Z. When the subtopics are displayed, click the plus sign next to zooming and then click the plus sign next to in and out.**

• **Click the Zoom in or out subtopic.**

Information is displayed about zooming (Figure B-8). Other subtopics relevant to the workspace are collapsed at the bottom of the page.

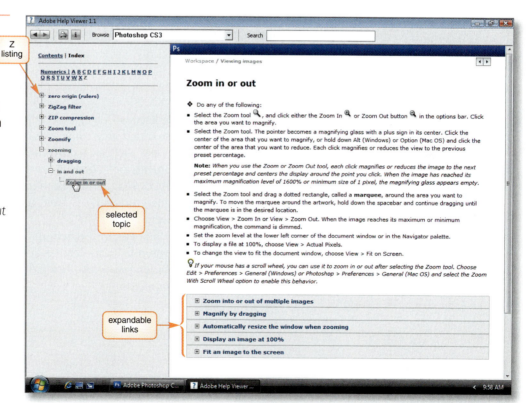

FIGURE B-8

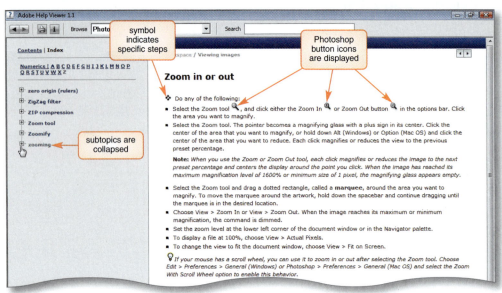

3

• **Click the minus sign next to zooming to collapse the topics (Figure B-9).**

FIGURE B-9

Adobe Help displays information that includes step-wise instructions with a special symbol. It also uses button icons as graphics in the help topics, to assist users in finding the appropriate button in Photoshop.

Using LiveDocs

A new help feature in the CS3 suite is called LiveDocs Help. LiveDocs includes all the content from Adobe Help that is provided with your installation, as well as updates and links to additional content on the Web. LiveDocs allows you to take surveys on certain aspects of Photoshop and add comments or questions on some topics. LiveDocs is a **wiki,** which is an online resource or Web site that allows users to add and edit content collectively. Comments and questions added to LiveDocs are moderated by Adobe Systems. To access LiveDocs you must be connected to the Web.

The user interface for LiveDocs opens in the default Web browser for your system and includes many of the navigational features from Adobe Help, such as Browse and Search boxes, and Contents and Index panes. Additional features include RSS feeds and e-mail notification of new comments.

Accessing LiveDocs

1

• In Adobe Help, click L in the Index pane.

• Scroll down to display the LiveDocs topic and click its plus sign. Click the Adobe Help resources subtopic.

Information about Adobe Help resources is displayed in the right pane (Figure B-10).

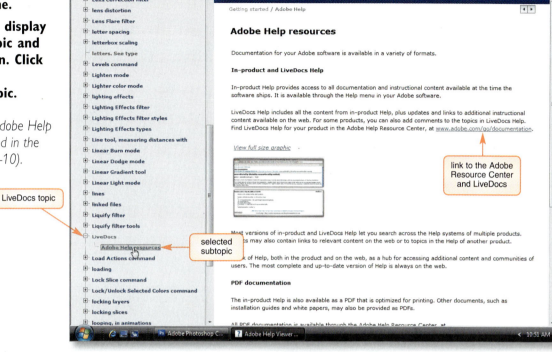

FIGURE B-10

2

• Click the link www.adobe.com/go/documentation in the right pane.

• When the Help Resource Center opens in a new window, click the Choose a product box arrow, and then click Photoshop in the list.

The Help Resource Center opens in a new window (Figure B-11).

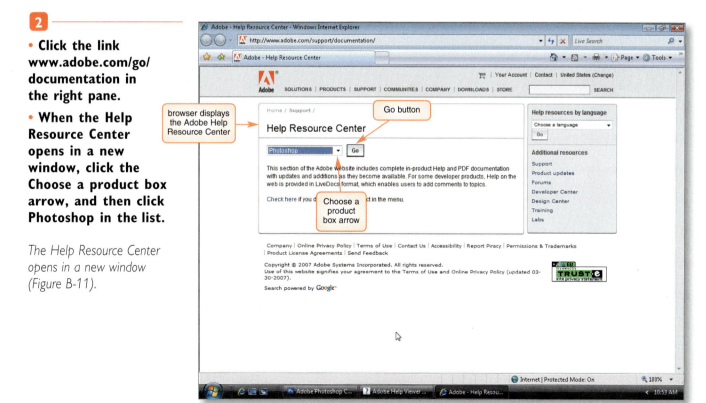

FIGURE B-11

3

• **Click the Go button.**

The Photoshop resources page is displayed (Figure B-12).

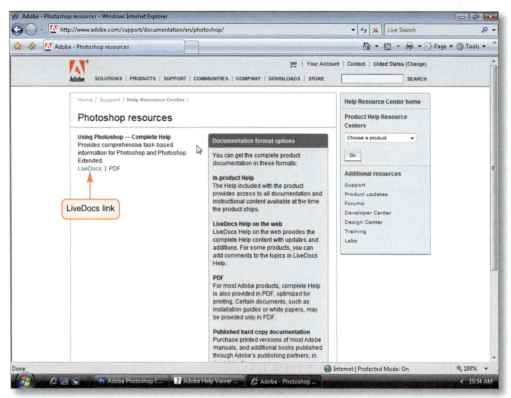

FIGURE B-12

4

• **Click the LiveDocs link.**

• **When the LiveDocs interface is displayed, using the Contents pane, click the plus sign beside the topic Opening and importing images. Click the plus sign beside the subtopic Image size and resolution, and then click View the print size on-screen.**

The LiveDocs page is displayed (Figure B-13). One comment has been added, however the number of topics you see may be different. LiveDocs displays links to take a survey, subscribe to an RSS feed, or receive e-mail comments.

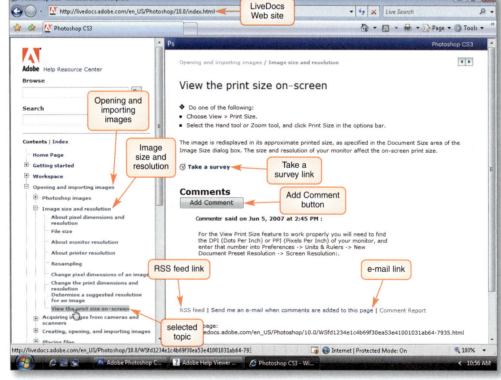

FIGURE B-13

Viewing a Video

Another feature of LiveDocs is the ability to view online videos and tutorials, as shown in the next steps.

To View a Video

1

• **With the topic View the print size on-screen displayed in the right pane, click the next topic button, twice.**

LiveDocs displays the topic about acquiring digital images from cameras (Figure B-14).

2

• **Click the link www.adobe.com/go/ vid0005 in the right pane. When LiveDocs opens a new window, double-click its title bar to maximize the window.**

LiveDocs begins a video about acquiring digital images from cameras. If your system is connected to speakers or headphones, narration will begin.

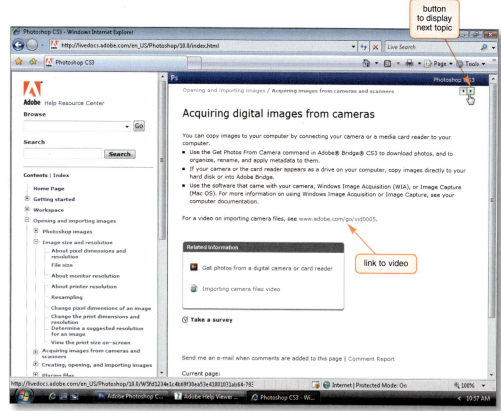

FIGURE B-14

Use Help

1 Using the Search Box

Instructions: Perform the following tasks using Adobe Help.

1. Type `pencil tool` in the Search box to obtain help on using the Pencil tool.
2. When the topics are displayed, click Paint with the Brush tool or Pencil tool.
3. One at a time, click two additional links and print the information. Hand in the printouts to your instructor. Use the Back to previous page and Forward to next page buttons to return to the original page.
4. Use the Search box to search for information on alignment. Click the Automatically align image layers topic in the search results. Read and print the information. One at a time, click the links on the page and print the information for any new page that is displayed.
5. Close the Adobe Help window.

2 Expanding on Adobe Help Basics

Instructions: Use Adobe Help to understand the topics better and answer the questions listed below. Answer the questions on your own paper, or hand in the printed Help information to your instructor.

1. Use Adobe Help to find help on snapping. Use the Search box, and enter `snapping` as the word. Click the search result entitled, Use snapping and print the page. Hand in the printouts to your instructor.
2. If you are connected to the Web, click the link to view the page on the Web. Use the next and previous topic buttons to view pages. If any page has comments, print the page. If any page has videos, watch the videos. Hand in the printouts to your instructor.
3. Return to Adobe Help on your system to find help on creating knockouts. Using the Index pane, click K. Then click the knockouts topic. One at a time, click each link and print the page. Hand in the printouts to your instructor.
4. Go to LiveDocs. Search for a topic that is of interest to you and take a survey or add a comment. Print the page and hand in the printout to your instructor. (Adding a comment may require you to register with Adobe. See your instructor for more details if you do not have an Adobe account issued with your software.)
5. In a browser, navigate to the Web page at www.adobe.com/designcenter/tutorials and then click the link for Photoshop. Navigate to a tutorial of your choice and follow the directions. Write three paragraphs describing your experience including how easy or difficult it was to follow the tutorial and what you learned. Turn in the paragraphs to your instructor.

Appendix C
Using Adobe Bridge CS3

This appendix shows you how to use Adobe Bridge CS3. Adobe Bridge is a file exploration tool similar to Windows Explorer, but with added functionality related to images. Adobe Bridge replaces previous file browsing techniques, and now is the control center for the Adobe Creative Suite. Bridge is used to organize, browse, and locate the assets you need to create content for print, the Web, and mobile devices with drag and drop functionality.

Adobe Bridge

You can access Adobe Bridge from Photoshop or from the Start menu. Both Adobe Bridge and Adobe Help can run independently from Photoshop as stand-alone programs.

Starting Adobe Bridge

The following steps show how to start Adobe Bridge from the Windows Vista Start menu.

To Start Bridge Using Windows

1

• **Click the Start button on the Windows taskbar and then click All Programs at the bottom of the left pane on the Start menu.**

Windows displays the commands on the Start menu above the Start button and displays the All Programs submenu (Figure C-1).

FIGURE C-1

2

• **Click
Adobe
Bridge CS3
in the list.
When the Adobe Bridge
window is displayed,
double-click its title bar
to maximize the
window, if necessary.**

*The Adobe Bridge window
is displayed (Figure C-2).
Your list of files and folders
may differ.*

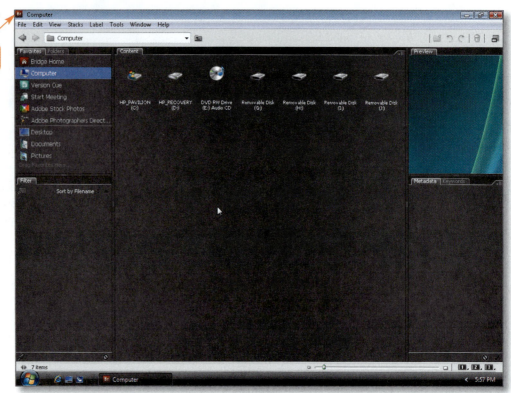

Adobe Bridge
window

FIGURE C-2

1. In Photoshop, click File on
   menu bar, click Browse
2. In Photoshop, click Go
   To Bridge button on
   options bar
3. Press ATL+CTRL+O

Setting the Default Workspace

To make your installation of Adobe Bridge match the figures in this book, you
will need to reset the workspace to its default settings as the following steps illustrate.

To Set the Default Workspace

1

• **Click Window on the
menu bar, and then
point to Workspace.**

*Bridge displays the Workspace
submenu (Figure C-3).*

Window
menu

Workspace
submenu

Workspace
command

Reset to Default
Workspace
command

FIGURE C-3

2

• **Click Reset to Default Workspace on the Workspace submenu.**

• **In the Favorites panel, click Computer.**

Bridge displays panels on the left, and the files and folders in Thumbnails view on the right (Figure C-4).

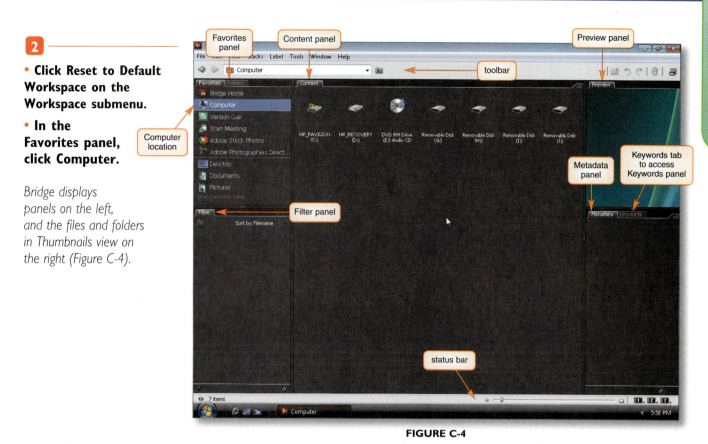

FIGURE C-4

The Adobe Bridge Window

The parts of the Adobe Bridge window are displayed in Figure C-4. The window is divided into panels and includes a toolbar and status bar.

The Panels

Several panels are displayed in the Bridge workspace in default view. To select a panel, click its tab. You can rearrange the panels by dragging their tabs. You can enlarge or reduce the size of the panels by dragging their borders. Some panels include buttons and menus to help you organize displayed information.

FAVORITES PANEL The **Favorites panel** allows quick access to common locations and folders, as well as access to other Adobe applications. Click a location to display its contents in the Content panel. If you click an application name, Windows will launch or open the application.

FOLDERS PANEL The **Folders panel** shows the folder hierarchy in a display similar to that of Windows Explorer. Users click the plus sign to expand folders and the minus sign to collapse them.

CONTENT PANEL The **Content panel** is displayed in a large pane in the center of the Adobe Bridge window. The content panel includes a view of each file and folder, its name, the creation date, and other information about each item. The Content panel is used to select files and open folders. To select a file, click it. To open a folder, double-click it. You can change how the Content panel is displayed on the Bridge status bar.

PREVIEW PANEL The **Preview panel** displays a preview of the selected file that is usually larger than the thumbnail displayed in the Content panel. If the panel is resized, the preview also is resized.

METADATA PANEL The **Metadata panel** contains metadata information for the selected file. Recall that metadata is information about the file including properties, camera data, creation and modification data, and other pieces of information. If multiple files are selected, shared data is listed such as keywords, date created, and exposure settings.

KEYWORDS PANEL The **Keywords panel** allows you to assign keywords using categories designed by Bridge, or you can create new ones. The keywords help you organize and search your images.

Toolbars and Buttons

Bridge displays several toolbars and sets of buttons to help you work more efficiently (Figure C-5).

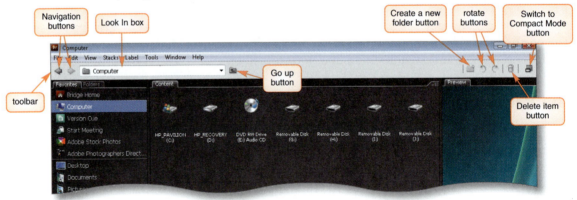

FIGURE C-5

MENU BAR The menu bar is displayed at the top of the Bridge window and contains commands specific to Bridge.

NAVIGATION BUTTONS Below the menu bar are navigation buttons that allow you to move back to previous locations and then forward again.

LOOK IN BOX To the right of the Navigation buttons is the Look In box. When you click the box arrow, Bridge displays the current folder's hierarchy, as well as favorite and recent folders. To the right of the Look In box is a Go up button to move up in the file hierarchy.

SHORTCUT BUTTONS On the right side of the toolbar are shortcut buttons to help you work with your files. The Create a new folder button inserts a new folder in the current location. The rotate buttons are active when an image file is selected in the Content panel. The Delete item button deletes the selected item. The final shortcut button switches to Compact Mode, which displays only the Content panel, and reduces the size of the window.

STATUS BAR At the bottom of the Bridge window, the status bar displays information and contains buttons (Figure C-6). On the left side of the status bar is a Show/hide panels Tab button followed by information regarding the number of items in the current location and how many files are selected, if any. On the right side of the status bar, the Thumbnail slider sets the size of the thumbnails. To the right of the slider are three workspace buttons to change the display of the Content panel, including **Default**, which is the view displayed in Figure C-5, **Horizontal Filmstrip** which displays the Content panel as a horizontal filmstrip, and **Metadata Focus** which displays the Content panel in thumbnail view, along with an enlarged Metadata panel.

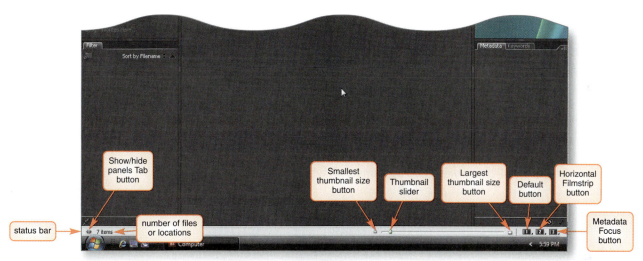

FIGURE C-6

Bridge Navigation and File Viewing

The advantages of using Bridge to navigate through the files and folders on your computer system include an interface that looks the same in all folders, the ability to see the images quickly, and the ease with which you can open the files in Photoshop or other image editing software. Besides the three kinds of displays represented by the workspace buttons on the right side of the status bar, Bridge offers three other configurations or layouts of the workspace accessible via the Window menu. **Light Table** displays just the Content panel for viewing files. **File Navigator** displays the Content panel in thumbnails, along with the Favorites panel and Folder panel. **Vertical Filmstrip** displays just the Content panel in a vertical filmstrip view.

The steps on the next page show how to navigate to a CD and view files. Your instructor may specify a different location for these files.

To Navigate and View Files Using Bridge

FIGURE C-7

1

• **Insert the CD that accompanies this book into your CD drive.**

• **After a few seconds, if Windows displays a dialog box, click its Close button.**

• **In the Content panel, double-click the CD icon associated with your CD drive.**

• **When the folders and files of the CD are displayed, double-click the Chapter01 folder.**

The photos in the Chapter01 folder are displayed (Figure C-7).

2

• **One at a time, click each of the workspace buttons on the right side of the status bar and note how the Content panel changes.**

• **Click Window on the menu bar, point to Workspace, and then click a workspace choice and note how the Content panel changes.**

• **Click Window on the menu bar, point to Workspace, and then click Reset to Default Workspace to reset the Content panel and other panels.**

Bridge is reset back to its default.

Other Ways

1. To view Light Table workspace, press CTRL+F2
2. To view File Navigator workspace, press CTRL+F3
3. To view Metadata Focus workspace, press CTRL+F4
4. To view Horizontal Filmstrip workspace, press CTRL+F5
5. To view Vertical Filmstrip workspace, press CTRL+F6

Managing Files

If you want to move a file to a folder that is currently displayed in the Content panel, you can drag and drop the file. The right-drag option is not available. If you want to copy a file, you can choose Copy on the Edit menu, navigate to the new folder and then choose Paste on the Edit menu. At any time you can press the DELETE key to delete a file or folder, or right-click and then click Delete on the shortcut menu. To rename a photo in Bridge, right-click the file and then click Rename. Type the new name.

The next steps illustrate copying a file from a CD to a USB flash drive using Bridge.

To Copy a File

1

• **With the Chapter01 folder contents still displaying in the Content panel, click the Flowers thumbnail.**

• **Click Edit on the menu bar.**

Bridge displays the Edit menu (Figure C-8).

FIGURE C-8

2

• **Click Copy on the Edit menu.**

• **In the Favorites panel, click Computer.**

• **When the Computer locations are displayed in the Content panel, double-click drive F or the drive associated with your USB flash drive.**

The contents of the USB flash drive are displayed (Figure C-9). Your list will vary.

FIGURE C-9

3

• **Click Edit on the menu bar, and then click Paste.**

Bridge displays the copy in its new location (Figure C-10).

FIGURE C-10

Other Ways

1. To copy, press CTRL+C
2. To paste, press CTRL+V

Bridge also offers a Duplicate command on the Edit menu (Figure C-8) that makes a copy in the same folder. Bridge renames the second file with the word Copy appended to the file name.

Metadata

A popular use for Bridge allows you to assign metadata. Metadata, such as information about the file, author, resolution, color space, and copyright, is used for searching and categorizing photos. You can utilize metadata to streamline your workflow and organize your files.

Metadata is divided into categories, depending on the type of software you are using and the selected files. The category **File Properties** includes things like file type, creation date, dimensions, and color mode. **IPTC Core** stands for International Press Telecommunications Council, which is data used to identify transmitted text and images, such as data describing the image or the location of a photo. **Camera Data (Exif)** refers to the Exchangeable Image File Format, a standard for storing interchange information in image files, especially those using JPEG compression. Most digital cameras now use the EXIF format. The standardization of IPTC and EXIF encourages interoperability between imaging devices. Other categories may include Audio, Video, Fonts, Camera Raw and Version Cue, among others. You can see a list of all the metadata categories and their definitions by using Bridge Help.

Assigning Metadata

The Metadata Focus workspace makes it easier to assign or enter metadata for photos, as shown in the following steps where a description and location are entered. In the Metadata panel, you can click the pencil icon to select fields of metadata, or you can move through the fields by pressing the TAB key.

To Assign and View Metadata

1

• **Click the Flowers thumbnail to select it.**

• **Click Window on the menu bar, point to Workspace, and then click Metadata Focus.**

• **In the Metadata panel, if necessary, click the right-pointing arrow next to IPTC Core to display its fields. Scroll down to the Description field.**

The Metadata Focus workspace widens the panel area (Figure C-11). Depending on your system's installed Adobe applications, your Metadata panel may display different fields.

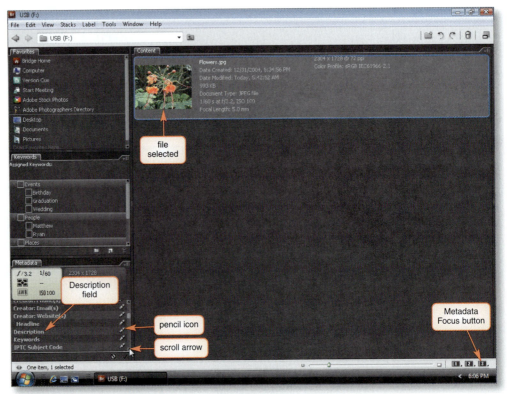

FIGURE C-11

2

• **Click the pencil icon to the right of the Description field. Type** Hawaiian Flowers **as the description.**

• **Scroll as needed and then click the pencil icon to the right of the Location field. Type** Kauai **as the location.**

• **Press the TAB key, Type** Kilauea **as the city.**

• **Press the TAB key. Type** Hawaii **as the state.**

The metadata is entered (Figure C-12).

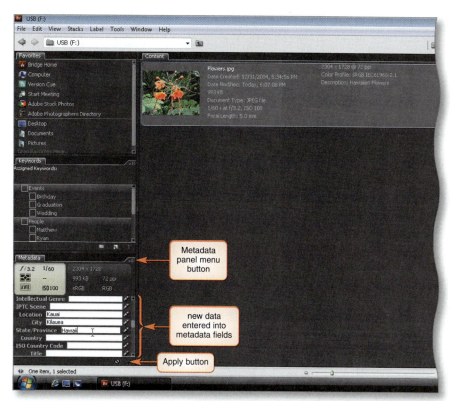

FIGURE C-12

3

• **Click the Apply button at the bottom of the Metadata panel.**

• **Click File on the menu bar and then click File Info (Figure C-13).**

• **Click the OK button.**

The metadata is applied, or stored, with the picture.

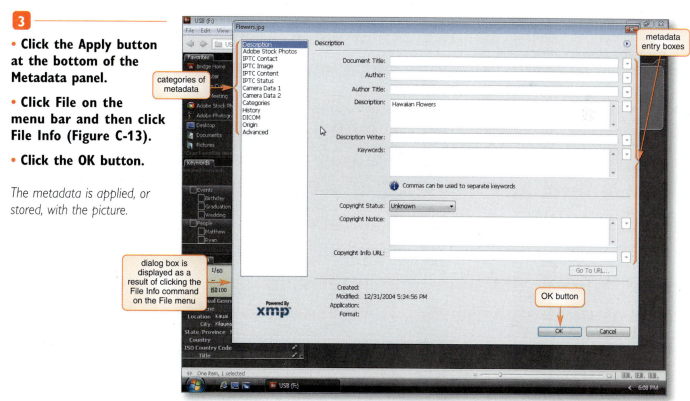

FIGURE C-13

Other Ways

1. Press CTRL+F4, enter data

The Metadata panel menu button (Figure C-12 on the previous page) displays options to increase or decrease the font size of the fields in the panel. Additionally, the menu displays options to set Metadata preferences as well as finding and adding new fields. For example, if your digital camera records global positioning system (GPS) navigational information, you can use the menu to append that data to the file.

A second way to enter Metadata information is to use the File Info command on Bridge's File menu. Figure C-13 on the previous page displays a dialog box to enter information about the Flowers image. As you click each category of metadata on the left, text boxes in the main window allow you to enter extensive metadata. This extended set of metadata is particularly useful for large businesses, such as the newspaper industry, which contracts with many photographers and must maintain photo history.

Keywords

The Keywords panel lets you create and apply Bridge keywords to files. Keywords can be organized into categories called **keyword sets**. Using keywords and sets, you identify files based on their content. Later, you can view all files with shared keywords as a group. To assign a keyword, you click the box to the left of the keyword in the Keywords panel. Buttons at the bottom of the Keywords panel allow you to create new sets and new words.

The following steps describe how to enter keywords associated with the Flowers image.

To Enter a New Keyword

1

• **With the Flowers image still selected, click the Keywords tab.**

• **Scroll down to display the keyword set named, Places.**

The Places keyword set is selected (Figure C-14).

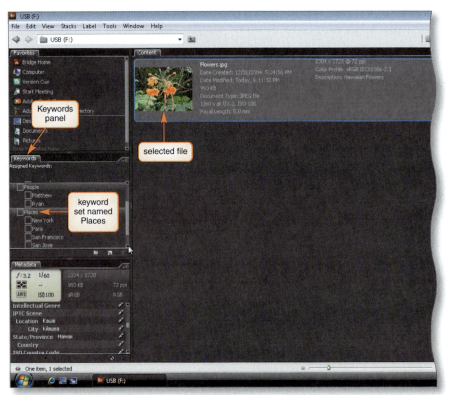

FIGURE C-14

2

• **Right-click Places and then click New Keyword on the shortcut menu.**

• **When the new field is displayed, type** Hawaii **and then press the ENTER key.**

• **Click the check box to the left of Hawaii.**

Bridge displays the new keyword and selects it (Figure C-15).

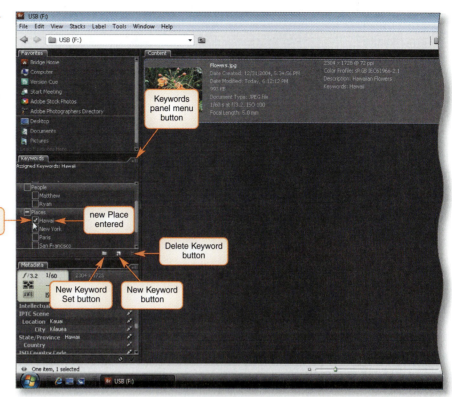

FIGURE C-15

To create a new keyword set, click the New Keyword Set button at the bottom of the panel. To remove a keyword assignment, click the box to the left of the keyword to remove its check mark. To delete a keyword permanently, remove its check mark assignment, select the keyword, and then click the Delete Keyword button at the bottom of the Keywords panel.

The Keywords panel menu button also displays options for new keywords, new sets, deleting, renaming, and finding keywords.

Rating Photos

A rating system from zero stars to five stars is available in Bridge to rate your images and photos. A rating system helps you organize and flag your favorite, or best, files. Many photographers transfer their digital photos from a camera into Bridge and then look back through them, rating and grouping the photos. You can rate a photo using the Label menu or using shortcut keys. Once the photo is rated, stars display below or above the file name depending on the workspace view. The step on the next page shows how to rate a photo.

To Rate a Photo

1

• **With the Flowers image still selected in the Content panel, press CTRL+3.**

Bridge assigns a three-star rating (Figure C-16).

FIGURE C-16

To change a rating, click Label on the menu bar and then either increase or decrease the rating. To remove all stars, click Label on the menu bar and then click No Rating. In some views, you can change a rating by clicking stars or dots that display below the thumbnail. You can remove the rating by clicking left of the stars.

Labeling Photos with Color-Coding

Another way to group photos in Bridge is to use a color-coding system. Bridge provides five colors for users to label or group their photos. The following steps describe how to add a green color indicating approval to the Flowers image.

To Label a Photo with Color-Coding

1

• **With the Flowers image still selected in the Content panel, click Label on the menu bar.**

Bridge displays the Label menu (Figure C-17).

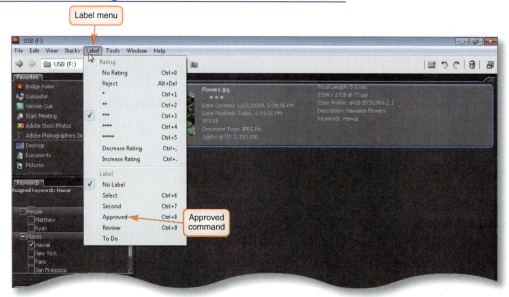

FIGURE C-17

2

- **Click Approved.**
- **If Bridge displays a dialog box, click its OK button.**

The color green is applied around the star rating in the Content panel, indicating approval (Figure C-18).

FIGURE C-18

Other Ways

1. Press CTRL+8

Color coding and ratings are permanent only when photos have embedded extensible markup platform (XMP) storage space. Otherwise, the colors and ratings are stored in your system's cached memory.

Searching Bridge

Searching is a powerful tool in Adobe Bridge, especially as the number of stored image files increases on your computer system. It is a good idea to enter keywords, or metadata, for every image file you store, so searching is more efficient. Without Adobe Bridge and the search tool, you would have to view all files as filmstrips in Windows, and then look at them a screen at a time until you found what you wanted.

Using the Find Command

In Bridge, you can enter the kind of data or field that you want to search, parameters for that field, and the text you are looking for using the Find command. For example, you could search for all files with a rating of three stars or better, for files less than one megabyte in size, or files that begin with the letter m.

The Find dialog box displays many boxes and buttons to help you search effectively as shown in the steps on the next page. You will look for all files with metadata that includes the word Hawaii.

To Use the Find Command

1

• **Click Edit on the menu bar, and then click Find.**

Bridge displays the Find dialog box (Figure C-19).

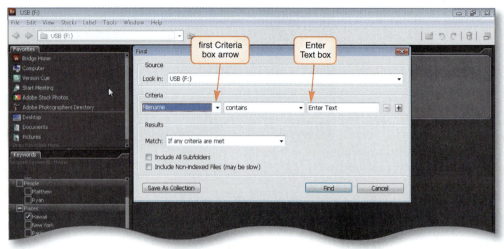

FIGURE C-19

2

• **Click the first Criteria box arrow, and then click All Metadata at the bottom of the list.**

• **Press the TAB key twice, and then type** Hawaii **in the Enter Text box.**

The criteria are entered (Figure C-20).

FIGURE C-20

3

• **Click the Find button.**

Bridge displays all files that have the word Hawaii in any part of the metadata (Figure C-21).

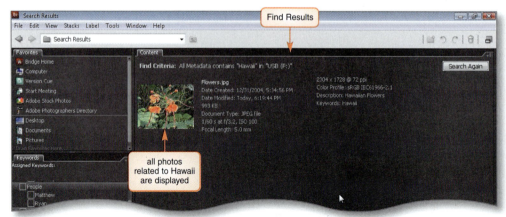

FIGURE C-21

Other Ways

1. Press CTRL+F

The plus button to the right of the search boxes in the Find dialog box allows you to search multiple fields. When you click the button, a second line of search boxes is displayed. For example, if you needed to find photos that were created last winter from your vacation in the Rockies, you could search for the date in the first line of boxes, click the plus button, and then enter the keyword to narrow your search even further in the second line of boxes (Figure C-22). When clicked, the Match box arrow allows you to match any or all criteria.

FIGURE C-22

Bridge offers you a way to save common searches as a **collection** for use later. For example, if you were working for a grocery wholesaler who stores many files for artwork in advertising, searching for pictures related to dairy products would be a common search. Looking through folders of images for pictures of milk or eggs or cheese would be very time consuming. Once you establish your search criteria, click the Save As Collection button (Figure C-22). Bridge then offers to name the search and store it. To display stored collections, click Collections in the Favorites panel. Then to perform the search again, double-click the collection. With metadata and collection searches, Bridge saves a lot of time.

The final step shows how to close the Search Results window, which quits Adobe Bridge.

To Close the Search Results Window and Quit Bridge

1 **Click the Close button in the Search Results window.**

Using Bridge

1 Assigning Metadata

Instructions: You would like to assign metadata to some of the photos you worked on in previous chapters in this book. The photos can be found on the CD that accompanies this book, or your instructor may direct to you to a different location. You will copy the photos from the CD to a local storage device and then assign metadata using Adobe Bridge.

1. Insert the CD that accompanies this book or see your instructor for the location of the data files.
2. Start Adobe Bridge on your system. When the Adobe Bridge window is displayed, on the Favorites tab, click Computer. In the right pane, double-click the CD that accompanies this book, or navigate to the location specified by your instructor.
3. Right-click the Chapter01 folder, and then click Copy on the shortcut menu.
4. Using the Favorites tab, click Computer, and then navigate to your USB flash drive or other storage location.
5. On the Edit menu, click Paste. After a few moments, the Chapter01 folder will display in the right pane. Double-click the folder to open it. If necessary, click the Default button on the Bridge status bar.
6. Click the first photo. In the Metadata pane, scroll down and click Description. In the description box, enter a short description of the picture. Click Description Writer. Enter your name.
7. With the first photo still selected, click the Keywords tab. When the Adobe Bridge dialog box appears, click Apply to apply the changes you just made in the Metadata pane. On the Keywords tab, click to place a check mark next to any keywords that apply to the photo.
8. Scroll to the bottom of the keywords list. If there is not an Other Keywords category, create one by right-clicking on the empty space below the last keyword, clicking New Keyword Set on the shortcut menu, and typing Other Keywords when the words Untitled Set are displayed. Right-click the Other Keywords category and then click New Keyword on the shortcut menu. When the words Untitled Keyword are displayed, type a new keyword relating to the selected photo.
9. Repeat steps 6 through 8 for each photo in the right pane of the Adobe Bridge window.

2 Rating and Categorizing Photos

Instructions: You would like to rate and categorize some of the photos you worked on in previous chapters in this book. The photos can be found on the CD that accompanies this book, or your instructor may direct to you to a different location.

1. If you did not perform exercise 1, Assigning Metadata, perform steps 1 through 5 from exercise 1 to copy images to your storage location.
2. With the photos from the Chapter01 folder displayed in the right pane of the Adobe Bridge window, click the first photo. Rate the photo on a scale from 1 to 5 with 1 being the worst photo in the group and 5 being the best photo in the group. On the Label menu, click the number of stars that corresponds to your rating. Repeat the process for each of the photos in the folder.
3. Click the first photo again to select it. Click Label on the menu bar. Choose a label setting, such as Approved. Repeat the process for each of the photos in the folder, choosing different label settings.

4. Choose your favorite photo in the folder and right-click the image. Click Add to Favorites on the shortcut menu.
5. Consult with at least three other members of your class to compare your ratings.

3 Copyrighting Photos

Instructions: You want to store title and copyright information about a photo you have created in preparation for using it on the Web. Title information appears in the Web browser's title bar when the image is exported with an HTML file. Copyright information is not displayed in a browser; however, it can be added to the HTML file as a comment and to the image file as metadata.

Using Adobe Bridge, you decide to enter author and copyright information and save it in a metadata template that you can use with future image files that you create. The following steps show how to add the copyright.

1. Start Adobe Bridge on your system. When the Adobe Bridge window is displayed, navigate to a photo that you have created from one of the chapters in this book, or a photo you took with a digital camera. Click the photo to select it.
2. On the File menu, click File Info. When Bridge opens the dialog box, enter a document title. Type your name in the Author box.
3. Click the Copyright Status box arrow and then click Copyrighted in the list.
4. In the Copyright Notice box, type `All rights reserved`. Type your name and then `Personal Copyright` and then type the year.
5. Click the Menu button in the upper right corner of the dialog box and then click Save Metadata Template in the list. When Bridge displays the Save Metadata Template dialog box, type Personal Copyright in the Template Name box. Click the Save button.
6. Click the OK button in the dialog box.
7. Navigate to a second photo that you have created or taken. Click the photo to select it.
8. On the Bridge menu bar, click Tools, point to Append Metadata, and then click Personal Copyright.
9. Close Adobe Bridge.

ADOBE

Photoshop CS3

Adobe Photoshop CS3 Quick Reference

In Adobe Photoshop CS3, you can accomplish a task or activate a tool in a number of ways. The following table provides a quick reference to each task and tool presented in this textbook. The first column identifies the task or tool. The second column indicates the page number on which the task or tool is discussed in the book. The subsequent three columns list the different ways the task or tool in column one can be carried out or activated.

Adobe Photoshop CS3 Quick Reference

TOOL OR TASK	PAGE #	MENU	MOUSE	KEYBOARD SHORCUT
Add to Selection	PS 93		Add to selection button	SHIFT+drag
Adjustment Layer	PS 166		Create new fill or adjustment layer button	
Auto-Align Layers	PS 74	Edit | Auto-Align Layers	Auto-Align Layers button	
Background Eraser Tool	PS 145		Background Eraser Tool button	E
Bridge	PS 51		Go to Bridge button	
Brightness/Contrast	PS 167	Layer | New Adjustment Layer | Brightness/Contrast		
Clone Stamp Tool	PS 174		Clone Stamp Tool button	S
Close Bridge	PS 52		Close button	
Close File	PS 46	File | Close	Close button	CTRL+W or CTRL+F4
Clouds	PS 171	Filter | Render | Clouds		
Color Layer	PS 133		Right-click layer name, click Layer Properties	
Commit Change	PS 77		Commit transform (Return) button	ENTER
Copy	PS 76	Edit | Copy		CTRL+C or F3
Crop	PS 31	Image | Crop		
Crop Tool	PS 30		Crop Tool button	C
Default Foreground/ Background Colors	PS 156		Default Foreground/Background Colors button	D
Default Workspace	PS 8	Window | Workspace | Default Workspace	Workspace button | Default Workspace	
Deselect	PS 39	Select | Deselect	Click document window	CTRL+D
Distort	PS 76	Edit | Transform | Distort	Enter rotation percentage or drag outside of bounding box	
Drop Shadow	PS 170	Layer | Layer Style | Drop Shadow		
Duplicate Layer (Group)	PS 171	Layer | Duplicate Layer (Group)		

Adobe Photoshop CS3 Quick Reference Summary *(continued)*

TOOL OR TASK	PAGE #	MENU	MOUSE	KEYBOARD SHORCUT
Duplicate Selection	PS 99			ALT+drag
Edit Menus	APP 8	Edit | Menus		ALT+SHIFT+CTRL+M
Edit Preferences	APP 5	Edit Preferences | General		CTRL+K
Elliptical Marquee Tool	PS 71		Elliptical Marquee Tool button	M
Eraser Tool	PS 145		Eraser Tool button	E
Exit	PS 55	File | Exit	Close button	CTRL+Q
Fill	PS 36	Edit | Fill		SHIFT+F5
Flatten Image	PS 177	Layer | Flatten Image		
Flip Horizontal	PS 76	Edit | Transform | Flip Horizontal		
Flip Vertical	PS 76	Edit | Transform | Flip Vertical		
Free Transform	PS 76	Edit | Free Transform		CTRL+T
Guides	PS 95		Drag from ruler	
Hide Layer	PS 135	Layer | Hide Layers	Indicates layer visibility button	
Keyboard Shortcuts	PS 106	Edit | Keyboard Shortcuts		ALT+SHIFT+CTRL+K
Lasso Tool	PS 83		Lasso Tool button	L
Layer Mask	PS 155		Add layer mask button	
Layer Mask Reveal All	PS 158	Layer | Layer Mask | Reveal All		
Layer Palette Options	PS 130		Layer palette menu button | Palette Options	
Layer Properties	PS 134	Layer | Layer Properties		
Layer Style	PS 168		Add a layer style button	
Layer via Cut	PS 127	Layer | New | Layer via Cut		SHIFT+CTRL+J
Levels	PS 165	Image | Adjustments | Levels		CTRL+L
Magic Eraser Tool	PS 145		Magic Eraser Tool button	E
Magic Wand Tool	PS 102		Magic Wand Tool button	W
Magnetic Lasso Tool	PS 83		Magnetic Lasso Tool button	L
Modify Border	PS 33	Select | Modify | Border		
Modify Smooth	PS 35	Select | Modify | Smooth		
Move Tool	PS 74		Move Tool button	V
Name Layer	PS 133		Double-click layer name	
New Guide	PS 97	View | New Guide		
Open File	PS 11	File | Open	Right-click file, click Open With	CTRL+O
Paste	PS 76	Edit | Paste		CTRL+V or F4
Pattern Stamp Tool	PS 177		Pattern Stamp Tool button	S
Perspective	PS 76	Edit | Transform | Perspective		
Photoshop Help	PS 53	Help | Photoshop Help		F1
Polygonal Lasso Tool	PS 83		Polygonal Lasso Tool button	L

Adobe Photoshop CS3 Quick Reference Summary *(continued)*

TOOL OR TASK	PAGE #	MENU	MOUSE	KEYBOARD SHORCUT
Print	PS 44	File | Print		CTRL+P
Print One Copy	PS 44	File | Print One Copy		ALT+SHIFT+CTRL+P
Quick Selection Tool	PS 101		Quick Selection Tool button	W
Quit Photoshop	PS 55	File | Exit	Click Close button	CTRL+Q
Rectangular Marquee Tool	PS 71		Rectangular Marquee Tool button	M
Refine Edge	PS 101	Select | Refine Edge	Refine Edge button	ALT+CTRL+R
Reset All Tools	PS 10		Tool Presets palette menu button | Reset All Tools or right-click tool button on options bar	
Resize Document Window	PS 84		Drag sizing handle	
Resize Image	PS 39	Image | Image Size		ALT+CTRL+I
Rotate	PS 76	Edit | Transform | Rotate		
Rotate 180°	PS 76	Edit | Transform | Rotate 180°		
Rotate 90° CCW	PS 76	Edit | Transform | Rotate 90° CCW		
Rotate 90° CW	PS 76	Edit | Transform | Rotate 90° CW		
Rulers	PS 28	View | Rulers		CTRL+R
Save a File	PS 39	File | Save		CTRL+S
Save a File with a New Name	PS 21	File | Save As		SHIFT+CTRL+S or ALT+CTRL+S
Save for Web	PS 46	File | Save for Web & Devices		ALT+SHIFT+CTRL+S
Scale	PS 76	Edit | Transform | Scale		
Screen Mode	APP 200	View | Screen Mode	Screen Mode button	F
Select All	PS 32	Select | All		CTRL+A
Select Bottom Layer	PS 131			ALT+,
Select Layer	PS 131		Click layer	
Select Next Layer	PS 131			ALT+]
Select Previous Layer	PS 131			ALT+[
Select Top Layer	PS 131			ALT+.
Show Guides	PS 97	View | Show | Guides		CTRL+;
Show Layers	PS 135	Layer | Show Layers		
Single Column Marquee Tool	PS 71		Single Column Marquee Tool button	
Single Row Marquee Tool	PS 71		Single Row Marquee Tool button	
Skew	PS 76	Edit | Transform | Skew	Enter width and height	Drag sizing handle
Smart Object	PS 131	Layer | Smart Objects	Layers palette menu button | Convert to Smart Object	
Subtract from Selection	PS 90		Subtract from selection button	ALT+drag
Thumbnail, change size	PS 131		Layers palette menu button | Palette Options or right-click thumbnail, select size	

Adobe Photoshop CS3 Quick Reference Summary *(continued)*

TOOL OR TASK	PAGE #	MENU	MOUSE	KEYBOARD SHORCUT
Transform Again	PS 76	Edit | Transform | Again		SHIFT+CTRL+T
Undo/Redo	PS 31	Edit | Undo/Redo		CTRL+Z
View Layer	PS 135		Indicates layer visibility button	
Warp	PS 76	Edit | Transform | Warp		
Zoom In	PS 24	View | Zoom In	Zoom In button on Navigator palette	CTRL++ CTRL+=
Zoom Out	PS 24	View | Zoom Out	Zoom Out button on Navigator palette	CTRL+-
Zoom Tool	PS 24		Zoom Tool button	Z
Zoomify	PS 46	File | Export | Zoomify		

Index